INDIA AND HER SUB-CONTINENT NEIGHBOURS

New Pattern of Relationships

INDIA AND HER SUB-CONTINENT NEIGHBOURS

New Pattern of Relationships

MEENU ROY

DEEP & DEEP PUBLICATIONS PVT. LTD.
F-159, Rajouri Garden, New Delhi - 110027

INDIA AND HER SUB-CONTINENT NEIGHBOURS
New Pattern of Relationships

ISBN 978-81-8450-277-0

Typeset by THE LASER PRINTERS, 8/15, 3rd Floor, Subhash Nagar, New Delhi-110027.

Printed in India at MAYUR ENTERPRISES
WZ Plot No. 3, Gujjar Market, Tihar Village, New Delhi - 110 018

Published by DEEP & DEEP PUBLICATIONS PVT. LTD.,
F-159, Rajouri Garden, New Delhi-110027. Phones: 25435369, 25440916.
E-mail: ddpbooks@yahoo.co.in • ddpubs@gmail.com
Sales Showroom: 2/13, Ansari Road, Daryaganj, New Delhi-110002
Phone/Fax: 23245122

Contents

PREFACE

The Indian sub-continent is linked by geography, history, culture, language and religion. But today the region is witnessing a dangerous pattern of action, reaction and escalation phenomenon which generates tension and arms race in the region. Religious fundamentalism, terrorism and violence are other threats which are being faced by all the nations of the sub-continent.

The post cold war period and liberalisation presented the changed scenario in almost all the areas which demands more economic, political, cultural, technological and educational interaction between the sub-continent's powers.

India's interests in the sub-continent are peace, development, peaceful co-existence, non-interference and security. No doubt, India is a sub-continent regional power among its small neighbours. Today the sub-continent is in a sorry state. So India is trying to move towards its regional neighbours to work for closer and greater economic, social, cultural and political cooperation. What are the areas of confrontation and cooperation, among the sub-continent powers, the book deals these emerging new pattern of relationships, which makes sub-continent power relations interesting one to study.

I am deeply grateful to my husband, Mukesh Bhargava whose constant support and encouragement was my strength throughout my writing. My special thanks are also to Mr. Gajendra Sharma for the computer printing and Mr. Bhatia of Deep & Deep Publications Pvt. Ltd., New Delhi, for publication the book.

Ajmer — Meenu Roy

Indian Sub-Continent and India's Foreign Policy

CHARACTERISTICS OF INDIAN SUB-CONTINENT

The term Indian sub-continent is used for the countries lying south of the Himalayas and surrounded by Indian Ocean from three sides. The countries of sub-continent are linked together in terms of religion, language, cultural traditions and racial ties. Despite the presence of a number of common factors, the countries of sub-continent are having strained relations. The whole Indian sub-continent in the past was treated by the British as one single unit. But after getting independence, the sub-continent region was carved out into several sovereign independent states with their separate identities.

As the whole region was under control of Britain, the people of one area moved freely into another. So we find ethnic groups into neighbouring states. For example Tamils from Tamil Nadu migrated to Sri Lanka in 4th, 5th centuries. Indian Hindus went to Nepal, Bangladeshi Muslims to India, Nepalese and Tibetans to India and Bhutan, Hindus to Pakistan and Muslims to India. This migration of population have changed the demographic character of region. The sub-continent powers bear certain specific features from the ethnic point of view. All the states of sub-continent are multi-ethnic societies, the ethnic map of sub-continent cuts across national boundaries. An ethnic group dominant in one country constitutes a minority ethnic group in another country. Concentration of an ethnic group in particular geographic region as a dominant community provides a base for its assertion for regional autonomy. Ethnic violence has become a major source of internal instability and ethnic conflict in all the states that have regional and extra-regional linkage.

Almost all the nations have been facing ethnic conflict and tensions. In the pre-independence era, ethnicity did not become a serious issue because of lack of social, political and economic mobilisation of various groups. But gradually ethnicity has assumed serious proposition. Its degree has ranged from demand for equitable distribution of resources, liberalisation of power structure, autonomy within the state to separatist movement and to terrorist acts. All these pose a serious threat to the integrity of the nation and peace of the region. The situation created by these movements is further aggravated due to cross-country affiliations of such ethnic groups and cross border terrorist activities. In fact because of racial, religious and linguistic overlaps between different states, the situation has been complex in sub-continent. Further the situation has become more serious with the emergence of terrorist organisations aided and abetted by foreign nations.

The territorial boundaries of the sub-continent are not clear because all are decided by the British treaties which are now not acceptable to states. This territorial disputes lead to conflicts. India was forced to fight four major wars with her neighbour on that count. The states of this region though belong to the same region, but they seem to have different systems that are contradictory-religious fundamentalism vs. secularism, democracy vs. monarchical rule, military vs. non-military governments.

Asymmetry in size, population, economy, military and technology is another characteristic of this region. If India is the largest in the size, Bhutan is the smallest. India enjoys democracy while others are monarchical or military regimes. This and other imbalance and asymmetry makes India a dominant power—a Big Brother in the region. Rather they find India dominating more and not like big brother. The disparity in power between India and its neighbours has given rise to suspicion, mistrust, fear among the nations. This is not unnatural and unjustified because of inherent asymmetry in the regional system.

The roots of differences among the sub-continent countries are grounded in perceptual differences. The contrary outlook of the powers is the product of their historical experience and the political culture in which their leaders have been educated, trained and working.

The historical background of Indo-Pak relations gave birth to an uneasyness in the relationship. The nuclear explosions by both India and Pakistan in May 1998 at Pokharan and Chagai and missile tests in April 1988 and 1999 have created regional tensions and insecurity in sub-continent. These tests have led to a new strategic situation that is bound to have lasting implications for both the countries, for the whole region of sub-continent and for the international community. This is resulted into a costly nuclear and missile race in sub-continent and has increased the risk of nuclear confrontation between India and Pakistan. It also resulted in a threat to peace and security in sub-continent in the new millennium.

With both the major countries of the sub-continent testing their nuclear and missile capabilities, the security scenario in the region has been radically transformed. The region that had witnessed three wars between India and Pakistan and one between India and China is the most likely area of the world to explode and wage a nuclear war in the new millennium. The escalation of tension and exchange of fire between India and Pakistan in Kargil areas of Kashmir in May-July 1999 was almost a war like situation. Both the countries are able to deploy nuclear weapons and they have developed ballistic missiles to carry the weapons to the selected targets. This nuclear and missiles race in the sub-continent constituted the greatest threat to the peace and stability of the region.

The region is witnessing a dangerous pattern of action, reaction and escalation phenomenon that generates tension and arms race in the region. Religious fundamentalism, terrorism and violence are another those threats which are facing by all the nations of the sub-continent. Cooperation in combating terrorism is in the national interest of every country in the region.

The post-cold war period and liberalisation presented the changed scenario in trade, commerce, investment, tourism science and technology which demands more economic, political, cultural, technological and educational interaction between the sub-continent and other nations.

THE SECURITY PERCEPTION

Security is the main goal of any country. The Latin word 'Securitas' referred to 'freedom from care'. Now security for a nation state is a multi-dimensional concept and encompasses various concepts. National security can be most fruitfully defined as the "ability of a nation to protect its internal values from external threats." But we may adopt a broad concept of national security, i.e. the preservation of the core values critical to the nation state from external and internal threats. Henry Kissinger has stated in his book "On Security" that the "national security in its widest sense comprises every action by which a society seeks to assure its survival or realises its aspirations internationally." The basic factors that govern national security is political, social, technological, military, economic and psychological.

Former Foreign Minister Jaswant Singh wrote in his book "National Security: An Outline of Our Concern", "National security is the presentation of the core values of our nation, the political, economic and social well being and preservation of our state, the inviolability of our territorial boundaries and the maintainance of national interests with in the strategic frontiers of India."

India has always approached the subject of security in its larger framework, beyond that implicit in defence and military forces. The concept of security has involved the preservation and perpetuation of the core values.

These are:

- Democratic political set-up.
- Secular state.
- Socialistic nature of the state.
- Attainment of egalitarian society.
- Maintainance of internal or external peace and security.
- Maintainance of political sovereignty and territorial integrity.
- Economic development and progress.

Kautilya, the great political thinker classified four threats to national security in his Arthashastra. They are:

- External threat with external complicity. Example: China and Pakistan.
- Internal threat with external complicity. Example: Problem of Mizoram and Nagaland.
- External threat with internal complicity. Example: The Kashmir issue.
- Internal threats with internal complicity. Example: The naxalite problem.

The roots of security problems in sub-continent are indigenous and threat perceptions in this region are sufficiently diverse to preclude a common approach for all. For India and the region, the major sources of threat continue to be Pakistan and China, despite the initiation of normalisation processes and formation of a regional organisation SAARC. For Pakistan and to a lesser extent, Bangladesh, Sri Lanka and Nepal, the main threats emanate from the Indian policy pursuits. Indeed, India is a dominant power in the region and as a result of this her policies affect the security perceptions of her immediate neighbours. However, Indian threat perception includes threats emanting not only from developments within the region but also from outside.

To evolve a common framework for ensuring system security is of vital importance. Systemic means—some basic values should be preserved by regime in power—such as secularism, democracy, non-interference, peace, etc.

It is impossible to realise the dream of prosperous sub-continent without addressing security concerns. The region as a whole is not safe from barbaric terrorist groups.

We must make bold efforts to combat terrorism in all its forms and manifestations. We should also address the root causes that lead to violent actions. There is a need to work jointly on a counter terrorism strategy for the entire region to defeat terrorism. The region should place great emphasis on eradicating terrorism and making sub-continent a safe place for the people.

INDIA AND THE SUB-CONTINENT

India's interest in the sub-continent are peace, development, peaceful co-existence, non-interference, security. India has to maintain good relations with all the neighbouring countries. India is a sub-continent regional power among these small countries. But India has always been a votary of regional cooperation in the sub-continent as sub-continent is linked by geography, history, culture, language and religion.

The presence of great powers in neighbouring nations is an alarm for the sub-continent. The United States and China's presence in the sub-continent and their military strategic relationship with Pakistan, Sri Lanka, Nepal, Bangladesh and Myanmar is the main concern for India. It is not only threatening the peace and development of the region, but also cornering the regional cooperation in sub-continent.

Though whatever happened in any country within the region, affects the neighbouring countries either individually or collectively, India does not want to interfere in the affairs of its neighbours.

Though initially India was a little apprehensive in joining the SAARC because India believed that the proposed forum could be used by the smaller neighbours affecting them collectively and individually in relation to India and that the regional association would encourage the neighbours to gang up against India. India came up over these fears and gave birth SAARC as a regional organisation of South Asian nations with the principles of equality of states, territorial integrity and non-interference in the internal affairs of each other.

Gujral Doctrine is also a step towards a good relations with neighbouring countries. India occupies an important position in sub-continent and in Asia. It links West Asia and South East Asia. India's primary importance lies in its strategic location in the great heartland of Eurasia. The Great Himalayas are in its north.

The Indian sub-continent is Indo-centric. India occupies the central position in the region from every point of view. India is definitely demographic, technological, ideological, political, economic, nuclear and military power among all the nations. It holds almost 70 per cent of area comprising south Asia. It touches all the countries of region while no two other countries have common borders. India is the largest of all states in the region in terms of all respects. India has fourth largest economy in the world and set to become the third by 2015 (Asia Development Bank Report).

The new balance of power is in the world and that is without military might. So India has a major responsibility for the peace, prosperity and development of the sub-continent. To achieve these goals, India has taken the steps for establishing NAM, SAARC, BIMSTEC. But no effective framework of regional cooperation can be successful in an environment of regional tensions. That is why the success of SAARC has a big question mark. India is now very much concerned with the security of Asia. India is a member of the Conference on Interaction and Confidence Building Measures in Asia (CICA), established in 1999, to promote permanent security system in Asia on the pattern of Organisation of Security and Cooperation in Europe (OSCE). To eliminate terrorism, it wants solidarity against terrorism.

India is an increasingly more important player in the global economic. And as a member of Asia continent, where half of the population of world resides, the responsibility of India is no less, India is also a member of Asia Cooperation Dialogue (ACD) established in June 2002 to expand cooperation among Asian nations in the fields of science, technology, tourism, resource management, energy security, transport and communication, infrastructure development and elimination of poverty.

INDIA—A BIG POWER

With the transfer of power in sub-continents, India envisaged a power relationship with smaller neighbours in which its historical pre-eminence entitled it to exercise a legitimate control over the foreign policy and security options of these states. This Indo-phobia created a fear psychosis in the neighbouring countries.

The search for security of the new states was also influenced by the cold war politics in which they were born. Above all their socio-economic underdevelopment, the British legacy and the geo-political developments were compelling them to take shelter under Western bloc. On the other hand India's pre-eminence in the region and leadership in Asia as well as an influential role in international politics through the policy of non-alignment and panchsheel were the considerate factors to be integrated their security and defence requirements with India. As they could not afford to be in different hostile camps. India was and is their immediate neighbour which could protect them from the maritime and landline frontiers

The emergence of Bangladesh in 1971 with the help of India established the dominance of India in sub-continent. After this the Simla Agreement of July 1972 was signed between India and Pakistan which further strengthened the Indian stand. It signed a cultural cooperation agreement with Dhaka on December 30, 1972, promoting and developing understanding between the two countries in the fields of culture, education and in science and technology. In 1974, India did her first nuclear explosion and thus became a nuclear power. But this nuclear capability gives rise to mistrust, suspicion and fear among the neighbouring countries. This fear had aggravated with acquiring nuclear capability by the Pakistan. India's liberal foreign policy approach towards her neighbours hence got a break.

Sooner the attitude of other sub-continental powers has changed. The nuclearization of sub-continent made other powers suspicious. India may be described the dominant major power, Pakistan as a significant and cohesive middle power, Bangladesh as a weak and dependent middle power, Sri Lanka and Nepal as weak small powers and Bhutan as mini state.

The Indian sub-continent has great similarities among the countries which help calling this mass of land as a region. Historically, economically and socially they are related, politically, ideologically and militarily they are asymetrical. Historically except Nepal and Bhutan all countries had the common experience of British imperialism, Economically this is a poor region. It accounts for about one third of total number of world's poor. This less developed region has slow industrial growth. Agriculture occupies an important position in the economies of sub-continent.

Alongwith the socio-cultural factors like religion, language and ethnicity play an important role in shaping the intra-regional relations in the sub-continent. Language like Tamil, Urdu, Punjabi, Bengali, Hindi, Nepalese are shared among different sub-continent countries. New Delhi has wisely moved away from the prickly border dispute with Nepal, Bangladesh, Pakistan and even China and instead sought to upgrade economic relations with all these countries.

The giant emerging Indian market exerts a gravitational pull for economic interest everywhere. The recent initiatives with

Pakistan have enhanced India's standing. While we may not share warm relations with all our neighbours, they realise that the Indian economy is capable of charging South Asia. With its high growth rate and large foreign exchange reserves, India is now proactively seeking markets as far a field as Africa in areas like energy and education. With the advantage of a large English speaking population, India has emerged as an IT powerhouse and favoured destination for outsourcing from the West. But to build on such positive trends, we must now have a broad foreign policy framework. New Delhi must document its long-term strategy. Mature democracies, especially those with global world views, clearly state and list their policy objectives from time to time after through debate and discussion. New Delhi now needs such a stated strategy both for its own benefit and for the world at large to understand its vision.

SUB-CONTINENT—A SORRY STATE

By 2025, the Indian sub-continent's population will reach two billion. Being a poor sub-continent already marred with the problems of poverty, unemployment, disease, unhealthy environment this is a worrisome fact. We do not have enough resources to look after so many people.

The Mumbai-based strategic Foresight Group has released a report called "The Second Freedom—South Asian Challenges 2005-25". Based on this study one comes to a pessimistic, but not unrealistic picture about the sub-continent's prospects.

In Pakistan and Nepal the institution that dominate life are respectively the military and the monarchy. Pakistan has had spells of rapid economic progress under its military rulers, but the benefits of that Ditto in Nepal, where links with the monarchy-dominated establishment pave the road to prosperity, while those outside this charmed circle are desperately poor. These conditions feed into general instability in both countries. As "the world's biggest democracy" Indians may like to think they are different, the one shining beacon of hope in South Asia. Unfortunately, the report shrade this complacency.

If Pakistan's military is its bane, the bureaucracy in India (and in Bangladesh) performs a similar role in distorting economies. India's inspector raj is billed to deliver $2,000 billion in missed economic opportunities and industrial growth over the next two decades.

Not only the Americans, but also the Chinese, Pakistani connections of these neighbours are looked upon with suspicion by India. It will be difficult to conceive of friendly ties between India and Pakistan as long as Sino-Pakistani military collaboration on India's sensitive Gilgit area continues. By seceding a disputed territory to China, Pakistan has broken the sub-continental solidarity.

The neighbouring countries have been accusing India for its hegemony. They accused India pursued a foreign policy of "befriend the far and attack the near." While India never interfere in their internal affairs or compel them to sign any treaty or never attack on any country. In fact a strong military and economic India is an important factor for peace and independence of its neighbouring states. Nepal and Bhutan like land-locked countries could not protect and defend themselves on their own.

The question of threat to territorial integrity and national sovereignty is a major point of tension in Indian sub-continent. There has been asymmetry in the perception of India and some of its neighbours. India is the largest state in the sub-continent. Hence, it has inherited the obligations of the ex-British India in terms of sub-continental approach to defence and foreign policy. Indeed, India since its independence has developed a sub-continental approach to the question of its security. But the tragedy is this, while India consider security in terms of the sub-continent, its neighbours have much restricted to their national security only. For example, Nepal is insisting upon its own zone of peace. They are not seeing towards India for their security, but is willing to act as an independent variable and willingly invites extra-regional powers in the security parameters of sub-continent. All the neighbouring countries are pro-China or pro-US. This is one of the reasons for India's refusal to sign a no-war pact with Pakistan as long as Pakistan does not assure India that it is not militarily linked to outside powers. The Pakistan's SEATO membership is the main reason for its continuous gaining military help from the US. This has harmed India's national interests. India objected the Indian Ocean Peace Zone (IOPZ) proposal of Nepal because this had not been discussed among the states before this was brought before the world forum.

CHANGING INTERNATIONAL SCENARIO AND INDIAN FOREIGN POLICY

The decade of the nineties came with many dramatic changes in the international politics. The disintegration of USSR collapsed the cold war bi-polar world. The break-up of Soviet Union was followed by the re-drawing of the map of Europe without a war. Further the forces of globalization and liberalization has given birth to a new world order, which is multi-polar, knowledge based and market oriented. The MNCs and TNCs have converted the world into a 'global village'. The 'geo-economics has become important in place of geo-politics. The sustainable development is now the force of new markets. The shrinking of national boundaries has boosted the new economic market forces.

In this changing international scenario, the economy of a nation has become a driving and determining force of politics. In the new emerging world order, India tried to adjust and re-arrange its priorities of foreign policy both at the global and regional level. India's policy of non-alignment, peace, harmony and friendship, mutual development has started a new era of friendship, peace and development in the history of sub-continent. India's Prime Minister Narasimha Rao said in the Parliament on December 20, 1991 that the Indian Government was prepared to adopt itself to the changing international environment. Now India's priorities in the region are peace, stability and development which can be secured only with mutual good faith and cooperation.

With the disintegration of Soviet Union, India left without a genuine and true friend. So India tried to move towards its regional neighbours to gain support and cooperation on regional and international issues and to build a climate of confidence and faith in the region. India realised that India's growth can be achieved on the basis of regional growth. The politics of violence and terrorism is a big threat for the security of the region. If its neighbouring countries are struggling with terrorism, fundamentalism, militarism, hunger and poverty, India could not become a stable and develop political and economic power. India's stability and security depends on the stability and security of the neighbouring countries.

Now the India's priorities in the region are: peace, stability, security, mutual economic development, transfer of technology.

India is trying to achieve these through the regional organisation of SAARC and BIMST-EC, free trade agreement, negotiations, visits, joint ventures, investment, etc.

India is now no longer interferring in the domestic affairs of its neighbouring countries but is interested in taking initiatives to improve relations. India took a number of initiatives which were aimed at resolving contentious bilateral issues and strengthening ties with the neighbouring countries.

Foreign policy is the content or a substance of a nation's efforts to promote its interests vis-a-vis other nations. According to Clement the distinction between domestic policy and foreign policy is misleading. In fact the foreign policy is merely an extension of nation's domestic policy. A state determines its foreign policy keeping in view its domestic compulsions.

Foreign policy is comprised of the means nations choose to achieve their goals in the arena of international politics. It is the determination of the best path to be taken to further these foreign policy stakes (objectives) that is the focus of a foreign policy.

The responsibility for foreign policy rests ultimately with the national leadership. Foreign policy is a composite of many perceptions and interests. Foreign policy is composed of 'ifs' mirroring the uncertainties of international environment.

Linkage is a foreign policy perspective that events, within one part of the international system or subsystems, are linked with events in other parts.

The foreign policy of a country is determined by a number of factors, which can be broadly divided into two categories—objective and subjective. The objective factors include the environmental factors within the framework of which the foreign policy of a country has to operate. The subjective factors are those specific developments or particular situations which influence the foreign policy of a country.

Foreign policy of a nation is closely linked with national interests of that country. One of the basic objectives of the foreign policy of any country is the promotion of its national interests. Thus the clashes of national interests give birth to conflicts.

Foreign policy is comprised of the means, nations choose to achieve their goals in international and national politics. Every nation want to achieve security, peace, economic sufficiency and national power and prestige. It is the determination of the best path to be taken to further these objectives that is the focus of foreign policy. The responsibility for foreign policy rests ultimately with the national leadership.

Foreign policy is based on the two time frames—long-term and short-term. The long-term, in which the situation can only be sketched in very broad terms. The long-term policy considerations are based on historic or ideological factors. The short-term often involves problems and crisis management. The dynamic circumstances affect short-term policy.

A large portion of foreign policy making is concerned with day to day problem solving as issue arise at home and abroad. Diplomats and foreign office officials are normally concerned with immediate mundane matters of narrow scope. However most governments also have some objectives that want to achieve. The objectives may be very specific, relating to a particular problem or general. Sometimes the term "national interest" has been used (or abused) as a device for analysing nation's objectives.

The idea of national interest may refer to some ideal set of purposes which a nation should seek to realize in the conduct of its foreign relations. In this sense the national interest may be regarded as those purposes which the nation, through its leadership, appears to pursue persistently through time. Apart from national interests, a foreign policy can also have 'core' interests and values. They are usually stated in the form of basic principles of foreign policy. 'Core' interests and values are most frequently related to the preservation of a political unit. There are short range objectives also which nations want to achieve in a short period.

The major four principals have played role in determining the foreign policy of India. They are national security, economic betterment, domestic politics and external interaction.

The demands of each of these four principal determinants of a sound foreign policy may conflict with each other. During the cold war, for instance, India's defence requirements called for close cooperation with the USSR, whereas our economic progress might have been better through greater cooperation with the west.

GEO-POLITICAL FACTOR IN INDIAN FOREIGN POLICY

The foreign policy and relations of India with its

neighbouring countries are determined by a number of factors. Geography is the foremost determinant of Indian foreign policy.

Foreign policy of a nation is determined by internal and external factors. In the category of internal determinants geo-politics is one factor among others such as economics, ideological and personality. India's strategic location in South Asia gives her a central position in Asian politics. Geo-politically India is in a strategic part of South Asia, set in the centre of Indian Ocean with intimate past and present connections with West Asia, South East Asia and Central Asia. Geography and geo-politics is important determinant of Indian foreign policy.

India's strategic location has placed it within easy reach of many sensitive areas including China, South-East Asia, West and centre Asia. India is surrounded with big powers like China and Russia on the one side and on the other hand Pakistan, Nepal, Bhutan, Sri Lanka and Bangladesh, Maldives are her small neighbouring countries. India has to maintain good relations with these countries. India is a sub-continent regional power among these small countries. It has to operate its foreign policy like this that it is protecting their neighbour's national interests also, not her interests only. India shows by her all actions that she is not trying to dominate their neighbours or interfering in their domestic affairs.

This strategic location makes it imperative for Indian foreign policy to work for closer and greater economic, social, cultural and political cooperation with other regional nations. It has a strong bearing upon India's security. Also India wants that no third party or big powers should come immediate interfere in this Indian sub-continent as this will be the direct threat to India. That's why India always is in the favour of peace and development of this region, trade and commerce within the region and regional cooperation between nations e.g. India wants to make SAARC more powerful and wanted to give birth to BIMSTEC. India's strategic location also make it a main trade route of land and sea. If we want to do trade with Far East we have to cross Indian Ocean. So India has got strategic location in South Asia. On the other hand, old land trade silk route was from Constantinople to China which should be revived again for cordial relations with Central Asia.

India's national interests are inseparably linked up with the Indian Ocean for the free trade and commerce. That's why Indian foreign policy's aim is to keep the Indian Ocean as a zone of peace and away from foreign intervention and naval exercises. India is against US to develop Diego Garcia as naval base. India's natural boundaries are linked with Pakistan, Nepal, Bhutan, Bangladesh and China. India's long coastal line and its security compels her to maintain a strong, well equipped, modern naval force.

The natural frontiers of the Great Himalayas and the Indian Ocean and the snow clad Himalayas make possible the entry of infiltrators from the Kashmir and sea side into India. The Siachen dispute is also the result of geo-politics. The construction and opening of the Karakoram highway by China-Pakistan is the security threat to India.

The defence of Himalayan frontier is a big factor in Indian security planning. Infiltrators come in a large number to India from Pakistan and Tibet after crossing Himalayas and create big problems for India. Terrorism in India is the result of cross border-sponsored by Pakistan. We can not vigil strictly our long border of 1500 km with Pakistan. Kargil war is the result of infiltrators who crossed Himalayas in large number. Pakistan, Burma and Nepal border also gives ample opportunity for smuggling arms, haroin, opium and goods also which create internal and external threats to India.

Chakma's problems with Bangladesh is also the result of our natural border with Bangladesh. Bangladeshis come India in Tripura, Meghalaya, Bengal and Assam to earn and then settle down in these states and now it is difficult to differentiate them with natives. Home Ministers asked time to time that these illegal Bangladeshis should quit India immediately. These illegal people are main irritant in Indo-Bangla relations. Same case is with the Tibetans. We gave Dalai Lama political asylum and from then many Tibetans are regularly coming India and do protest against Chinese policies, this caused irritants in Indo-China relation.

Importance of normal and good relations with Nepal and Bhutan is largely due to be their belongingness to the Himalayan kingdom. Law, disorder and extremist activities of Maoists is a worry for India. The importance of relations with Nepal and Bhutan has been largely due to their strategic location in the Himalayas. After 1962, India realised the importance of these Himalayan states. The influence of Himalayan frontier was clearly reflected in the speech of Nehru in 1961, when he observed, "If it is breached, the way to Indian plains and ocean beyond would be exposed and the threat to India would then likewise be a threat to the other countries of South and South East Asia. India's determination to resist aggression and retain her territorial integrity is therefore, a vital factor in the safeguarding of peace and stability throughout this whole area.

GOOD RELATIONS WITH NEIGHBOURS IS IMPORTANT

The neighbours of India are strategically important for India as K.M. Pannikar said:

> "India like every big power has her own area of primary and strategic importance around her intrusion into which by a foreign power would be considered by India as a threat to her own safety and this area included Nepal, Burma and in a way Sri Lanka. India had made it clear to the big powers that she would not tolerate their interference into the affairs of these countries."

Though India's foreign policy interests have a global dimension, but the sound relations with our immediate neighbours is the starting point. To that is linked our security, our prestige, our economy, our stability. It is a necessary pre-condition for a meaningful role on the wider international stage. Know thy neighbour is the first dictum of a successful foreign policy.

Nehru's Speech broadcasted on September 2, 1946 after the Installation of the Provisional Government is a reflection of India's friendly foreign policy:

> "We hope to develop close and direct contacts with other nations and to cooperate with them in the furtherance of world peace and freedom . We are of Asia and the people of Asia are nearer and closer to us than others. India is so situated that she is the pivot of Western, Southern and South East Asia. In the past her culture flowed to all these countries and they came to her in many ways. Those contacts are being renewed and the future is bound to see a closer union between India and South East Asia. . . . We want to be friend every country so that our circle of friendship may grow and

become wide and cooperative and peace may thrive. What kind of friendship is that which envisages enmity with others? We should be friend all and stretch out our hands to all. . . . The preservation of peace forms the central aim of India's policy that is why we have chosen the path of aggression and non-alignment. We believe in non-aggression and non-interference by one country in the affairs of another.

Even before the independence India had faith in peace and friendship with their neighbours which was reflected in the Congress Resolution adopted at the Haripura Session of 1938. The resolution said:

"The people of India desire to live in peace and friendship with their neighbours and with all other countries and for this purpose wish to remove all cause of conflict between them. In order therefore, to establish world peace on enduring basis, imperialism and the exploitation of one people by another must end. We want to befriend every country so that our circle of friendship may grow and become wide and cooperation and peace may thrive. The preservation of peace forms the central aim of India's policy. We believe that each country has not only the right to freedom but to decide its own policy and way of life. We believe, therefore, in non-aggression and non-interference by one country in the affairs of another and the growth of tolerance between them and the capacity for peaceful co-existence."

The above principles were the exposition of India's foreign policy, made in a speech broadcast after the installation of the Provisional Government (September 2, 1946). T.N. Kaul, in his book "Diplomacy in Peace and War" beautifully analysed:

"We should avoid the mistakes as we made in Nepal and not take smaller countries for granted or act as their big brother. They are sensitive, even touchy on small things, proud and easily hurt. We must respect their sensibilities, honour their national aspirations and win their trust and confidence. They are subject to many pulls and pressure, stresses and strains internally and cannot bear these long without understanding and respect of a friendly neighbour like India."

POLICY OF GOOD NEIGHBOURHOOD

The Prime Minister of United Front government, Indra Kumar Gujral went for the policy of good relations with neighbouring countries in 1996. Gujral emphatically believed that there was a need to adopt a liberal attitude towards neighbours. Giving an interview to Frontline, Gujral stressed on regionalism as a major component in the foreign policy. Now Gujral was focused on neighbouring countries. He paid a visit to Bangladesh and admitted that relations with Bangladesh were the most difficult dimension of India's regional policy. Gujral also paid a visit to Nepal in 1997. India used track II and track III diplomacy in mending fences with Pakistan.

The BJP-led NDA government also emphasized on good relations with the neighbouring countries. Vajpayee took fresh initiatives in the form of Lahore Bus diplomacy and the running of Samjhauta Express. Sonia Gandhi called it a 'step forward in cementing the cordial relations between India and Pakistan and putting an animosity of the past behind them. Lahore-Amritsar bus service began on January 29, 2006, joined two proud cities of undivided Punjab. But the Kargil conflict in 1998, thwarted this peace process. The Agra Summit between General Musharraf and Vajpayee in 2001 also failed and relations between these two neighbours got strained. The cross border terrorism made the situation more worse.

But gradually the economic diplomacy took over political diplomacy. And now the India's relations with its neighbouring countries including Pakistan are taking shape. The key of this is mutual benefit.

REGIONALISM AS PRINCIPLE OF INDIA'S FOREIGN POLICY

One of the cornerstones of India's foreign policy has been to build a strategically secure, politically stable, culturally harmonious and economically cooperative neighbourhood. The foreign policy of India in the international milieu rest on the national interests which are the predominant consideration for any country. The first Prime Minister Jawahar Lal Nehru said in his speech in the Constituent Assembly on December 4, 1947 that the art of conducting foreign affairs lies in finding out what is most advantageous to the nation. This is precisely the basis of India's foreign relations.

The geo-politics of the sub-continent poses constant interaction between India and her neighbours. It imposes on India and other states too, friendship as a "geographical imperative".

India is a meeting point of East and the West. The India's geographical location makes it an important land and sea route for trade and commerce. Everyone has to pass through the Indian Ocean if one wants to trade from Europe, Africa and Gulf to East Asian countries.

India as a core country of the region has a vital role to play. For this it has to win the confidence and trust of its smaller neighbours.

INDIA'S REGIONAL POLICY: DEVELOPMENT AND DIMENSIONS

The Indian foreign policy, during Pt. Nehru's time had no place for neighbouring countries. It was quite ambitious. India wanted to play a bigger role in world politics. The Nehruvian approach did not want to join either of the two blocs. He decided to follow the policy of non-alignment and through it, India got opportunities to play a significant role in the conflict resolution. Nehru granted greater importance to international issues in comparison to regional issues. The cold war ridden world politics gave India's non-aligned attitude a prestigious standing at world level and a limited role to play in the region. India overlooked the needs and possibilities of strong regional ties and bonding.

In fact the British legacy of such-continent left a number of unsettled issues between the nations of the region. As a result, India had regional policy and perceptions. India's role in the region lacked clarity, coherence and continuity. On the question of Kashmir, India had no clear standing. On the MacMahon line, India did not compel China to clear the clouds. Tibet we just gave it to China on a platter. The tiny Himalayan states of Sikkim. Bhutan and Nepal had pre-conceived nations of India's big brotherly attitude and hegemony. These countries began to propagate that they were being over shadowed by India and that their identity, independence, and sovereignty were at stake.

Though India tried to consolidate its relationship through bilateral friendship treaties. But this did not reduce their threat perception. And they began establishing politico, strategic and economic relations with the extra regional powers. The cold attitude of Indian political leadership, lack of experience and maturity in India's diplomacy gradually created the climate of suspicion and ill faith which resulted into bilateral border and trade problems.

After 1962 India was compelled to review its foreign policy priorities and perceptions. As during the attack of China, India found herself isolated. No support was particularly received from the neighbouring countries. None of them condemned the Chinese aggression. After 1962 India laid emphasis on cordial relations with her neighbouring countries. With Nepal and Sri Lanka, India tried to improve its relations and follow an accommodative approach to some extent. But the major differences did persist between India and other countries. Especially Pakistan and India was deeply involved in conflicts over Kashmir and Sir Creek, India was involved in war with Pakistan in 1948, 1965 and 1971. The year of 1971 brought a dramatic change, as a new nation emerged on the sub-continent. Initially both Bangladesh and India had a very cordial relations, but the relations deteriorated with the time.

The establishment of military regimes in the neighbouring countries of Pakistan and Bangladesh, which India brought on the world map, had a very sharp differences with India. With Nepal also, India did not agree on its proposal of zone of peace which annoyed that country also. The question of Indian citizens converted the mutual understanding into mutual ill faith.

Under the leadership of Prime Minister Rajiv Gandhi, India's relations with Sri Lanka reached to a critical stage. India had to call its IPKF which she sent to Sri Lanka for peace keeping. In 80's India followed a policy of assertion and accommodation towards its neighbouring countries but could not succeed in gaining their support and faith on the regional and international issues.

DIMENSIONS OF INDIA'S REGIONAL POLICY IN RECENT YEARS

No doubt the sub-continent is India centric, but India does not want to dominate and manipulate the politics of sub-continent. In recent years India's foreign policy has become quite mature. The dimensions of India's regional policy can be described as following:

Strong Bilateral Relations

India has emphasized on strengthening bilateral relations with the neighbouring countries. India lays stress on the solutions of bilateral contentious issues through bilateral negotiations, summit, visits whether it is border or trade or river water.

Non-Intervention

India has followed a policy of non-intervention in the regional affairs in the post cold war era. India has preferred handling of internal problems by these countries on their own. This non-interferring policy of India has build up a climate of confidence among the neighbours. India wants that Sri Lanka should itself find the solution of its ethnic problem. It does not want to play any mediatory role. India did not interfere in the Nepal's domestic royal issue.

Policy of Economic Cooperation

India, a fourth emerging economic power in the world economy, can play a significant role in the growth of sub-continent region. India alone share border with all the countries of the region. So it can attain economic prosperity through greater economic integration at the regional level. India has shown interest in South Asia Union on the lines of EU during 2002 SAARC Kathmandu summit.

STRESS ON SUB-REGIONALISM

Recently India has shown interest in sub-regional cooperation. The BIMST-EC which involves Bangladesh, India, Myanmar, Sri Lanka and Thailand is given birth. It is against these historical back-ground that the sub-continent powers currently attempt to find a common ground for negotiations, agreements and treaties.

The interdependence of states has become a reality, but steps towards finding cooperative solutions to mutual problems have been small, hesitant and in consistent. There is widespread recognition today that the application of power has limitations because of the risk that conflict anywhere might lead to a confrontation and this might lead to a war.

National leadership play a vital role in shaping the relations. The leaders do have impact on the direction of foreign policy. It is essential for national leaders to be politically strong enough within their nations to arouse the support needed for appropriate action. Despite this, it is impossible to separate perceptions of a leader form the nation. An effective leadership steer the nation on a fairly consistent foreign policy course.

PROBLEMS AND CHALLENGES BEFORE SUB-CONTINENT

The Indian sub-continent belongs to a concept of Third World—a group of developing countries. Unlike other region, this sub-continent did not experience the full impact of cold war diplomacy and it has not been the theatre of deep conflicts and sharp confrontations of great powers. Though India and Pakistan had fought three wars but the major forces determining the relationship in this sub-continent are internal and emerged out of situations majorly following the partition of India in 1947 and disintegration of Pakistan in 1971. Minorly the problems of migration, infiltration, border demarcation, smuggling, arms and human trafficking are the results of no clear boundaries, which are the legacy of British India.

In the sub-continent, India is sharing common borders with Pakistan, Nepal, Bhutan, Bangladesh, Myanmar and Sri Lanka. There is no clear border with anyone so border disputes are going on with everyone. The border disputes are the legacy of British India, as all were previously part of British Empire. Britain had done the border demarcation through treaties, which are now not acceptable to these nations.

India and Sri Lanka are only a democratic state in the sub-continent. While Bhutan is enjoying monarchical government, Pakistan has military rule. Bangladesh has an elected government.

Decline of democracy is worrisome fact. India wants to spread and restore democracy in the sub-continent as military regime is pro-Islamic values and against democracy and human rights. India's basic values are secularism, democracy and mixed economy. It is against religious fundamentalism.

Socially it is a backward region plagued with poverty, illiteracy, disease and above all corruption. Most of the people are living under poverty line, which have no basic amenities. Illiteracy is the main hurdle in development.

India always says that it want improve her relations with all our neighbours. But statements are not enough, actions are more important. Trust deficit is the main reason for the conflicts in the region.

CHALLENGES BEFORE INDIA'S FOREIGN POLICY—DOMESTIC CHALLENGES

Foreign Policy of every country is a mirror reflection of domestic corelationship of social forces. If the state is a critical factor in political process, the foreign policy is pursued by the politicians, the bureaucrats and the army generals.

Indian Foreign policy has completed 60 years, yet it has failed in achieving its goals and objectives. Many challenges were are before it in the past and present. It need perspectives to face the challenges of 21st century.

1. Social Forces

Foreign Policy of India on the one hand has been hijacked by dominant classes and social groups for the promotions of their immediate economic interests, on the other a new dimension has been added by the emergence of the forces of Hindutva in the political process of India. From Babri Masjid to protest against visit of Pope to Godhra and to conversion. The forces of Hindutva have brought to the international focus the issue of status of minorities and Human Rights in plural society of India.

2. Political Instability and Weak Leadership

An internally fragile, unstable, fragmented coalitional political process cannot face the new challenges of the emerging new world order.

3. Power Challenge

In the present international system a country without power—whether economic, military or technological is in no position to play an active role. India has failed to become power.

4. Identity Problem

India failed to acquire power commensurate to its size and capacity. This irrational behavior of India with all its smaller neighbouring states has developed a mixed feeling of fear into its neighbours. They have become suspicious of India's size, potential and its lack of will to acquire power. Some of India's neighbours bringing the influence of external powers into the sub-continent. India's identity problem is whether it is a major power and actor with initiative in the international system or a medium power subject to the pressures and pulls of other major powers.

5. Kashmir and Pakistan

Solution of Kashmir issue and normal relations with Pakistan is a big challenge before Indian foreign policy. Pakistan is a big threat to its peace and internal security.

EXTERNAL CHALLENGES BEFORE INDIAN FOREIGN POLICY

Today Indian foreign policy is facing many external challenges and threats—border violations, internal disorders and subversive acts, economic, techno and scientific threats etc. The mass border crossing of foreign nationals from Bangladesh, Pakistan, Nepal and Sri Lanka have changed the demography of India. This demographic changes deteriorate law and order situation in the country and helps spying and espionage against the country and provides the base for terrorists and other nationals engaged in subversive activities. Many terrorist organizations like LTTE, PWG, Harkat-ul-Ansar, J-e-M, Hurriat, Jammu Kashmir Liberation Front and others are engaged in internal crimes and sustained subversive actions like serial blasts, hijacking, mass killing of pilgrims and massacres of people in the name of revolutionary action against bourgeoise exploiters.

Securing our boundaries is as important as securing our democratic values, culture, natural resources and trade and economic interests which are based on the correct balance of our foreign policy. A wrong foreign policy can jeopardize national security. Indian national security has been under threat in the past. We should be come over the threat perception without military power, the economic development can be snatched away from us. The state of north-east states and Jammu and Kashmir, terrorism and separatism are the complex issues of our foreign policy.

To get the techno scientific know how is the demand of time to develop India's technical and scientific capacity. Cooperation in frontier areas like 'PSLVs', remote sensing, weather and seismic forecast, nuclear and non-conventional power generation technologies, nano technology, artificial blood, genetic engineering, etc. is beneficial for India in particular and humanity in general. For this we need collaboration for establishing close ties with advanced countries as well as neighbouring countries.

Economically also we are facing many challenges in the area of trade and commerce.

INDIA-PAKISTAN RELATIONS : IRRITANTS AND PROSPECTS OF PEACE

Foreign policy of a nation is determined by many factors e.g. geography and history then comes is economic and commercial needs. A nation can choose its friends, but cannot choose its neighbours. Thus Geography is the mother of diplomacy. Since independence the relations between Pakistan and India are always bitter. India and Pakistan are two nations that have experienced war with each other in 1947 over Kashmir, the Punjab border area in 1965 and the Multan-Sind-Kutch region in 1971 and a conflict in Kargil region. The Indo-Pakistan relations are a big threat to South Asian region. Further the nuclear proliferation of these two countries have endangered the security of South Asia. Both India and Pakistan are the victims of history.

INDO-PAKISTAN RELATIONS IN HISTORICAL PERSPECTIVE

During the period of 1947-65, many problems and issues were raised which determined the nature of Indo-Pakistan relations. After the partition, about 12 million migrated from Pakistan to India and India to Pakistan, as Pakistan decided to be an Islamic republic and India as a secular state. The influx of refugees became an important reason for communal riots and later on for December 1977 war between India and Pakistan. The problem of recovery or compensation for the abandoned properties of the refugees was also related with the problem of migration. In April 1955, an agreement was signed at Karachi and the dispute related to immovable property was resolved. In January 1956, the two governments agreed for the transfer of evacuee Bank Accounts, Lockers and Safe Deposits. The division of assets and trade relations too kept the Indo-Pakistan relations tense and strained. The river water dispute over Indus, Sutlej, Beas and Ravi resulted into Indus Water Treaty of 11 September 1960. The Treaty gave India the full right to utilise the waters of three rivers Sutlej, Beas and Ravi and accepted the right of Pakistan to use the waters of Jhelum, Chinab and Indus.

In 1965 Pakistan attempted a military solution of Kashmir through its attack on India in September 1965. On September 23, 1965 both accepted the UNSC resolution for cease fire after 18 days war.

After the war the Soviet Russia offered her land (Tashkent) for holding negotiations for peaceful settlement of differences. After a series of meetings from 4 to 10 January, 1966, the two leaders Zulfikar Ali Bhutto and Lal Bahadur Shastri signed on the Tashkent declaration. But it could not change the stance of India and Pakistan over the Kashmir issue.

The development of crisis in East Pakistan led to December 1971 war of liberation of Bangladesh and Bangladesh came as an independent sovereign state on the world map.

THE IRRITANTS IN INDO-PAKISTAN RELATIONS

- Kashmir
- Siachen
- Sir Creek
- Wullar Barrage/Tulbul Project
- Iran-Pakistan-India Gas Pipeline
- Cross Border Terrorism

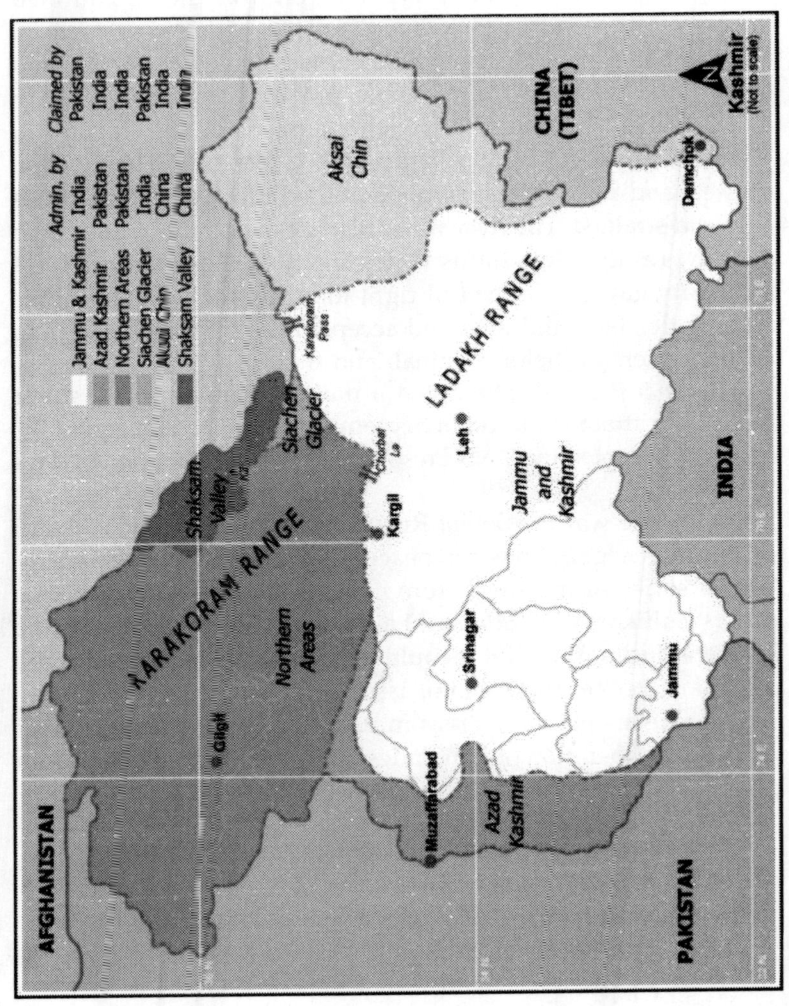
Admin. by Claimed by
Jammu & Kashmir India Pakistan
Azad Kashmir Pakistan India
Northern Areas Pakistan India
Siachen Glacier India Pakistan
Aksai Chin China India
Shaksam Valley China India
AFGHANISTAN
PAKISTAN
INDIA
CHINA (TIBET)
Aksai Chin
Karakoram Pass
Siachen Glacier
Shaksam Valley
KARAKORAM RANGE
Northern Areas
Gilgit
Muzaffarabad
Azad Kashmir
Srinagar
Jammu
Jammu and Kashmir
Kargil
Leh
LADAKH RANGE
Demchok
Kashmir
(Not to scale)

I. Kashmir : The Core Issue

Accession of Kashmir to India

On August 15, 1947 India became independent and in accordance with the Cabinet Mission Plan of May 1946 the state of Jammu and Kashmir like any other native state, had the option of "entering into a federal" relationship with the successor government or governments in British India or failing this, entering into particular political arrangements with it or them. But following an invasion of his state by tribesmen from Pakistan, Maharaja Hari Singh sought help from India and signed an Instrument of Accession on October 26, 1947. Lord Mountbatten, the Governor General of India indicated his acceptance in the following words: "I do hereby accept this Instrument of Accession, dated this twenty-seventh day of October nineteen hundred and forty-seven."

This Instrument of Accession was in no way different from those executed by some 500 other states. It was unconditional, voluntary and absolute. It bound the state of Jammu and Kashmir and India together legally and constitutionally. The execution of the Instrument of Accession by the Maharaja and its acceptance by the Governor General finally settled the issue of accession of the State of Jammu and Kashmir in India.

To drive the invaders out of the state now became the task of the Dominion of India and the request and warnings by the Government of India to the Government of Pakistan to deny assistance and bases to the invaders met with no response. India, therefore, decided to lodge a complaint to the Security Council against Pakistan by invoking Article 35 of the charter of United Nations.

On January 27, 1948, India and Pakistan submitted draft proposals to the President of the Security Council on the appropriate methods of solving the Kashmir dispute. In this proposal India agreed to the holding of a plebiscite in Kashmir as the ultimate determinant of Kashmir's status as soon as peace has been restored.

But the plebiscite was never held because according to India, Pakistan did not withdraw its troops which was a pre-requisite for holding the plebiscite. Pakistani troops and tribesmen did not vacate the territory. Thus the cease-fire of January 1, 1949 was of no avail. India did not succeed getting the territory vacated even now.

After the execution of the Instrument of Accession on 27 October, 1947, and adoption of the Indian Constitution on 26

January 1956 the state of Jammu and Kashmir was irrevocably brought under the territorial and constitutional jurisdiction of India. A special provision, Article 370, was made for it in the Indian Constitution. Article 370 enjoined it with special status and autonomy with its own flag and constitution. The centre had control over three subjects-defence, foreign affairs and communication.

The Kashmir, was a part of India, quite lawfully, was even admitted by the US representative, Warren Austin, in the security council on February 4, 1948, "With the accession of Jammu and Kashmir to India this foreign sovereignty (of Kashmir) went over to India and is exercised by India and that is why India happens to be here as a petitioner." It is noteworthy that the Kashmir dispute did not arise from the partition process. There is no conflict of jurisdiction over Jammu and Kashmir Pakistan acquired a locustandi in Kashmir by virtue of its aggression. Nawaj Sharif once described Kashmir as the unfinished business of 1947.

Pakistan's Standing on Kashmir

- It considers the acquisition of Jammu and Kashmir the unfinished project of partition.
- Pakistan's claim to Kashmir is firmly rooted in the two nation theory.
- It desires to invalidate the provisions of the India Independence Act and the Instrument of Succession.
- To organise international interaction and pressure on India to make India cede Jammu and Kashmir to Pakistan through some process of international arrangement or UN resolutions.
- It is in the favour of plebiscite, as it still considers Kashmir a disputed territory and not part of either India or Pakistan. Its final disposition is to be accomplished through a UN conducted plebiscite.
- The Line of Control as stated by the Simla Pact is not a permanent arrangement-Line of Control is not an international boundary.
- The wishes of the people of Jammu and Kashmir are in favour of Pakistan and consulting the wishes of the majority is a democratic and secular principle, not a communal one.

- Pakistan from the very beginning is propagating the theory that Kashmiries wants 'azadi' from India. Kashmir should be given the right of self-determination to opt either to join India or Pakistan. Islamabad's contention is that this right the people of Kashmir given under UN resolutions.

Successive governments of Pakistan including the present one, have believed that Pakistan objectives would be met by a combination of covert military operations, support to the terrorist operations (Jehad) and international pressure, intervention or mediation. Prime Minister Nawaj Sharif described terrorist activities in Kashmir as a "legitimate struggle for freedom".

Pakistan does not accept India's interpretation of the Simla Agreement that all outstanding problems between the two countries should be resolved only bilaterally and that recourse should not be taken to any other means. That is why Pakistan raises the Kashmir issue at international forums to seek a solution.

Important segments of the government itself and certainly its main political supporters indulged in strong anti-India rhetoric. In Pakistan, Benazir Bhutto's moves to normalise relations brought about allegations of being soft on India. To secure her position she has also resorted to bellicose rhetoric and talks about 1000 year war like her father Zulfikar Ali Bhutto. The question of relations with India is basically linked with the internal politics of Pakistan. When Pakistan found the central government of India weak, it raises the Kashmir issue to create the atmosphere of instability and anxiety in India. Pakistan military governments have made anti-India attitude and confrontation with India their profession. To get legitimacy in their country they use the Kashmir problem as a tool. It is an open fact that the Kashmir policy's architect is Army and not political leadership.

Pakistan internationalises the Kashmir issue against the spirit of Simla Agreement. It raises the Kashmir issue at UN meetings. Pakistan newspapers are filled with reports on Kashmir and with advertisements in support of the "freedom movement" inside Kashmir. Also Pakistan approaches the Islamic countries to persuade them to exert pressure on the Indian government to solve the Kashmir issue on the basis of the UN Resolutions. Pakistan view is that the option given to the people of Kashmir under the UN agenda was to choose between India and Pakistan and India had occupied Kashmir "against the wishes of the people of Kashmir. So the fate of the people of Kashmir should be decided by the plebiscite. It is noteworthy that for Pakistan "self determination" in Kashmir does not imply an independent Kashmir.

Islamabad has over the years never really missed an opportunity at any international forum to speak against India's alleged violation of human rights in the Kashmir Valley. The Pakistan military dictatorship is always considered India a hostile country. The military rulers of Pakistan are always indulged in strengthening their legitimacy by creating a fear of Indian aggression and by justifying the need to strengthen the military power of Pakistan.

Indian Perception on Kashmir

1. India sees Kashmir as an integral part of India. India considers the Accession of Kashmir to India is like the annexation of Texas by the US. In 1844 the Government of Texas, threatened by the menace of predatory incursions from Mexico, requested the Government of the US to annexe the state. After the Kashmir accession, many elections have been hold in Kashmir and the people of Kashmir have given their clear opinion through these elections. In these conditions, the question dose not arise on the review of Kashmir accession. More over Pakistan has occupied a big part of it illegally.
2. India does not want any outside 'intervention' in the region. New Delhi has never looked favourably at persistent offers by Washington, London and even Tehran to mediate in the Kashmir dispute. As Pakistan can not see Sind or Pakistan Occupied Kashmir (POK) separate from Pakistan, India also can not see Kashmir separate from India.
3. Pakistan has been pressing for a plebiscite in Jammu and Kashmir saying the Kashmir people should be given their inalienable right to self determination. India has categorically told Pakistan that Kashmir is an integral part of the country and such actions tantamount to blatant interference in her internal affairs.

4. The Simla Agreement of 1972 is a positive development and should be used for resolving disputes between the two countries. India is against the internationalisation of Kashmir issue, instead it wants to resolve it through bilateral talks.
5. India has no interest in altering existing boundaries; we are a status quo power.
6. Pakistan should immediately stop infiltrations and terrorist activities in Kashmir as violence is no solution of any problem. India's relations with Pakistan can never improve as long as Islamabad continues to promote terrorism in India.

The urge for change comes from Pakistan. The fact remains that Pakistan had steadily extended its jurisdiction beyond the point where the LoC was left dangling. It unilaterally, drew its line not "north to the glaciers" but north-east to the Karakoram pass. It authorised foreign expeditions and even US maps showed the area on the Pakistan side.

No doubt, the whole state is legally and constitutionally an integral part of India. The dispute regarding Kashmir since 1948 has been that Pakistan has not vacated parts of India under its occupations.

It had agreed to do so while accepting the UN resolution of August 1948 which mandates Pakistan to vacate the state in its entirely, for India to retain its military and political presence in the state, and ensure normalcy, Pakistan aggressions across the Cease-Fire Line in 1965 and 1971 destroyed the UN resolutions and the Simla Agreement finally nullified it.

II. Siachen—A Cartographic Aggression

The fighting for control of this 75 Km long glacier is going on since April 1984.

Siachen is a politically explosive and militarily sensitive issue. For four decades now the two countries have been clashing for the control of this strategic glacier on the Hindu Kush. Pakistan intruding there does not wish to lose the foothold it has gained on these icy ridges. Although a full scale war has not broken out, the intermittent firings and terrible climatic conditions have taken a heavy toll of human lives. The casualty rates have been very high largely on account of the climate. The dispute created a war zone in Siachen.

The Siachen confrontation is the world's most insane, cruel, strategically absurd and highest altitude war. It is being fought at elevations exceeding 6000 meters over a dispute on an undemarcated border beyond a point technically known as NJ 9842 which is eminently amenable to a negotiated solution.

Lying between 3800 m and 7500 m above sea level the Siachen glacier, located in the Karakoram is the highest battlefield of the world. Siachen has immense ecological, geographical and political significance in South Asia. The area is rich in unique biodiversity. The Karakoram region is the 'water tower' of Asia.

Pakistan occupies the southern slopes whereas India occupies the northern slopes in Siachen. Neither India nor Pakistan showed any strategic interest in this region before 1984. The Siachen glacier was neither included in the cease-fire line drawn according in Karachi Agreement of 1949, nor in the Line of Control as drawn at the Simla Agreement of 1972. In both instances the line ended at a point known as NJ 9842. A summary verbal reference in the 1949 agreement said only that beyond this point the line went "north to the glacier". Going to the north-west of the Siachen glacier at Dzingrulma—as it does at present—the line moves from NJ 9842 through Bilafond, Saltoro Kangri, Sia La, Baltoro to join the central part of the Shaksgam area of Jammu-Kashmir which Pakistan illegally ceded to China. But if it were to go north-eastward of the Siachen glacier from Dzingrulma, the line would move on to join the India-China boundary between the eastern corner of Pakistani-ceded Shaksgam and the western corner of Chinese-occupied Aksai Chin. This is where the strategic Karakoram Pass is situated. India took umbrage when Pakistan chose to draw a line due north from NJ 9842 to the Karakoram pass and claim all areas west including Siachen as part of its domain. While India claims that all Siachen should be under India's control.

Put in another way, the LoC would, if it went north-east of the Siachen glacier, keep the Karakoram Pass out of the Indian-administered side of Jammu and Kashmir and within Pakistani control. After India realised this, and learnt of Islamabad's presuming to give permission to foreign expeditions in Siachen, it raced Pakistan to occupy it. Pakistani maps had begun to show it as part of "Azad" Kashmir.

It all began with efforts to promote Himalayan tourism with the result that Islamabad licensed climbers of foreign teams to the glacier from the Pakistan side from around 1975. New Delhi viewed this as a bid to establish an unwanted territorial claim.

Seven Indo-Pakistan meetings held on the Siachen glacier in the last 10 years—the last in November, 1988—have failed to persuade agreement. Since 1983 the troops of both sides are holding positions on the Saltoro ridge, which is west of the Siachen glacier.

A military confrontation on the Saltoro ridge is costing India for more than it does to Pakistan because of the terrain altitude factor and the much longer logistics line on the Indian side. It is therefore in our interest to end the military confrontation in the area as early as possible.

The core issue is here is not the withdrawal of forces, but the need to ensure that the frontier is accepted and treated as inviolable. This requires that the LoC be clearly defined and respected. The best way is to extend the LoC (agreed upon under the Simla Agreement). Lt. General M.I. Chibber once said that the glacier is of no strategic consequence. The only reason why India occupied the icy waste was to prevent what New Delhi viewed as cartographic aggression by Pakistan.

De-militarisation of Siachen, therefore only means that India would withdraw its military. The withdrawal of forces by both sides from their present positions along the Saltoro ridge, however can be achieved subject to a bilateral agreement on the demarcation of the line of actual control. This can be possible by extending the existing LoC.

III. The Issue of Sir Creek

After 1965 war, Pakistan claimed that Sir Creek (60 miles long estuary in the marshes of Rann of Kutch) half of the Rann along the 24th parallel belonged to it. India also claimed on it. India says that since the allocation, delimitation, demarcation and administration of Sir Creek have been a settled issue since 1914 and 1925. Pakistan should formally accept the mid channel boundary as the border. Pakistan's view is that the Green line of the map appended to the 1914 document (lying on the eastern edge of the Creek) should be transposed on the ground. India says it is unnecessary since the line is only a symbolic representation of the mid-channel boundary.

Pakistan considers the LoC in Sir Creek controversial. India considers the old boundary of Sind and Gujarat province international boundary on which there stands old pillars also, known by G-Pillar. But Pakistan is adamant that the international boundary starts with the land and watery area of Sir Creek is of Pakistan. India's Jawans are doing security round till G-Pillar.

With the exploration of crude oil and minerals in the area of Sir Creek, Pakistan is again focused in Sir Creek. It is oil and natural gas rich area. Also it is a rich area in fisheries too. Fishermen of both countries like the area.

India has proposed in 1998 that maritime boundary in Sir Creek can be marked from seawards, stalling from the exclusive economic zone limit and proceeding landwards upto a mutually acceptable limit. Pakistan's stand, however was that the maritime and land boundary issue would not be delinked but had to be addressed together.

IV. Wullar Barrage/Tulbul Project

The Wullar Barrage dispute arose when Pakistan objected to India's proposal to build the barrage on Jhelum at the mouth of Wullar near Sopore in Jammu and Kashmir in 1948 to make the river more navigable in summer and to regulate the discharge of water into Jhelum, which eventually runs into Pakistan. India says the Wullar project is for navigation purpose only. Pakistan says that it violated the 1960 Indus Water Treaty, India is not allowed to store the Jhelum's water. It also fears that the project would empower India to control the flow of the river and release large flows of water during hostilities. Pakistan is against the construction of barrage on the Wular, while India's concern is only of ensuring navigation.

The project is on hold since 1987 without any solution.

V. Tulbul Navigation Project

Tulbul project is an effort of making good the capacity of Mangla Dam on Jhelum river lost due to siltation and would also restore substantially the loss in Ralsi irrigation utilisation. India wants that during the lean winter months (December to February) the mean flow of Jhelum at Mangla would increase substantially if the water level in the Mangla reservoir make higher. Pakistan has already constructed Mangla Dam on river Jhelum with a live storage capacity of about 5.5 MAF (Million Acre Feet). But as a result of siltation the capacities of Mangla Dam has already been lost to the extent of 0.46 MAF and more would be lost in due course of time.

Pakistan had objected to India's taking up of the project on the premise that this was a storage work and that this was not permitted on the main stream of Jhelum river and that by taking up this project India isolated the Indus Water Treaty. According to India the controlled structure was not a storage work as defined in the treaty and India did not, therefore, violate it.

With a view to setting the issue bilaterally the Government of India took up the matter with Government of Pakistan in February 1987. However Pakistan put a pre-conditions for the stopping of work for having Government to Government discussions on this issue. Accordingly since October 2, 1987, the work is lying suspended. An expenditure of Rs. 18 crore was incurred by India on this project till the work was stopped. Above all the construction cost is raising day by day.

VI. Baglihar

There had been persistent differences between Pakistan and India over the Baglihar Hydro-electric project which is under construction on the river of Chenab in Doha district in Jammu and Kashmir.

Pakistan is against construction because it finds it against the Indus Water Treaty. Pakistan is also against the design of dam. Pakistan objection is that India after constructing the dam, will be able to collect more water. The secretary level talks even could not find a solution. Then to solve the deadlock Pakistan showed its readiness on the mediation of World Bank under the clause 9(2)(A) of the Indus Water Treaty of 1960. The treaty is on the distribution of water of six rivers which are flowing from India to Pakistan and treaty is convened by the mediation of World Bank. The World Bank told that it is not the guarantor of Indus Water Treaty. So it suggested to refer the dispute to a neutral observer. The World Bank appointed in 2005 a Swedish neutral expert professor Raymond Lafitte to give point of differences.

After 20 months of proceedings, Professor Lafitte has given his findings on those points of differences in 2007.

The differences over Baglihar now stand resolved by the neutral experts findings. India is claiming moral victory over the settlement of the Baglihar dam dispute where a World Bank appointed neutral expert has ruled that India had not violated the Indus Water Treaty. Pakistan, too has claimed victory since the ruling ensures that one of their objections—reduction of the dam height— has been upheld. It is, however, one of the rare instances where both countries have accepted a mediated solution to a festering problem.

VII. Gas Pipeline

The proposed gas pipeline from Iran to India through Pakistan, would be beneficial for the economy of the region. The five billion gas pipeline project may generate $ 500 million in annual transit fee for Pakistan. The 2670 Km pipeline will originate in Southern Iran, pass by Pakistan's Multan city and terminate at Bhuj in Gujarat.

Pakistan would like to pursue Iran Pakistan-India gas pipeline as a "peace pipeline" that would prove to be a stepping stone for ushering peace and stability in the region.

VIII. Terrorism—Pakistan War by Proxy

In the last two decades, Pakistan has emerged as the principal bully terrorist nation and main promoter of Islamic fundamentalism in the region. Its premier intelligence agency, the ISI attempted to create a separate Khalistan state in India. And from 1989 Pakistan waged an unrelenting proxy war in Jammu and Kashmir. The ISI ex-infiltrated trained terrorists back into the state. Pakistan spread a "hate India-destroy India" message amongst its own people. Their objective is to de-link Kashmir from India and grab it and this gradually has become its single most persistent political, military and territorial objective.

India has shown a map to Pakistan authorities in which the 46 places camps were shown where the terrorists are being given training for the activities of sabotage, killing, etc. Evidences, documents and maps are exhibited to the world also that Pakistan is interfering in our internal affairs. It is a open secret that with the connivance of the army a number of training centres have been established in different parts where Pakistan and other youths are living, given latest arms and training.

No man's land is existing between two countries, but there are many villages lying very near to border where to cross the border is just like to cross a lane. Pakistan utilises these villages and villager's huts as a 'Reception Room' for welcoming the terrorists who wants to cross the border.

IX. Drug Trafficking

Hidden behind this terrorism and insurgency is the smuggling of narcotic drugs which are bound for western countries, generally through Britain. India lies in the middle of the Golden Crescent (Afghanistan, Iran and Pakistan) and the Golden Triangle (Burma, Thailand and Laos). Terrorists engaged in drug trafficking have been increasingly using India as a transit point.

X. Militant Groups

The funds from these smuggling operations are being used by Pakistan to prop up militant groups in Kashmir. Though there are about 150 such groups, the main among these are just a few, the HM, JKLF, Jamaat-i-Islami, Muslim Janbaz force, Al-umar-Mujahideen, the Allah Tiger.

Of the 105 training centres set-up by Pakistan to indoctrinate the militants, 48 are in Pakistan, 49 in Pakistan occupied Kashmir (POK) and 8 on the Pakistan-Afghan border. Training is handled entirely by the Pakistan army and the ISI. There are many confessions by militants about their training in Pakistan.

For the past several years, Pakistan has pursued an aggressive policy towards India. Pakistan recruiting and equipping tens of thousands of Mujahideens and her agents infiltrate them into India. These insurgents are supplied by Pakistan with sophisticated weapons including AK-47 rifles, rockets, rocket launchers and now human bombs also.

The aim of the insurgents in Jammu and Kashmir is to secede from India and help Pakistan to annexe the state. As a result, India has suffered enormous losses and recently a war like situation in Kargil area. Thousands of innocent Indians and brave soldiers have lost their lives. The material losses are incalculable.

PAKISTAN'S GAME PLAN

The Pakistan game plan is clear. It wants to make soft noises with India, mainly to satisfy the international opinion and give the impression that it wants to have good relations with New Delhi but the military establishment and the ISI have instructions to keep Kashmir, especially the LoC, at boiling point. It would not be content to have peace in Kashmir because then the issue that gives the ruling establishment in Pakistan the reason to continue in power have little appeal.

The other part of Pakistan's game plan is to keep Kashmir disturbed.

The internal security of India deteriorated over the past two decades primarily due to "cross border terrorism" sponsored by Pakistan. When Pakistan realised that it could not win a direct war against India, it took recourse to cross border terrorism to destabilise India and spread terror among the people by exploding bombs here and there.

Islamabad wants to keep on disturbing the LoC. As it has done in the Kargil area, it wants to keep on occupying strategic points on the Indian side of the LoC. This helps Pakistan manage to occupy more land by disturbing the LoC and cut off as many strategic links on the Indian side as possible. During the Kargil war it obviously wanted to snap the Srinagar-Leh road link.

Islamabad "aiding, abetting and encouraging" terrorism in the Kashmir Valley is clearly a violation of the Simla Agreement.

WAR IS NOT A SOLUTION

Pakistan fought four wars with India of which three were directly over Kashmir in 1948-49, in 1965 and in 1971 and the last Kargil (1999) a covert war which has produced more casualties than all the others taken together. But no war could solve the Kashmir problem. But this is also true that any future war with Pakistan is unlikely to be localised along the border and within a limited theatre as was the case in the three earlier conflicts of 1947-48, 1965 and 1971. It is no secret that every successive regime in Islamabad uses the Kashmir situation to try and deflect attention from trouble at home and from its own debility.

But neither the people of India nor those of Pakistan want

war. Indeed the time has come for New Delhi to examine its policy in relation to Pakistan and to make it clear that while improvement of relations between the two countries is the obvious and desirable goal, it cannot be pursued at the expense of more vital national interests.

THE NEW EQUATIONS IN INDO-PAKISTAN RELATIONS

The new environment is marked by five features. *First,* there is a strong popular sentiment for peace in both countries and new stakeholders for peace have emerged. *Second,* there is a manifest sense in both countries that there is no military solution to the Jammu and Kashmir dispute or other problems. *Third,* there is recognition at both popular and official levels that neither country can achieve its full economic potential, or achieve prosperity for its people, while engaged in confrontation. *Fourth,* the two countries realise that they need to carefully manage their relations in a nuclearised environment. *Fifth,* globalisation is unleashing new dynamics and creating imperatives for cooperation, reshaping Pakistani and Indian political perceptions. *Six* positives have emerged so far from the diplomatic engagement of the last two years. First, the cease-fire on the LoC has continued to hold. Second, there has been unprecedented people to people contact. Third, two rounds of the composite dialogue have been completed uninterrupted; the third round started in January 2006. Four, a number of CBMs have been agreed to and implemented. The fifth positive is the willingness to discuss economic cooperation signalled by continuing talks on the multinational Iran-Pakistan-India gas pipeline project. Sixth US after 9/11 is soft towards India. Can this be consolidated and further enlarged?

COMPOSITE DIALOGUE

The composite dialogue means engage in dialogue to resolve political issues through talks.

On June 23, 1997, the foreign secretaries of India and Pakistan drew up an eight item agreed agenda for dialogue in a purposeful and composite manner.

The following eight issues are decided to be detailed with at the levels indicated below under dialogue:

1. Peace and security including CBMs : foreign secretaries
2. Jammu and Kashmir : foreign secretaries
3. Siachen : defence secretaries
4. Wullar Barrage/Tulbul Project: water and power secretaries.
5. Sir Creek : additional secretaries (defence)
6. Terrorism and drug trafficking : home secretaries
7. Economic and Commercial Cooperation : commerce secretaries
8. Promotation of friendly exchanges : cultural secretaries

The dialogues between the two countries were held time to time. But the consensus was not made on Siachen, Sir Creek and Wullar. In the mean time the December 13, 2001 attack on the Indian Parliament worsened the situation. But Delhi-Lahore Bus, Thar Express cool down the situation.

The 14 foreign secretary level talks . . . were held between India and Pakistan with no results. Discussions were held on CBMs. and peace and security. Since the 50s, the two sides have talked to each other about their problems but nothing is resolved to mutual satisfaction till now whether it is Kashmir, Siachen or terrorism

LAHORE BUS DIPLOMACY

The NDA Government head A.B. Vajpayee took bold initiative to improve Indo-Pak ties by starting bus service from New Delhi to Lahore in early 1999. Vajpayee himself traveled to Lahore on the first day of the service. This peace initiative was widely acclaimed as a move to bring the two estranged neighbours close in the interest of peace, security and development.

LAHORE DECLARATION

After a long discussion between 14 to 20 February, 1999 the Nawaz Sharif and Vajpayee signed on the Lahore Declaration on 21st February, 1999.

- give prior information of missile experiments,

- no attack on ships and planes,
- negotiate on security concepts and principles to ignore war,
- no illegal use of nuclear arms,
- no further nuclear experiment, and
- increase level of communication facilities.

The Lahore declaration says that the two leaders share a vision of peace and stability between their countries and of progress and prosperity of their people. They are aware of the need "to devote their energies for a better future." And they are resolved to take immediate steps for reducing the risk of accidental or avoidable use of nuclear weapons.

The Lahore summit has achieved much more.

First, the dialogue between the two countries has now been raised to the political level and will take place at three levels the Prime Ministers, foreign ministers and senior government officials record. The dialogue has now a much enlarged agenda, including discussions on security concepts, nuclear deterrence, disarmament, non-proliferation, WTO-related matters and information technology, apart from the perennial bilateral issues covered under the "composite and integrated dialogue process". This will help in maintaining the momentum of the dialogue.

VAJPAYEE DECLARED UNILATERAL RAMZAN CEASE-FIRE

On December 2, 2000 Vajpayee Government declared a unilateral cease-fire, for the holy month of Ramzan towards normalisation of relations. During the six month period of non-initiation of combat operations by the security forces, the militants had expanded their grounds network.

MUSHARRAF-MANMOHAN TALK

During the NAM summit in Havana both the leaders agreed on to set-up a joint mechanism to counter terrorism and to resume dialogue.

AGRA SUMMIT

Indian Prime Minister Vajpayee took another peace initiating in July, 2001 by inviting Pakistan President Parvej Musharraf for talks in Agra. Unfortunately Agra Summit proved a total failure with no results.

PAKISTAN FLEXIBILITY ON KASHMIR

In the SAARC Islamabad Summit both were agreed to hold a composite dialogue. Islamabad had said it is willing to look at options other than UN resolutions to settle the Kashmir problem but has no plans to abandon Kashmir. Now Pakistan wants to cash in on the feel good factor to create a peaceful SARRC.

Demilitarisation of the region, establishment of some form of self rule by the Kashmiris on either side and joint supervision of the border, no war pact are some of the proposals suggested by Pakistan time to time.

Parvej Musharraf offered to drop a 50 years old demand for a UN mandated plebiscite over Jammu and Kashmir and ready to meet India. He seems 'bold and flexible in an attempt to resolve the Kashmir dispute.

You cannot choose your neighbours and Pakistan happens to be India's. The destinies of the two countries are thus interlinked. Their was no option but to keep the dialogue alive.

The Indo-Pakistan relations are down since the blasts in Mumbai. The two leaders decided in Havana (17 September 2006) on the early resumption of foreign secretary level talks as part of the composite dialogue. They stated that the "peace process must be maintained". The joint statement said, 'The leaders decided to continue the joint search for mutually acceptable options for a peacefully negotiated settlement of all issues between India and Pakistan including Jammu and Kashmir in a sincere and purposeful manner".

MUSHARRAF VISIT TO INDIA

April 2005 was very important for India when India received two important leaders of two important neighbours. From 9-12 April President of China and from 16-18 April Pakistani President Parvej Musharraf invited India.

However he came to New Delhi to see the sixth one day match of India-Pakistan Cricket series, but he discussed bilateral issues with Indian leaders. Before this he came to India in 2001 for Agra summit.

Peace Process : Joint Statement of 17 points

- Both the countries are agreed on this that it is not possible to go back from the process of peace.
- Continue talks on Jammu and Kashmir.
- Increase frequency of Srinagar-Mujaffrabad bus service. Allowing trucks for trade on road.
- Search possibilities for starting new bus services—Punch-Rawalkot, Amritsar-Lahore to Nankana Sahib and other holy places.
- Consulate General at Mumbai and Karachi.
- Continue talks on Sir Creek and Siachen.
- Talks on pipeline between the petroleum ministers.
- Re-active of joint economic commission.
- Cooperation in gas pipeline.
- Organise quickly the meetings of Joint Business Council.

This was the third joint statement of two head of states during last 16 months. First joint statement was issued on January 6, 2004 by Musharraf and Vajpayee in Islamabad, second was issued by Parvej Musharraf and Manmohan Singh on November 24, 2004 in Islamabad and third one was issued on April 18, 2005 in New Delhi.

THE CBMs—NEED TO BUILD UP CLIMATE OF CONFIDENCE

The Confidence Building Measures (CBMs), the defecto solutions to international irritants, have played a significant role in preventing wars across the world. The CBMs have prevented tensions from escalating into war. The CBMs are the best pragmatic solution to the vexed issue.

India and Pakistan—the two nuclear weapon states need desperately to start discussing and adopting CBMs to avoid conflicts which can escalate into a nuclear war. We need CBMs to build trust between adversaries or we need trust for formalising CBMs. The Joint Study Group (JSG) do talks for CBMs to push peace process between the nuclear armed rivals. Mutual flexibility, should be displayed, which is very important for achieving success.

Nuclear CBMs

The next stage in the discussion of nuclear CBMs should be the deployment of nuclear weapons and the nature and size of the nuclear deterrent. Here one hopes that Pakistan would realise that what it should aim at is security and not necessarily parity. Because of the need of providing for the exigency of the threat to our security from China, it may not be possible for India to concede parity with Pakistan. Besides, Pakistan should also recognise that consistent with its commitment to no-first use. India would require a deterrent which is fairly well diversified in terms of its delivery systems. Finally, the two countries must start discussing mutual reductions in conventional arms which is not only essential for diverting resources for development but could determine the very nature and size of their deterrent.

Economic CBMs

The mutual benefit of a united economy for both the countries would be strong enough to pull down the wall of hostility that has come up between us. The effects of economic unity, of one market for goods and services, of free movement not only of people but also of capital can change the life pattern of many people. Faced with these changes, all artificial boundaries based on sectional, obscurantist divisions could easily crumble. The European Union is a living example of such economic unity among different nations. Admittedly, India cannot offer unlimited aid to Pakistan, as the West Germany did to East Germany. But we can offer a regime of asymmetric free trade and investment to Pakistan which can be of immense benefit for Pakistan, and potentially also for India.

If the European Union could make France and Germany, once traditional enemies, turn out to be close friends and partners why can not be India and Pakistan.

- India has produced 50 proposals for economic and trade cooperation, some of which are to open Wagha-Atari boundary for trade,

- extend relations in the field of agriculture, banking, IT, telephone, civil aviation and navy etc., and
- control piracy of Indian music and films, supply of petro products to Pakistan, grant MFN status to India by Pakistan.

The India-Pakistan CEO Business Forum has identified trade and investment, manufacturing, services and communications as cover key areas for enhancing trade between the two nations.

India has already granted Most Favoured Nation (MFN) status to Pakistan. Islamabad, however, has not reciprocated so far.

In simple terms, the MFN arrangement would mean that India would offer to Pakistan an immediate free market for trade and investment, in return for Pakistan doing the same for India, more gradually, say over five to seven years. This means that Pakistan should be able to export any of its products to India freely without any tariff or non-tariff barriers. Similarly, Pakistan will have free access to the Indian capital market, so that any Indian should be able to invest in Pakistan or any Pakistani should be able to borrow or sell shares to Indians.

At first, this may appear to be rather discriminatory for India, but the cost of that would be quite tolerable for us. We have accepted in India the desirability of free trade which we would like to achieve fully over a few years. It is a small price to pay for transforming our relationship. We are after all a much bigger country, and if weaker states of India can have free trade for goods produced in stronger states, they can also have free trade from Pakistan. Receiving cheaper products from competitive producers forces adjustments in the activities of the producers, but enhances the welfare of the consumers. Free access to products from Pakistan will only hasten that adjustment, and not distort or disrupt them.

For Pakistan, the benefits could be enormous, considering just the differences in the size of the two economies. With the opening up of the Indian market to Pakistani producers, new factories will come up in Pakistan, with new channels of trade, transport and communication. If these are also supported by new investments from India, they will lead to a much greater integration of Pakistan's economy with ours. Overt and legitimate trade between India and Pakistan has been virtually discouraged by Islamabad since 1965. The trade between India and Pakistan would reduce the transport cost and quick deliveries would lead to small inventories and less damage to goods in transit. If India and Pakistan allow free trade between them, they will have a combined market of 1.1 billion consumers, second only in size to China and an economy with a combined GDP around 300 billion dollars. A combined Indo-Pakistan market offers sever advantages crucial to attracting foreign investment such as low inflation rates, a good industrial base, abundant raw materials, a skilled labour force and modern financial systems.

It is argued that as bilateral trade expands and both economies progressively integrate, policy makers of both the countries will show the required political will towards amicable resolution of Indo-Pakistan disputes.

There is an enormous amount of talent in the two South Asian countries. India is one of the leading industrial nations on the earth, while Pakistan is technologically the most advanced and most skilled Muslim country in the world. India is ahead of Pakistan in reprocessing technology. While Pakistan has the edge on India in uranium enrichment. If we could pool our sources, in the same direction, there is no limit to what we would achieve. Infact the sky is the limit.

MFN is a small step with a great potential and kickstart for a composite Indo-Pakistan dialogue. MFN means no discrimination in trade India.

India has given to Pakistan tariff concessions on 393 items but Pakistan has provided to India on 248 items. However on 73 out of 248 cannot be imported from India as they are on banned list.

Currently Indo-Pakistan trade volume is less than $250 million a year. Indirect trade between two is through third countries like UAE and Singapore and cross border smuggling are estimated over $ 1.5 billion a year. This trade gives loss of revenue to both sides and higher costs of imports. Both India and Pakistan are members of WTO and a basic WTO tenet is that all its 140 odd number nations must provide each other MFN status.

From bicycles to textile machinery and automotive parts to consumer goods, Pakistan is forced to buy from a third country although these products could be easily sources from India. The

Pakistan government has kept these items under the negative list which entails items that can not be imported from India. There is a wealth of business opportunities for both the countries. Despite of being neighbours both the countries are unable to top each others mar bets. India and Pakistan can work together as a huge out sourcing centre for multinational companies. South Asia perhaps the only region left in the world where there is no regional trade specifically because of disputes between India and Pakistan.

India and Pakistan on 22 September, 2008 agreed to start trade across LoC on two routes, the Srinagar-Muzaffarabad route and the Poonch-Rawatkot route while a third one the Kargil-Skardu route is still under negotiation.

India's Trade (export + import) with Pakistan (and Sri Lanka)

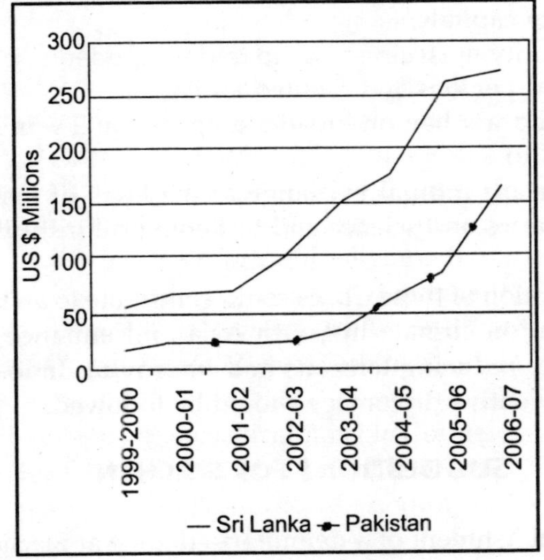

Opportunities

- Recorded trade between India and Pakistan low however trade through third country like Afghanistan, Dubai, Gulf States, and illegal channels is quite significant.
- Potential for intra industry trade exists in engineering goods, transport equipment, agricultural goods, Pharmaceuticals, chemicals and textiles.

Problems

- Absence of MFN status to India.
- Restricted positive list of items of imports from India.
- Non-tariff barriers in India
- Indian trade regime considered to be more restrictive than Pakistan.
- Politics

Cultural

Cultural exchanges and cross border movement improve the perception of the people about their common interests.

The Berlin Wall between East and West Germany had crumbled in the same way not by design, nor by militant up, but by the spontaneous using of popular will.

The two countries should relax the free movement of people with simplified travel documents. This will help people of the divided state to have one to one interaction which will help strengthen social, political and emotional bonds and people from both sides will tend to have stake in peace.

For people to people contacts we need—

- to liberalise process of visa, establish visa camps apart from capitals,
- priority in issuing visas to traders, students, journalists, aged persons and reputed artists,
- withdraw ban on broadcasting Indian TV in Pakistan, and to,
- increase mutual exchange at the level of institutions, libraries and science and technological institutions

The adoption of these CBMs could contribute to an improved non-proliferation climate in South Asia and enhance regional security while reducing tensions and improving Indo-Pakistan relations. Preventive diplomacy should be followed.

SUGGESTIONS FOR SIACHEN

- Establishment of a demilitarised zone at Siachen,
- Authentication of military dispositions,
- Delimitation of the LoC northwards of NJ 9842,
- Redeployment (i.e. withdrawal) of troops to mutually agreed positions, and
- Convert it into peace park.

Visiting the Siachen glacier, Prime Minister Manmohan Singh said that he wants to make, the world's highest and coldest battlefield a peace mountain.

Demilitarisation of Siachen will serve as a catalyst in the preservation of the Himalayas ecosystem also.

OPTIONS ON KASHMIR

A number of "options" have been put forward from time to time.

I. Since Pakistan has been violating the Simla Agreement in letter and spirit in recent years, one option is that we could revert to the pre-Simla Agreement position that is the whole state should be reunified within the Indian Union.

II. The concept of the LoC as the border was implicit in the 1949 cease-fire that saw all of Kashmiri speaking and Hindu dominated area under Indian control and Pakistan holding those that were vital for its defence. In 1972 India's suggestion of converting the cease-fire line into a LoC was the first stage in converting it into an international boundary. Given that neither side will give up territory voluntarily, the most logical step is to make the LoC the international border. Dr. Farook Abdullah also advocated that the current LoC be turned into the international border.

    It is unrealistic to expect Pakistan to accept such a solution unless it is forced to do so. We are in no position to force this solution on Pakistan.

III. A third option with the LoC as its border could be, to place the state on par with other states if the Indian Union, by abolishing Article 370. There is merit in the argument that the special status has been a major cause of the sense of separateness and alienation of the people.

IV. There has been some talk abroad of a fourth option constructed around placing the Kashmir Valley under a third party (UN) control for a specified period of, say, ten years, after which its final status could be decided. However there would be no legal, constitutional and political validity of this approach, it would legitimise expansionism through proxy war and terrorism. On the other hand, there is a high risk of a communal resurgence and violent backlash in the rest of the country. This is a risk that no one interested in peace and stability in the region, can even advocate.

V. These very reasons and more, will not permit the fifth

option that is, of a secession resulting from a plebiscite or other formula. This, of course, would be the optimum option that Pakistan would seek to enforce. The plebiscite, as envisaged in the UN Resolution of 1947 and 1948, has virtually lost its relevance as a solution to the Kashmir problem.

VI. The sixth option is to shift the LoC eastward, in what has been termed as the "James Had" proposal. This would call for a division of the Valley. Pakistan would no doubt opt for such a scheme since it would give it a foothold inside the Valley. But here is no rational or objective basis for such an arrangement. The state and its people are not just so much of real estate and commodity to be divided and redivided on abstract concepts.

The first option is in favour of India, as Pakistan is required to vacate the state not merely because the UN resolutions required it, but because its continued occupation of Indian territory is in gross violation of international law and good neighbourliness. The second option would only be a position of last resort and the others to be rejected outrightly.

TOWARDS NORMALISATION

- On 16 October, 2002 India had withdrawn those extra armymen who were deployed on international boundary after attack on Parliament. Now the position of army is as before December 13, 2001. Pakistan also announced of withdrawal of armymen on October 17.
- Exchange of news about nuclear centres doing it since 1992. Both the countries exchange news on January 1 every year according to 27 January, 1991 agreement.
- Revised shipping services protocol signed an accord on nuclear risk reductions in February, 2007.
- Established a noting between the coast guards of the countries.
- Pakistan has opened up the Katasraj temple for Indian devotees.

- India and Pakistan have eased restrictions in March 2007 on movement of each other's diplomats, allowing them to travel beyond the respective capitals without permission. As per the understanding, Indian diplomats in Islamabad can go to Taxila and Hassanabad (Panja Saheb) and Pakistani diplomats can go to Noida and Gurgaon.
- Bus service started on January 20, 2006 between Amritsar and Lahore.
- Thar Express started on February 18, 2006.
- Another bus service started between Amritsar and Nankana Sahib on March 24, 2006.
- India and Pakistan both are exchanging the informations related to nuclear projects since 1992 under the nuclear agreement of 1988.
- After the December 13, 2001, terrorist attack on Parliament, India cut off all air, road and rail links with Pakistan, From January 1, 2004 the flights resumed.
- India and Pakistan for the first time on October 1, 2008 allowed trucks to carry goods into each other's territory marking a milestone in direct trade between the two countries.

PRIME MINISTER SHOUKAT AZIZ VISIT

The Pak Prime Minister came to India for two days on 23 November, 2004. It was an important visit as after a gap of 13 years, a Pakistan Prime Minister paid a visit to India after Nawaj Sharif visit in 1991. Prime Minister Manmohan Singh made clear that any change in boundaries is not acceptable to India. The Pakistan did not seem ready to grant MFN status to India. He linked it with the issue of Kashmir. The Pakistan Prime Minister stressed on to talk first on Kashmir. Iran-Pakistan-India gas pipeline was also discussed. Prime Minister said that Pakistan was determine on it whether India would not ready to join the project. The Prime Minister also extended an invitation to New Delhi Prime Minister to visit Islamabad which was accepted by Manmohan Singh readily.

TALKS ON KASHMIR

The fourth round of the composite dialogue between India and Pakistan held in Islamabad (March 2007) for two days at the foreign secretary level.

The talks were held on two issues of Jammu and Kashmir and peace and security.

Though they did not come out with a joint statement. But both were agreed to speed negotiations for an agreement on prevention of incidents at Sea; another to conduct quarterly flag meeting; a framework agreement on speedy return of inadvertent line crossers; conclude an agreement on no development of new posts and defence works along the LoC, and new border control guidelines on the international border.

India again stressed on that any solution to the Jammu and Kashmir issue would be with in the parameters of the constitution. If Pakistan looked at Kashmir as an issue of sovereignty/territory, then it would be a zero sum game. It could be done if a people centric approach was adopted.

NEED TO MORE CONFLICT MANAGEMENT TO CONFLICT RESOLUTION

On Jammu and Kashmir it is important that we how move from CBMs to dispute resolution. Parvej Musharraf has given three ideas on the resolution of the Kashmir issue—demilitarisation, reduction of military force and freezing of missile programs by both.

India has rejected it on this ground that its security needs cannot be linked to Pakistan alone.

COOPERATION IN EDUCATION

The joint commission working group on education met in Delhi on 21 February, 2007 and identified six areas in education in which collaboration would be possible.

- Exchange of books between NCERT and the National Book Foundation of Pakistan.
- Institutional linkages between India's UGC and the Higher Education Commission of Pakistan.

- Cooperation in the areas of economics, business administration, agriculture, health, law, IT, science and technical education.
- Joint workshops, seminars, symposia, seminars.
- Collaborative research.
- Exchange experiences of educational policy in both countries.

ANTI-TERROR MEET

During the September 2006 NAM meeting in Havana, Prime Minister Manmohan Singh and General Musharraf decided to put in place an India-Pakistan anti-terrorism institutional mechanism to identify and implement counter—terrorism initiatives and investigations.

In this process the first meeting on anti-terrorism mechanism was held at Islamabad on 7-8 March, 2007. At the meet India gave an another 'most wanted' list to Pakistan and asked for help from Pakistan in tracing specific individuals involved in the Varanasi blasts of March 2006. Pakistan was disappointed that India shared no information about the Samjhauta blast (February 19). Rather Pakistan alleged 'interference' by Indian consulates on the Afghan border inside Pakistan and India's involvement in the insurgency in Balochistan. India denied all these allegation saying India has nothing to do with developments in Balochistan.

After two days (7-8 March, 2007) of talks on anti-terrorism, at Islamabad, both agreed to meet every three months to review progress on terror cooperation. The two sides agreed to exchange information for investigations into terrorist activities and prevention of violence and terrorist acts in both countries.

TALKS ON SIACHEN

The Defence Secretary level talks was held in Rawalpindi in April 2007 (7 and 8th April) on Siachen Glacier, Saltoro Ridge issue. Pakistan has offered a package deal and asked India a "time bound" troop withdrawal to pre-conflict positions as quid pro-quo. India has occupied almost all the dominating heights on the Saltoro Ridge since 1984 and would like to see international legal diplomatic safeguards before it vacated them if Pakistan changes on the agreement and moves its troops into the positions vacated by Indian troops.

Though both India and Pakistan agreed on the need to demilitarise the forbidding glacier heights way back in 1989, the exactmodalities for the disengagement and redeployment of troops has been the bone of contention ever since.

Despite many quarters describing Siachen as a "barren frozen wasteland" India considers it to be vitally important strategically.

IRAN-PAKISTAN-INDIA (IPI) GAS PIPELINE

Proposed gas pipeline from Iran to India through Pakistan, which would be beneficial for the economy of the region. The 5 billion gas pipeline project may generate $ 500 million in annual transit fee for Pakistan. The 2670 Km pipeline will originate in Southern Iran, pass by Pakistan's Multan city and terminate at Bhuj in Gujarat.

Pakistan would like to pursue Iran Pakistan-India gas pipeline as a "peace pipeline" that would prove to be a stepping stone for ushering peace and stability in the region.

In the first week of April 2007, Indian Petroleum Minister Murli Deora went to Pakistan to sort out differences over transit fee for the $ 7 billion IPI gas pipeline. The transit fee reorained a theory issue between the two countries.

Iran wants to sell natural gas to India and Pakistan at $ 4.93 per million British thermal unit (Btu at $ 60 per barrel crude oil price). Pakistan wants a transit fee of per cent 0.49 per million Btu (10% of the gas price) and a transportation tariff of $ 1.57 per mBtu, making the delivered price of gas at India-Pakistan border per cent 7 per mBtu. Islamabad had sought 10% of the gas price as transit fee to deliver the gas at Pakistan-India border to provide right of way, security and safety to the pipeline as well as taxes and other expenses. While India is willing to pay a maximum of 15 cents per mBtu.

India wants Pakistan to take into consideration the fact that Islamabad would also utilise the gas from the same pipeline and any calculation of transit fee should take this into consideration. Since Pakistan itself will be a beneficiary of the pipeline it should not ask for transit changes higher than international rates.

The IPI is an Asian energy lifeline for wheeling natural gas from Iran through an overland pipeline.

Difference on SAFTA

Pakistan's non-compliance with SAFTA provisions has created differences between India and Pakistan in the field of trade. According to India, Pakistan is isolating the SAFTA by continuing to allow India access for only a small number of duty-free goods. India wants a larger positive list of goods from Pakistan.

US FACTOR IN INDO-PAKISTAN RELATIONS

US Kashmir Policy

The Kashmir policy of United States is a significant part of American diplomatic strategy in South Asia. However initially United States accepted the validity of Kashmir accession to India on 27 October, 1947. But later on under the pressure of cold war politics changed its stand. The United States accepted the view following the United Nation's resolution of January 17, 1948 that the accession was incomplete and Kashmir was a disputed territory.

United States aims behind supporting Pakistan lay in its cold war politics strategy in South Asia. It realised the importance of Pakistan for its geo-political location for establishing air bases for countering the USSR. Pakistan becomes the partner and ally of United States by becoming the member of SEATO and CENTO (originally Baghdad Pact) and need military aids and weapons from the United States. Under these pacts, Pakistan got the military aid immensely and were used against India during 1965 and 1971 war. United States aid to Pakistan was responsible for armament in South Asia.

The United States helped to pass resolution on Kashmir-United Nation Security Council Resolution Numbers 47, 51 and 80 which embodied the plebiscite through which the final disposition of the state of Jammu and Kashmir to India or Pakistan be made. Above resolution could not passed without United States consent. On the whole United States Kashmir Policy is pro-Pakistan and meantime offered mediation on Kashmir which India is strongly criticising and rejecting continuously.

Change in United States Policy

From the early 90s, a significant change developed in United States in favour of India on Kashmir, although it was not fully favourable. In place of plebiscite the United States began favouring bilateral negotiations or by other peaceful means mutually agreed upon. It was decided that LoC, resulting at the time of ceasefire on 17 December, 1971, should be respected by both nations. In March 1991, United States cleared that the United Nations previous resolution on plebiscite in Kashmir were no longer relevant and United States now in favour of bilateral negotiations under a Simla Agreement.

Post-Cold War United States Kashmir Policy

End of cold war in 90s changed the internal scenario. United States again declared Kashmir as "disputed" with three contending parties-India, Pakistan and Kashmir. Pakistan sponsored terrorism is a main concern of India, but United States does not consider Pakistan a terrorist state. The attack on the World Trade Centre on 9/11 pressurise USA to take action against terrorism which resulted into Afghan war and attack on Iraq. But United States is not ready to consider Pakistan a terrorist state. Simply the United States-Kashmir policy is based on double standards.

America is adopting policy of appeasement. For economic purposes India is more important for United States and for strategic purposes Pakistan. The globalisation factor increased India's role for American economy and Afghanistan and Iraq war enlarged the place of Pakistan. America declared Pakistan as an important ally against terrorism.

There are three basic principles that govern the United States position on Kashmir:

- The United States considers all of Kashmir to be disputed territory on both sides of LoC.
- The issue should be settled peacefully between India and Pakistan.
- The United States is prepared to be helpful in this process.

The United States under Clinton leadership was willing to offer itself as a mediator, if all the disputants agreed to United

States mediation. The India is against the mediation as it does not consider Kashmir a disputed area but an integral part of India. The only significant change in United States policy is this that on Kashmir, the United States is no longer talking of a referendum or plebiscite.

Pakistan is always a most favoured nation for United States. The United States had designated Pakistan as major non-Nato ally in 2004. Pakistan has become a major United States ally after 9/11 against Islamic terror. India got only $85 million aid in comparison to Pakistan which got $700 million, while Afghanistan got $929 million in 2005. Pakistan whose economy is roughly $1/8^{th}$ of India's gets eight times as much United States aid as India. The United States fully backed Pakistan during all the wars against India.

Pakistan under the cover of its nuclear weapon capability which it had acquired with Chinese help by January 1987, launched a proxy war in Kashmir in 1988-89. The United States which knew that Pakistan had acquired a nuclear weapon capability, invoked the Pressler Amendment to deny economic and military aid to Pakistan only in 1990, after Soviet troops had withdrawn from Afghanistan in 1989. After a brief period of indifference, the United States again found itself supporting Pakistan. The United States expresses concern over Pakistan's involvement in terrorism in Kashmir but not willing to designate Islamabad as a state sponsoring terrorism. President Clinton had suggested a formula of four—Rs—restrain, respect for LoC, reduction of violence and resumption of dialogue for the solution of Kashmir problem.

Conclusions

It is clear that United States-Kashmir policy revolves around its diplomatic interest in South Asia. During cold war period, it has given open support to Pakistan. Post cold war era, known for world economy, has inspired United States to change the policy and it has started favouring India. Clinton had adopted Pro-Indian Kashmir policy. During Afghanistan and Iraq war Pakistan again become more significant for United States.

Present Kashmir situation is the result of various factors and United States is main factor among them. Military and economic aid of United States help to Pakistan and political support in

United Nations encourages Pakistan to internationalise the Kashmir issue and not to resolve it through bilateral negotiation. If USA stop to support Pakistan on diplomatic, military and economic front, should declare Pakistan as a terrorist state, then the Kashmir problem can be solved peacefully.

America raised voice for human rights in Kashmir. But United States must show its concern of human rights in Pakistan Occupied Kashmir (POK) also. If United States is concerned terrorism in USA, then it must stop Pakistan's terrorist activities in India and Kashmir also. United States must avoid its double standard Kashmir policy otherwise history never forgive it.

WHY PAKISTAN IS FOR PEACE?

Today Pakistan is in favour of establishing peace between the two countries. Why it is so?

- Pakistan use of terrorism as an instrument of foreign policy finally recoiled on them when 9/11 happened. US started anti-terrorism war.
- Pakistan adopting wrong priorities, has look out in terms of economic growth as well as social and political advancement. Pakistan development depends on peaceful interaction with South Asia.
- Pakistan geo-strategic importance cross out of its proximity to the three largest nations of the world—China, India and USSR and its commanding the oil sea lanes from the Gulf. But in a unipolar world with no active tension among these three major powers and the US, that geo-strategic location has lost much of its significance.
- Pakistan source of financial support is Saudi Arabia which is now under US scrutiny.
- US pressure was responsible for u-turn of Pakistan. Now faced with the US war against terrorism and developing international alignments, pressurised it to give up the policy of confrontation with India and embark on sub-continental economic cooperation is vitally needed to prevent Pakistan from becoming a failed state.

In an interview to Gulf News, General Musharraf said he wants to go down in history as the one who finally brought peace to Kashmir. But the real peace could mean not just the absence of violent conflict, but also a secure environment, prosperity for all, harmony between communities. Construction of peace could not possible without reduction of violence that has so deeply, scarred the Kashmiri psyche. Islamabad would stop using violence as an instrument of its policy towards India in Kashmir. The need to bridge the gap in perception and reality in India-Pakistan relations is essential in order to secure a better future for the two countries in particular and the South Asian region in general.

It is a need to create and develop the climate of confidence in these two trouble torn border states. India and Pakistan cannot be considered "friends", as the word is perceived in international usage, because they are "brothers" and "blood brothers". At times, brothers can squabble even fight. But they would continue to remain brothers. It is this perspective, we need to develop. "Bilateralism" has always a casualty in India-Pakistan relations. Problems should have been solved either through wars or peaceful negotiations without any role for a third party. The Tashkent Agreement of 1966 was the super power intervention at the diplomatic level. The Simla Agreement of 1971 was the only serious effort at "bilateralism".

We both need a vision larger than the sum of our problems. India's preference has been people to people relations, trade, economic cooperation, cultural exchanges, and so on. In each field Pakistan has a problem. A peaceful solution to the Kashmir problem through mutual consultation between India and Pakistan is the need of the time.

The confidence between the neighbours can not be generated unless the Pakistan's sponsored actions are stopped, including firing across the LoC, infiltration, tension. What is required of is first an assurance that Pakistan would not isolate the territorial status quo with violence and second condemnation of terrorist violence in the Valley and elsewhere in India.

HIGH AND LOWS IN INDO-PAK TIES

1947. Britain divides its Indian empire into secular but mainly Hindu India and Muslim Pakistan, triggering one of the greatest and bloodiest migrations of modern history.

1947/48. India and Pakistan go to their first war over the disputed Himalayan region of Kashmir. The war ended with a UN-ordered ceasefire and resolution, seeking a plebiscite for the people of Jammu and Kashmir to decide whether to become part of India or Pakistan.

1965. India and Pakistan go to war over Kashmir. Fighting ends after United Nations calls for ceasefire.

1971. Pakistan and India go to war a third time over East Pakistan, which became independent Bangladesh.

1972. Pakistani Prime Minister Zulfiqar Ali Bhutto and Indian prime minister Indira Gandhi sign agreement in Simla to lay principles meant to govern relations.

1974. India detonates its first nuclear device.

1990. Indian Army opens fire in Kashmir's summer capital Srinagar during protest against crackdown on separatism, killing 38 and spurring a revolt. India accuses Pakistan of arming and sending Islamist militants into Indian Kashmir.

1998, May. India carries out five underground nuclear tests and announces plans to build a nuclear arsenal; Pakistan conducts six tests of its own in response.

1999, Feb. Indian Prime Minister Atal Behari Vajpayee makes a historic bus ride to Pakistan for summit with Pakistani counterpart Nawaz Sharif.

May. The two countries stand on the brink of their fourth war after India launches major counter-strike against Pakistani intruders dug in on mountains in Kargil in Indian Kashmir. 2000-01.

July. Summit between General Pervez Musharraf and Vajpayee in the Indian city of Agra ends in failure.

Dec. Militants attack Indian parliament. Fourteen people, including the five assailants, are killed. India blames Pakistan-based Kashmiri separatist groups Lashkar-e-Toiba and Jaish-e-Mohammad

	and demands action against them..
2003 Feb.	Both countries expelled emboss odours from their countries.
April.	Vajpayee extended the hand of friendship. Historical declaration of Srinagar.
May.	Delhi-Lahore bus service reassured.
Nov.	Agreed for cease fire.
Dec.	Air flights resumed from January 1, 2004
2004 Jan.	Vajpayee-Musharraf meeting during SAARC Summit held at Islamabad.
Feb.	Re-start of Indo-Pak talks after a gap of three years..
Sept.	Meeting of Indo-Pak Foreign Ministers in New Delhi.
	Vajpayee-Musharraf meeting at New York during UNSC session.
Nov.	Initiative to reduce number of Indian armymen.
2005 April.	Srinagar-Muzafarrabad bus service started on April 7.
	Musharraf visit to India during 16-18 April to see cricket match.
2008, July.	India says Pakistan's ISI intelligence agency was behind a bomb attack on the Indian embassy in Kabul that killed 58 people.
Nov.	Mumbai attacks bring tension to its highest level since the weeks following the December 2001 attack on India's Parliament.

Issues and Dynamics of India-Nepal Relations

India and Nepal are two closely related neighbours, sharing a special friendship and multi-dimensional relations. Both are tied by geography, history, culture and religion with the open boundaries. "In language and religion, gods and goddesses, food and clothing, writes M.S. Rajan, "two countries have more in common with each other than with any third country of the world." Nepal is special for India, as Nepal is a Hindu state. The Kingdom has immense religious importance for India. It was in the context of these deep rooted socio-cultural interactions that the border between the two countries was maintained open. The Chinese aggression of 1962 have made India realise the importance of Nepal as a front line buffer state. Today India has open border with Nepal and both are the members of SAARC. Nepal's stability, peace, progress and friendship is vital for India's peace, stability and progress and on the whole for South Asia's peace, stability and progress. Being a landlocked country, Nepal is also interested in India for the trade and economic relations. The deep socio-cultural connections, economic interdependence and geo-strategic importance gives the uniqueness of bilateral relations.

No doubt, Nepal has a geographically strategic location but Nepal was historically never considered as a buffer state. The Britishers accorded Tibet the status of a buffer state. After Tibet

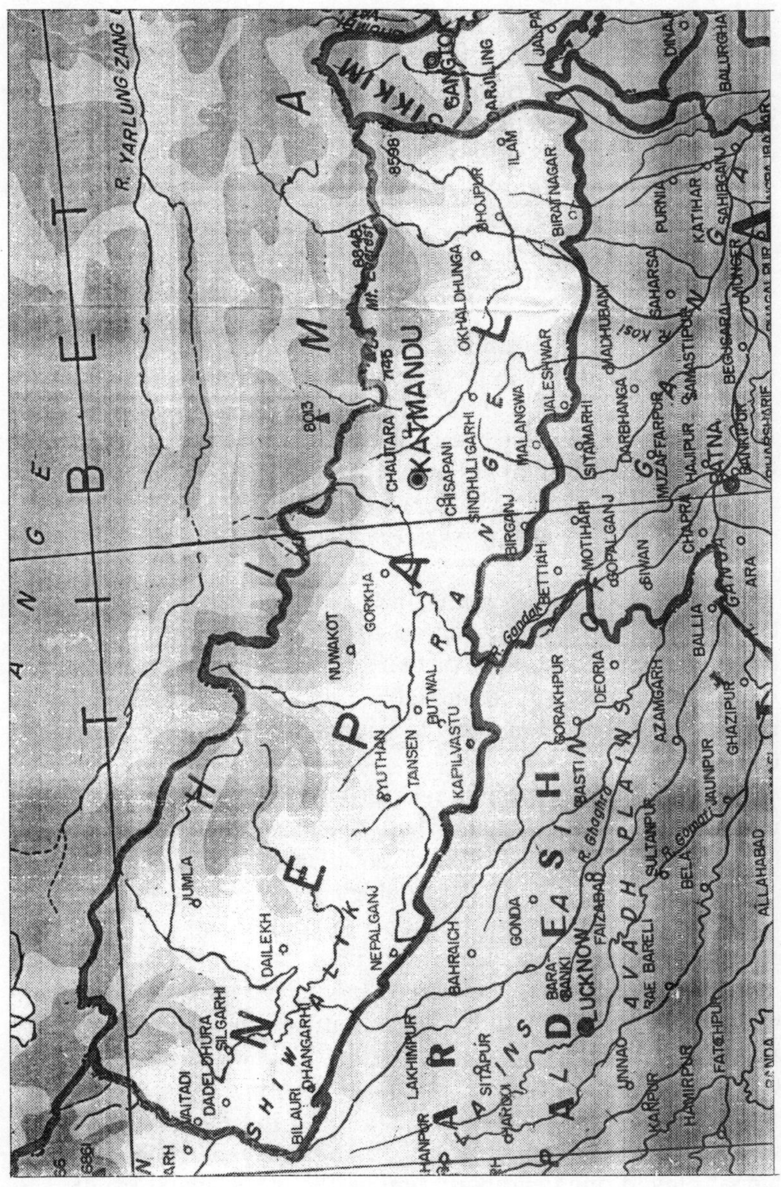
T I B E T
R. YARLUNG ZANG
N E P A L
KATMANDU
CHAUTARA
CHISAPANI
SINDHULI GARHI
OKHALDHUNGA
BHOJPUR
ILAM
BIRATNAGAR
JALESHWAR
MALANGWA
BIRGANJ
GORKHA
NUWAKOT
BUTWAL
TANSEN
PYUTHAN
KAPILVASTU
JUMLA
DAILEKH
NEPALGANJ
DHANGARHI
BILAURI
DADELDHURA
SILGARHI
BAITADI
8598
8848
Mt. Everest
8013
DARJILING
GANGTOK
SIKKIM
LUCKNOW
BARA BANKI
FAIZABAD
GONDA
BAHRAICH
BASTI
GORAKHPUR
DEORIA
AZAMGARH
GHAZIPUR
JAUNPUR
BALLIA
SULTANPUR
RAE BARELI
ALLAHABAD
SITAPUR
LAKHIMPUR
HARDOI
KANPUR
HAMIRPUR
FATEHPUR
BETTIAH
MOTIHARI
GOPALGANJ
SIWAN
CHAPRA
HAJIPUR
MUZAFFARPUR
SITAMARHI
DARBHANGA
MADHUBANI
SAMASTIPUR
SAHARSA
PURNIA
KATIHAR
SAHIBGANJ
BEGUSARAI
MUNGER
PATNA
ARA
BALURGHAT
R. Gandak
R. Kosi
R. Ghaghra
R. Gomati
G A N G A
A V A D H
S H I W A L I K
H I M A L A Y A
G A N G E S   P L A I N S

occupation by China, Nepal's border in the north has come directly in touch with China. This border is though natural and hazardous but not difficult to cross through passes in between the Himalayan ranges. China has direct access right up to the border with Nepal by constructing strategic roads all along. Thus Nepal occupies an important strategic position in India's northern security system. Nehru in his speech, had emphasised Nepal strategic importance thus:

> "It is clear that the interests of India and Nepal are inevitably joined up. It is not possible for any Indian Government to tolerate any invasion of Nepal from anywhere. It is not necessary for us to have a military alliance with Nepal. But apart from any pact or alliance, the fact remains that we cannot tolerate any invasion from any foreign country on any part of the Indian sub-continent or whatever you may like to call it. And any possible invasion of Nepal would inevitably involve the safety of India."

India has many economic interests in Nepal. Because of open border, Indians are playing an important role in economy of Nepal. Nepal's economy is primarily based on tourism only. It has immensely dependent on India. Nearly 90 percent of Nepal's trade is with India. There are many Indians who are running hotels and trade in Nepal.

The multi-dimensional relations between the twos have also made them uneasy partners. There is vast asymmetry between the two countries in terms of size, population, resources, levels of development, capabilities, technological advancement, etc. Nepal as a small neighbour has developed a kind of fear psychosis and an inferiority complex also.

As a result Nepal has often misperceived India's attitude towards Nepal as the Indian hegemony or India's big brotherly attitude. Hence despite so much dependence on India, it has tried to assert upon its identity and independence by way of going against India. The Indo-centric nature of the region and India's vastness against a small neighbour has played a negative role. Nepal played one neighbour against the other which resulted in ups and downs in the relations between the countries.

Nepal and Bhutan are important for India's security and its

defence needs, as these two are independent and sovereign states of the Himalayan region. Despite this, India's four states—Uttarakhand, Uttar Pradesh, Bihar and West Bengal are sharing border with Nepal which is open too. Any unrest in these Indian states can generate many security problems. Rise of communism in China and its successful assault on Tibet forced India to reconsider its northern security strategy. Making roads on Tibet border by China and recently linking Beijing to Lhasa by rail link have added a new dimension to India's security in the north. Increasing interest of US in South Asian affairs in general and Nepal in particular was also a concern for India.

Political instability in the state was and is always crucial for India for its own security considerations. In considerations of all factors, India and Nepal signed the Treaty of Peace and Friendship. The two governments under this treaty agreed to respect each other's sovereignty and independence to consult mutually on matters relating to security and exchange of information. It was also stated that Nepal will take India's assistance and agreement in case of import of arms from a country other than India.

Nepal-India boundary was demarcated and delimited after the Anglo-Nepal war of 1814-16. Treaty of Sugauli (1816) shaped Indo-Nepal border in which Mahakali River formed the western boundary in the east along with the ridges in the Darjeeling hills and Sikkim. The southern boundary of Nepal along the Tarai region borders Uttarakhand, Uttar Pradesh, Bihar of India. The Tarai is a transitional region between the Hills of Nepal and the Gangetic Plains of India. Most of this area is covered by agricultural fields, forests and river, so geographically it is difficult to distinguish the boundaries.

Since Britishers, the problem of border demarcation between Nepal and India is existed. In 1829 under an agreement the pillars were erected to demarcate the border between the border of two. But these pillars are destroyed with the time which created demarcation dispute between the two neighbours. The Tanakpur barrage and Kalapani issues are another border issues between two.

The open border is a source of intimacy and irritants both. While it makes people to people contact easy, it creates many problems also. India-Nepal relationship is a people-centric relationship and government should honour this traditional and natural bond. The Nepalese students always look towards India for their education. This is the most basic and widest people to people relationship built at an impressionable age. The Gurkhas serving in the Indian army are also a potential source of socio-cultural interactions between the two countries. The Nepal Himalayas have a religious importance and is tied up with India's history, tradition, faith, religion, beliefs, literature and culture.

THE UPS AND DOWNS IN INDO-NEPAL RELATIONS

The relations between these two Hindu nations have seen many ups and down, cooperation and differences since 1947. Following the old treaty of 1923, India, Bhutan and Nepal entered into a new treaty of Peace and Friendship in July 1950. Both of them gave recognition to each other's sovereignty and independence and agreed to hold mutual consultation of each other's national security. Neither country shall tolerate any threat to the security of other by a foreign aggression.

Respecting the sovereignty of Nepal, India forwarded all economic aid and help to Nepal for its development and economic stability, Accepting and respecting Nepalese monarchy, India never tried to impose democracy in Nepal. India took interest in Nepal's economic development, administrative reorganisation, social upliftment, restructuring of armed forces and political stability.

India's policy from Nehru time is to strengthen democracy. So India always wanted in Nepal that there should be no confrontation between popular elements and the army Royal to the king. As this confrontation would have an effect on India's security, due open border and the intricate closeness of people level ties between two countries. That is why Indian government have followed strengthening Nepal's small armed forces with support and arms.

In 1952 King Tribhuvan requested India to train and reorganise the Royal Nepal Army (RNA). An Indian military mission was established in Kathmandu, which stayed there till 1970. In 1963, King Mahendra asked India to re-equip the RNA. Then again in 1990, India undertook the modernisation of the force with a Rs. 500 crore equipment package. After the Maoists attacked the RNA in its barracks at Dang in 2001, the package was revived in a big way. The Indian Army's training and re-equipment assistance together with the formation of the India-Nepal bilateral group on security are the cornerstones of RNA's conversion from a ceremonial army into a counter insurgency force.

The Indian Army has 43 Gorkha battalions, almost as large as the RNA infantry. Besides, there are nearly 1,50,000 Indian ex-servicemen of Nepali origin in Nepal, who together with the families of serving soldiers make a strong pro-India constituency. The Indian Chief of Army staff is an honorary General in the RNA and vice-versa. In short, the military-to-military relations are long standing and abiding. One can say the RNA is a clone of the Indian Army.

The RNA is firmly loyal to the King. Its officers agree that they have not known democracy the way the Indian Army has. They nurse a 'healthy disrespect' for the political class. But despite a lackluster operational record, they have a job to do: to fight the Maoists, seen as a common threat by both countries. The Maoists are unlikely to seize power in Kathmandu any time in future, nor are they likely to join the newly formed Maoist groups in India and become a part of the Compact Revolutionary Zone from Nepal to Andhra Pradesh. Yet, they control 80 percent of territory in Nepal and have a political stalemate.

The supplies and training for RNA cannot be blocked indefinitely, as it would require new weapons and ammunition soon. Under treaty obligated and MoUs Nepal is obliged to seek arms from India. Should India continue to maintain the freeze on supplies, Nepal would be forced to seek weapons from China and/or Pakistan. Besides, we would lose the goodwill of the RNA and our leverage over it. It would adversely affect RNA's operational capacity and morale.

A change in Nepali perception towards India began to take place after 1955. King Mahendra had a soft corner for China. The anti-India demonstration and criticism of India's big brother attitude further deteriorated the Indo-Nepal relations. King Mahendra's objective was to reduce Nepal's dependence on India. He raised the bogy of Indian hegemony and began to provide a new thrust to Nepalese nationalism based on anti-India. Nepal persuaded a policy over emphasizing its identity and independence. The war with China in 1962 resulted in a considerable change in India's regional policy.

The non-cooperation from the neighbouring countries at the time of crisis, realizing India that it should give priority to regional policy in its foreign policy calculations. So India followed a reconciliatory approach towards Nepal. Nepal demanded the withdrawal of Indian telephone operators and security guards from Nepal-China border. India has to accept these without any alternative system.

During the King Birendra's time India's emergence as a strong regional power after the emergence of Bangladesh compelled Nepal to not to follow the policy of playing one neighbour against the other. During the regime of King Birendra in 1975 a demand for declaring Nepal a 'Zone of Peace' was raised. India found it against the Peace and Friendship Treaty.

Since 1955, the Nepalese had been raised the demand for withdrawal or revision of the 1950 Treaty of Peace and Friendship. But India finds it suitable for its security concerns.

In 1975, during King Birendra's coronation ceremony, the idea of declaring Nepal a 'zone of peace' was put forward so that no any country could use the land of Nepal for military activities. The world was with Nepal on this proposal, but India did not accept this proposal. It became an objective of the Nepalese foreign policy overlooking and disregarding India's security interests in the Kingdom. India was not in favour of this proposal. India's contention was that it already had a peace and friendship treaty which ensured protection of national interests of the two countries. In the absence of support of India, Nepal had to quit this proposal. Then Nepal started purchasing arms from China in 1986. It was a clear violation of the agreement of 1965. It was clear that Nepal was avoiding the security interests of India.

In 90s India's relations with Nepal started getting normal. In October 1992, Indian Prime Minister Narasimha Rao paid a visit to Nepal. With his policy of economic liberalisation, he encouraged Nepal's exports to India and emphasised on the need to accommodate Nepal's economic interests.

During the communist regime, after 1990, the Nepal Government put again and again the demand of reviewing the Treaty of 1950. Nepal considers this treaty based on inequality and irrelevant in present time, because of the changing regional security and political circumstances. India always consider the treaty mutually beneficial.

During the communist regime Nepal's Prime Minister Man Mohan Adhikari visited India in April 1995 and pointed out in one of his statements that:

> "With India our relations are more intimate at the people's level. As such it will not be proper to link our relations with China to our relations with India."

Nepal's purchasing of arms from China and ignoring India's security sensitivities made India-Nepal relations once again uneasy. Nepal introduced the Work Permit System (WPS) for the Indians who wanted to enter into a job in Nepal in 90s. In fact it made difficult for the Indian migrants to find out a job as the process of obtaining the WPS was very cumbersome.

Gujral visited to Nepal in June 1997. It was his first foreign visit after becoming Prime Minister. Many accord were signed. Both the nations confirmed the Mahakali River accord in which both the countries will complete the Pancheshwar hydro electric project in equal partnership. The civil aviation, Ruxol-Sirsiya rail project, etc. were the other successes of Gujral's Nepal visit.

During Gujral visit India accepted Nepal's long standing demand for an alternative trade route to Bangladesh through Indian territory in Phulbari. It was indeed a significant goodwill gesture on the part of India. On the issue of revision of 1950 Treaty, India agreed to initiate discussions. India tried to follow a policy of good neighbourly relations under Gujral Doctrine. Under the Gujral Doctrine, Prime Minister Gujral emphasized that India should adopt an accommodative attitude towards the neighbours and need not to look for the reciprocity.

In September 1999, Indian foreign minister Jaswant Singh's visit to Nepal developed a closer understanding between the two neighbours. The cross-border terrorism was the main issue of talks. The presence of Pak's ISI agents in Nepal with an objective to encourage terrorist activities in north-eastern Indian states were the main concerning issues for India.

Nepal assured to not to use its territory against India's interests. India also assured Nepal that the Maoist terrorists will not be allowed to use Indian territory for operating terrorist activities against Nepal. It is noteworthy here that both the countries has an extradition treaty.

Indo-Nepal relations were strengthened with the visit of Nepalese Prime Minister Sher Bahadur Deuba to India in April 2002. The issues of mutual concerns were discussed. India's main concern was the use of Nepalese territory for anti-India activities. The Nepalese Prime Minister assured that Nepal will not allow the land to be used against India. Nepal's basic concern was to seek India's cooperation in bringing the Maoist insurgency under control. India agreed to provide military equipment to Nepal government. India also assured Nepal that it would not allow Maoist insurgents to take shelter in the Indian territory. King Gyanendra paid a six days visit to India on 23rd June 2002 after becoming the king. He also pleaded for India's cooperation in controlling the Maoist problem in Nepal.

To make strong bilateral relations and to gain Indian support to tackle Maoist problem, Prime Minister Deuba came to India on a five days visit in September 2004. This was his last visit before the dismissal of his Government by King Gyanendra in March 2005. The main issue of talks was the Indian military aid, as Nepal was in dire need of financial aid and grant for purchasing Indian arms and ammunitions.

To encourage India's investment in Nepal, the Nepal Prime Minister addressed a meeting of Indian entrepreneurs. The agreements on the forecast of weather and cooperation in the field of culture and sports were also signed. India offered help in establishing internet facility in Nepal for weather forecast.

King Gyanendra had a program of eleven days visit of India, but due to death of ex-Prime Minister Narasimha Rao, he had to cancel his visit. Later on he was coming India on 23 December, 2004, but could not come as Indo-Nepal relations became sour on the dismissal of democratic government.

DISMISSAL OF DEUBA GOVERNMENT

On February 1, 2005 King Gyanendra, after dismissing the seven month old Deuba Government, announced an emergency and took all the powers in his hands. This action of King was discarded world over. India, against this undemocratic action of King, withdrew all the military aid. India was giving 70 percent subsidy to Nepali army for purchasing arms and helicopter from India and tackle Maoist rebel problem.

After the pressure of US, India had to again started the military aid to Nepal, but India is in favour of restoring democracy in Nepal. The anti-India demonstrations, over an alleged remark made by Bollywood actor Hrithik Roshan, made the relations disturbed and difficult.

Despite the difficult moments, the visit diplomacy made easier to communicate, seek cooperation and overcome difficulties. There was President Narayanan's state visit to Nepal. Prime Minister Vajpayee also went to Nepal. These visits and official level dialogues about mutual concerns have helped put the unpleasant incidents. They have now reached a stage of meaningful dialogue.

FACTORS DETERMINING THE RELATIONS

India and Nepal are two closely related neighbours which have multi-dimensional relations. The open border and deep socio-economic cultural connections, economic interdependence and geo-strategic importance gives the uniqueness of bilateral relations.

Strategic

Nepal has a strategic location in Himalayas, situated at the southern slopes of the central Himalayas. It separates Tibetan Plateau from the Indian plains. Its south east and west region forms border with Uttaranchal, Uttar Pradesh, Bihar and West Bengal states of India. Hence Nepal's strategic importance is immence for India. The role of geography in Indo-Nepal relations has to be considered. That is why the Treaty of Peace and Friendship was signed in 1950 by twos. Nepal's northern frontier includes number of passes.

The possibility of an invasion through these passes cannot be totally rules out and this makes Nepal all the important for India. The development of roads has also been another geo-strategically important factor in Indo-Nepal relations. The construction of Kathmandu-Kodari road in 1961 and link roads from Sinkiang-Tibet Highway reaching the borders of Nepal, Bhutan and Sikkim by China and recently rail link from Beijing to Lhasa clarifies the Nepal's strategic position in India's northern security system.

Open Border

The unrestricted, uncontrolled and open common border between two is responsible for free-movement of people, smuggling of goods, narcotic drug trafficking, arms smuggling, poaching, etc. There have been increased terrorist and fundamentalist activities on Indo-Nepal border. Some madrassas are also running on Indo-Nepal border. The open border facilitates illegal migration between the two countries and no quota system is there to determine number of migrants crossing the border Tarai region.

Economic

India has many economic interests in Nepal such as the utilization of water resources, promotion of trade, promotion of private capital investment, development of joint ventures. The landlocked position of Nepal, makes it excessive economic dependent on India. India has given 21 transit points to Nepal apart from port facilities at Kolkata. Kandla and Mumbai. India has been the single largest trading country with Nepal. The issues of trade and transit have determined relations between the two. Nepal does offer opportunities for Indian investment and also provides a market for the Indian products.

Personalities of Political Leadership

Personalities of political leaderships determine the foreign policies of any country. Nepal is an only Hindu state with dominant Hindu culture and Hindu kings. Therefore there is always a special relationship between two Hindu states. Nehru considered Himalayas as a main defence line of India's northern frontier and regarded Nepal important in India's security system. During Indira Gandhi's regime India played an important role in Nepal's economic development. Rajiv Gandhi's assertive and dynamic attitude brought him into personality clashes with King Birendra of Nepal. King Mahendra had a soft corner for China, this attitude of him deteriorated Indo-Nepal relations. King Gyanendra's time Indo-Nepal relations was towards deterioration.

The ambitions of the Nepalese power elite and quest for

power and authority has often resulted in a misperceived perception about India. The Nepalese ruling elite believes that India's natural alliance and sympathy is with the democratic forces. Hence they did not trust India's quest for stability in Nepal. Nepal's political leadership always take India as a kind of a guardian and then blamed India for interfering in Kathmandu and for "doing too much or too little."

DYNAMICS OF INDO-NEPAL RELATION

With the disintegration of Soviet Union, India lost a dependable ally. Hence, India started to consolidate relations with the neighbouring countries. Globalisation and liberalization also emphasized upon establishing regional economic cooperation. Hence India followed a policy of accommodation and adjustment. India liberalized its economic policies towards Nepal. 'One Window' policy was adopted. The two countries also cooperated in river water resources development.

Tanakapur Barrage agreement and Mahakali river valley were the results. Nepal has already enjoying the facility of Calcutta Port, later on the facility to use Khandla and Mumbai Port was also given to her. Nepal is demanding 70 km land for transportation to Bangladesh, on which India is still not agreed. But in 1997 India agreed to provide transit facilities to Nepal for its trade with Bangladesh via Phulbari in West Bengal.

Nepal does offer opportunities for Indian investment and market for Indian products. Pipeline diplomacy is set to tie New Delhi and Kathmandu into a permanent energy relationship. Nepal government with the joint venture with Indian Oil Corporation is ready to lay a pipeline to wheel Petro products from India and two plants to bottle cooking gas in the state.

INDIA AND NEPAL: SHARING OF RIVER WATER

India and Nepal are blessed with Himalayas and Himalayan rivers. Nepal is the second richest country in the world in water resources. The utilization of these river water for irrigation, hydro-power generation, fisheries, navigation, flood control require close cooperation and understanding between Nepal and India. Nepal is rich in water resources. Nepal's three major rivers—Kosi,

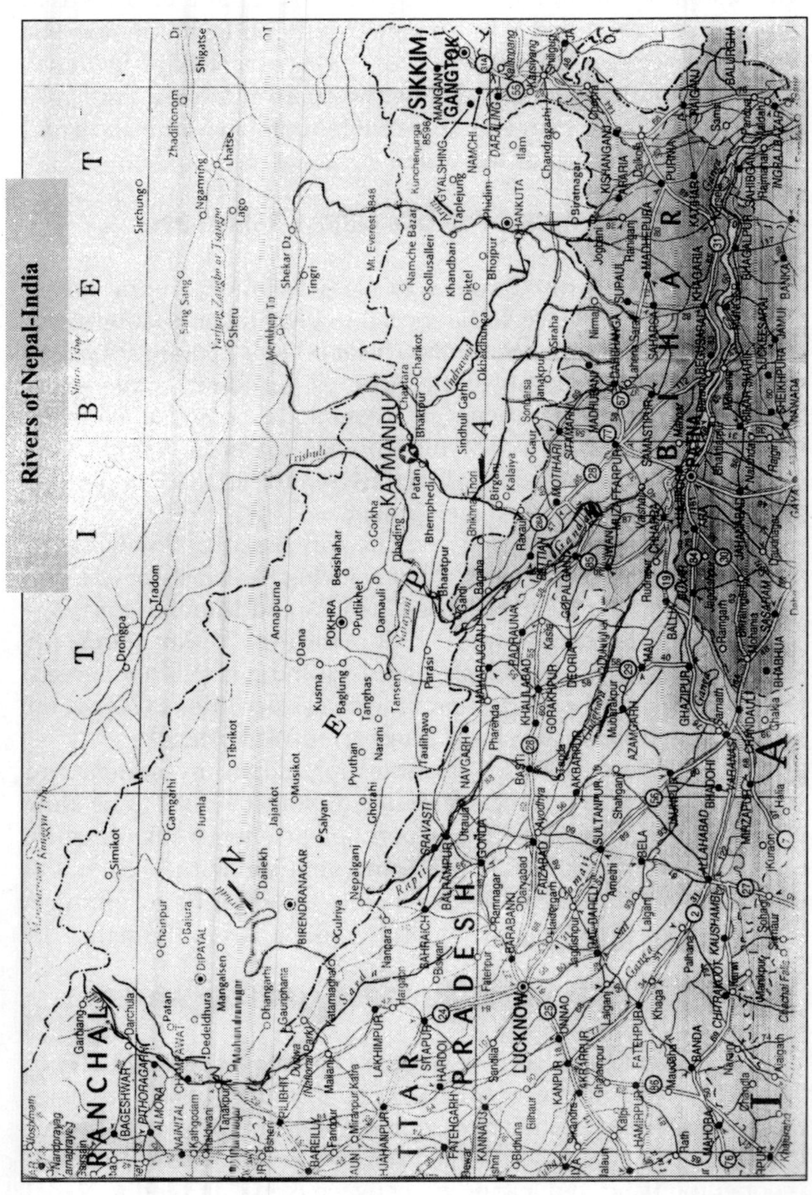

Rivers of Nepal-India

Gandak and Karnali originate from Nepal and join Ganga in the Indian territory, after crossing over the Tarai region of Nepal. Other main tributaries of these rivers are—Kali Bheri, Rapti, Trisuli, Panar, Kamala, Bagmati.

Nepal has rivers but no capital and technology to exploit the river waters. Thus it needs Indian help to harness the river waters. Since early 50's India has been giving capital and technology aid to Nepal for sharing of river's waters. India comes forward for joint cooperation for mutual benefits. India is interested in surplus hydro power. The problem of floods and sedimentation caused in Uttar Pradesh, Bihar and West Bengal also requires joint cooperation in water management. Kosi, Gandak, Trisuli, Devighat projects between two and some small hydro power projects like Surajpur, Kalariya are part of India-Nepal cooperation on water resource development.

But the sharing of river water is not going smoothly. Nepal keeps low profile in the negotiations for tapping river water. Viewing India's interest in managing river waters as it faces the problems of floods, sedimentation, etc., Nepal wants to bargain with India on this to secure more concessions in other sectors. Recently Tanakpur barrage controversy and Mahakali Treaty is raised a dispute with the deterioration of political relations. Nepal charges on India that the joint projects give benefits to India more and Nepal is not given its due share. King Birendra himself once remarked that Nepal had been cheated by India in the case of Kosi and Gandak river projects. But Nepal should realise that the rational utilisation of water resources is in the interest of preserving ecology in the Himalayas, controlling floods, soil erosion and power generation. And these problems can be solved only through mutual cooperation. Nepal is rich in the water resources and we have to utilise them professly for tackling the vast unemployment problem and expedite the development of the country.

Water released from the rivers in the neighbouring Nepal country is the main reason for the annual floods in eastern Uttar Pradesh and Bihar. The recent Kosi flood in north Bihar is the worst example of this. So Centre should initiate a dialogue with the Nepal Government for finding a permanent solution to the floods which ravage large areas of Uttar Pradesh and Bihar every year.

Under the Mahakali Pact of 1996 between the Indian and Nepalese government it was decided to build the Pancheshwar project on the Sharda river, the Karnali embankment project on the Ghagra and the Namure/Bhalubhang multi-purpose project on the Rapti river. But no substantial progress has been made in the last 12 years.

A small state syndrome and a cultivated anti-India attitude among the Nepali political class have prevented Kathmandu from exploiting its immense water resources for national benefit in cooperation with New Delhi. The recent Kosi flood in northern Bihar in 2008 cleared a simple fact that more modern methods of river water management in the eastern Himalayas is needed.

INDIA-NEPAL JOINT VENTURE

Nepal a small land locked country in the southern slopes of the Himalayas with a population of 24.8 Million (in 2000) is one of the poorest countries of the world. Being a land locked country, it has excessive economic dependence on India even for most essential commodities. India provide transit facilities to Nepal for its trade with the overseas countries. India has been biggest aid donor and partner of Nepal since very beginning. In 1964 India undertook the construction of Sanauli-Pokhara highway. India helped Nepal in rural development, education, industrial development, construction of highways, telecom. For improving the trade imbalance, India came with joint ventures. The joint venture an effective way of economic cooperation through which India and Nepal are sharing capital, technology and managerial responsibilities as well as the profit.

With liberal economy, the two are sharing skills, technology and resources to seek equitable benefits through joint ventures. Joint ventures are mostly in the field of manufacturing sectors, hotel, tourism, electricity, railway and civil aviation. During the Gujral regime, both the countries were agreed on joint Pancheshwar hydro electric project. India has vast opportunities to expand its investment in Nepal. The economic collaboration can be increased in the areas of leather, jute, carpet, cement, textile, pharmaceuticals, food processing, etc. No doubt, Indian business community is playing a significant role in the mobilisation of the Nepalese economy.

THE GULF WIDENS

Indo-Nepal ties was on a boil since February 1, 2007 royal coup. Delhi mounted international pressure on King to restore democracy in Himalayan Kingdom. India also cancelled its arms supply to Nepal. The worsening economic situation in Nepal triggered a fresh wave of migration into India. India has a 1,880 km border with Nepal. Some one million Nepalese have moved to India because of violence and instability. To demonstrate India that Nepal can do without India, Nepal did a Rs. 100 crore deal with China to supply arms and ammunition to Nepal. India does not want Beijing to provide arms to Kathmandu and China is trying to increase its influence in Nepal affairs. India's concerted campaign against King's royal coup and the western nations growing disenchantment with Kathmandu over Human Right, concerns has prompted China to quietly extend support to the King and offered him the much needed arms supply.

Another worry for India is the role of Pakistan intelligence agency-ISI. Islamabad was trying to capitalise on the crisis by offering arms to Nepal. But inspite of all these, Nepal offered its support for India's bid for a seat in the United Nations Security Council (UNSC).

Uttarakhand is very much concerned about the security on the Indo-Nepal border. The Uttarakhand Chief Minister B.C. Khanduri recently urged the Central Government in April 2008 to set-up a joint technical committee in order to fix the border line between the two countries along Champawat and Udham Singh Nagar districts of the state. The state was facing problems due to position of two pillars on Indo-Nepal border. Because of this problem Uttarakhand cannot have a clear 'No Man's land or under take removal of encroachment.'

TERRORISM AND MAOIST ACTIVITIES

In recent years, India's major concern is that Nepal territory is being used by the terrorists for launching anti-India activities like hijacking, smuggling of arms, women and narcotics. It is believed that the terrorist organizations supported by Pakistan's intelligence agency-ISI. On Indo-Nepal border, some madrassas are also running. Today the Pakistan's ISI has chosen Nepal for anti-India activities, because of the open Indo-Nepal border and the adjoining area of Indo-Nepal border is densely populated land and industrially developed. India's north east area is already struggling with instability and terrorism. And Pakistan wants to take benefit of this. The activities of ISI is neither in the interest of Nepal nor India. The major concern for India is that Kathmandu has become a asylem city of criminals. The terrorists of Kashmir take benefit of the Indo-Nepal open border and do the illegal arms smuggling and plane hijacking business. The hand of ISI is suspected behind these. The ISI wants to use terrorist's ambition to take the proxy war beyond Kashmir and into country's hinterland. In a status report on internal security presented to Parliament in December 2006, Home Ministry has said that ISI is there against the anti-India jehadi gangs.

After having used the western border for years, Pakistan-based groups like Lashkar-e-Taiba and Jaish-e-Mohammed have opened new fronts for India to guard, using Bangladesh and Nepal as launching pads for its cadres. The status paper says: "The current strategy of these groups is to maintain a continuous flow of finances to sustain terrorist network, target vital installation and economic infrastructure, recruit and train local modules, attack soft targets like market places, public transport system, places of worship and congregation.

ISI has chosen Nepal for anti-India activities mainly because of the open border of Indo-Nepal and secondly Nepal has become a passage of purchasing and selling of smuggled and illegal arms. And lastly, the adjoining area of India bordering Nepal is the tarai region of dense population. These activities are against the security and stability of India. Cases of kidnapping and extortion targeting Indian businessmen in Kathmandu and its neighbouring areas is increasing. This has created a sense of fear and insecurity among the Indian business community in Kathmandu. The continuous threats to Indian businessmen may force them to quit the country and return to India.

MAOIST PROBLEM OF NEPAL

Maoist problem in Nepal is a decade long. The Maoist movement in Nepal is a biggest security threat to India, as thousands of Nepalese including Maoists and pro-democracy activists have sneaked into bordering areas of Bihar and Uttar Pradesh About 170 Indians districts are already under Naxal influence. Nepali Maoists who are taking refuge in the bordering states of India could very well engage in bloody territorial clashes with rivals like MCC and PWF. Outlawed KLD in North East is developing links with Nepalese Maoists and ULFA.

Maoists menace in Nepal is India's biggest security threat. Maoists activities are increasing day by day in Nepal. But India did not interfere in it, always considered it as an internal affair. The Maoists in Nepal came against the King Gyanendra openly.

They wanted to restore democracy, as King Gyanendra assumed absolute power after sacking the government in February 2005. The King dismissed the Deuba government and took over power directly, declared emergency and put most political leaders under house arrest. But the entire country was in favour to achieve democracy. After all king bowed to public pressure, reinstated democracy on April 25, 2006. The Seven Party Alliance (SPA) elected Koirala as interim Prime Minister. The Maoists called unilateral ceasefire and agreed to work with SPA.

After 9/11 King Gyanendra declared Maoists "Terrorists" in the hope of coining Washington's sympathy. The United States also told India not to supply arms to Nepal King. India, United States and Europe protested against King seizure of absolute powers and did recall of their ambassadors.

The Maoists activities in Nepal is a cause for concern for India. Increasing unrest in Nepal compelled thousand of Nepalese including Maoists and pro-democracy activists to take shelter in the bordering areas of Bihar and Uttar Pradesh. This can lead to an increased security threat in the Indian state.

So India to solve the crisis, sent Karan Singh and foreign secretary Shyam Saran to Kathmandu. India played a major role to get King to back off and also gave an economic package to Nepal. New Delhi prefers a political settlement of Nepal's Maoists problem rather than a military one.

Though after pressurising from United States, India delivered the arms to Nepal. After February take over, Maoists leader Prachand and Prime Minister G.P. Koirala signed the landmark accord on 21 November, 2006. This was the end of 238 years old feudal system and after 11 years of civil war, King Gyanendra ultimately left the Kingship and Maoist leader Prachand became the PM in September 2008.

India is also interested in a representative and responsive political system in Nepal, as the political stability and establishment of democracy in Nepal is in favour of India. In the 1990 movement in Nepal many Indian political leaders openly supported democratic forces of Nepal. Since then India's approach has been to support democratic regimes.

NEPAL LOOKS TO PAKISTAN AND CHINA FOR ARMS

Pakistan and China between whom this small land locked state is sandwiched have more direct interest in Nepal. Nepal's growing military linkages with China and Pakistan is the subject of India's worry. Since 70s and 80s, Nepal is involved in purchasing arms from China and Pakistan. With the accession of King Mahendra to the throne, the principle of 'special relationship' with India was rejected and concept of 'equal friendship' with both of her neighbour India and China was adopted. King Mahendra visited China in 1961 for a three week which was resulted into a construction of a highway linking Kathmandu with the Tibetan border town of Kodari with Chinese assistance.

Recently Nepal has turned to China and Pakistan for military help after India and US imposed arms embargo in the wake of February 1 dismissal of the Deuba Government by King Gyanendra. Nepalese army chief Pyar Jung Thapa took a week long visit to Pakistan. Beijing also sent 18 truck load of arms and ammunition to Royal Nepal Army (RNA) during Maoist insurgency. Before King Gyanendra grabbed absolute power, most needs of the RNA were met by India. India did partially left the embargo on May 10, 2006 but only for "non-lethal supplies" like bullet proof jackets, hand held thermal imagers and night vision devices.

There is a new turn in Nepal-Pak relations in trade also. Pakistan wants to reach a free trade agreement with Nepal as soon as possible. Pakistan wants to give Nepal more access to its markets. For this a demand has been raised that India should provide a corridor to facilitate bilateral trade between Nepal and Pakistan. But this will be against the interests of India. Instead India stresses on compliance SAFTA in South Asia.

NEED FOR MORE CORDIALITY BETWEEN TWO

Beyond obvious ties of history, culture and soft borders, lie deeper new realities of Indo-Nepal relations that both countries need to face up to. These realities have been taking shape over many decades but have largely been ignored.

It is a fact that destiny has put India and Nepal quite close to each other. But a vast asymmetry between two in terms of size, population, resources, level of development, capabilities has caused complexities. India's security concerns in Nepal and Nepal's excessive dependence upon India has resulted into fear attitude of Nepal. Nepal often misperceived India's attitude as Indian hegemony or Big Brother attitude as so Nepal has tried to assert upon its identity and independence by way of going against India. There are a number of relatively small steps which India has taken or has agreed to take to improve Indo-Nepal relations—Opening a consulate in Birganj, Power Trade Agreement which aims to promote private sector participation in developing. Nepal's potential for generating hydro power. Nepal has a commercially exploitable potential of 25,000 MW, but it now produces hardly one percent of this. Recently India and Nepal renewed their 11 years old trade accord for another five year in February, 2007.

India has entered into Nepal's power sector with a Power Purchase Agreement (PPA) for the Asian Development Bank (ADB) promoted 750 MW West Seti Hydro-electric Power Project in Nepal. A total of 135 km of transmission line from the project site upto the Indo-Nepal border would be laid from the Nepal side and another 100 km to Atamanda, near Bareilly on the Indian side. 90 percent of the power will be bought by India. In India, the likely beneficiaries of the project would be Uttar Pradesh, Haryana, Punjab and Delhi.

India is also keen to strengthen the intelligence sharing mechanism between forces Sashastra Seema Bal (SSB) of India and Seema Suraksha Prahari (SSP) of Nepal guarding the border on either side.

EQUITY MUTUAL INTERESTS: BASIS OF COOPERATION

There is a need to develop mutual trust between twos. The

Nepalese ruling elite believes that India's natural alliance and sympathy are with the democratic forces. Hence they do not trust India's quest for stability in Nepal.

Nepal plays the game of one neighbour against the other. Respecting the Gujral doctrine, India should not interfere in the internal affairs of Nepal and that India did during the King Gyanendra time and recently during the movement of restoration of democracy in Nepal.

- India and Nepal need to fall into a pattern of behaviour that they follow with any other country. New Delhi needs to give up its 'Monroe Doctrine' apply to Kathmandu. Nepal, in turn needs to realise that sovereign affairs cannot have extra territorial responses or solution.
- India should review its border policy. Open border gives the security ramifications. We should have border check posts and regulate the entry of Nepalese nationals. We should try to stop increasing China's influence in Nepal.
- The terrorist problem needs to be looked on a priority basis. More patrolling is needed to control illegal movements of people and goods across the border. Controlled border rather than closed border is the only solution for further strengthening the India-Nepal friendship.
- Both the countries can enter into more cooperation for mutual gains in the field of river water resources development and hydro electric power. This is where the key to prosperity lies for both countries. Nepal has rich water resources which could be developed to meet energy requirements of both countries and also help combat perennial problems of flooding and inundation. Nepal's natural water resources can not be only a source of disaster along the border. We must frame a policy for preventing natural calamities and harnessing Nepal's rivers for energy. This would mean income for Nepal and power for India.
- On trade, as the bigger partner, India has to be more accommodating than it has been so far. The primary thrust has to be on investment.

Trade with Nepal

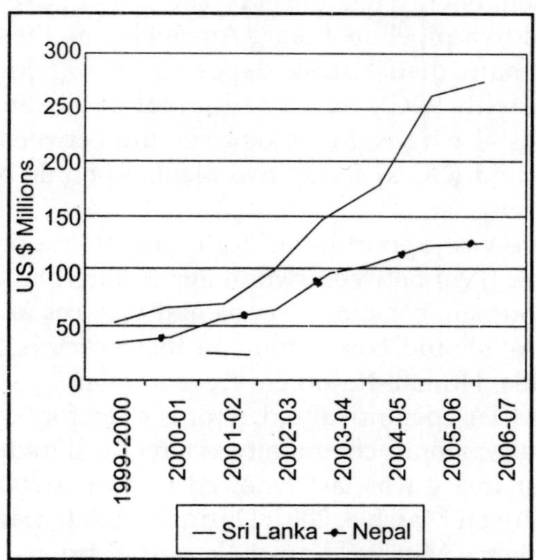

Opportunities

- Due to limited domestic production of manufactured products and increasing demand, India can export transport vehicles and communication equipments; agricultural machinery, tools and fertilizer; medicine, medical equipment and tools, etc.
- Joint venture opportunities in tourism industry, investment in hydro-electric power, telecommunication, civil aviation and infrastructure (road and airport) construction.
- Joint ventures potential for Indian manufacturing mainly for exporting exists in consumer durables, non-durables, garments and carpets, apparel, etc.

Problems

- Limited natural resources, difficult topography, poor infrastructure, weak human capital base and labour union excesses supported by Maoist.
- Though Nepal open to foreign direct investment, implementation of policies often distorted by bureaucratic delays and inefficiency. Investors in Nepal face a non-transparent legal system.
- On the Indian side Nepal traders face non-tariff barriers, corruption, politically motivated business and border closures, high transaction cost like submission of unnecessary documents, administrative hassles at customs office.

Indo-Nepal oil pipeline can tie New Delhi and Kathmandu into permanent energy relationship. The Nepal government has given its nod to a pipeline linking Amalekhganj, the Himalayan Kingdom's main distribution depot about 175 km south of Kathmandu with IOC's supply terminal at Raxaul in Bihar. Kathmandu is also agreed to a joint venture between Nepal Oil Cooperation and IOC to set-up two plants to bottle cooking gas in the kingdom.

There are vast opportunities for economic cooperation and Joint Ventures (JVs) between two in agriculture and agro-based industries, tourism, consumer goods and services and ancillary industries. We should concentrate on these sectors ignored all these years like Human Resources Development.

With SAPTA operationalised, door is open for South Asia to join the global economic community as a regional trade grouping. The five year treaty was last renewed in March 2002 and was going to expire on March 5, 2007. During the Kathmandu visit of Indian Commerce Minister Kamal Nath on February 25, 2007 to attend the SAARC meeting, the treaty was given extension of five years. Both the government and the private sector in Nepal wanted an automatic renewal of the treaty. As both governments are working out a comprehensive economic package, Nepal wanted the treaty to be renewed to buy time till the package is complete.

An extension of five years of Indo-Nepal Trade Treaty is a welcome step. But it is a need of signing a comprehensive economic partnership treaty between Nepal and India to further expand trade relations between the two countries. Economically advanced India will automatically increase Nepal's trade opportunities.

As the Kingdom of Nepal is currently going through an acute power crisis, the Nepalese government has been easing investment policies to seek joint ventures in the power sector with Indian investment. With relief and rehabilitation being the focus of the current government policy in Nepal, the seven party ruling alliance is looking for India's assistance in infrastructure and hydro power.

The Indo-Nepal investment protection talks are also on track now. After remaining buried for over three years, the Bilateral Investment Protection Agreement (BIPA) draft between India and

Nepal has been finally resurrected in January 2007 to the relief of Indian investors. Though Nepal has BIPA with four countries and India with over 60, the two immediate neighbours surprisingly do not have one though India is Nepal's biggest trading partner. The need was felt in the nineties, and in 1998, India forwarded a proposal. Though expected to be signed in 2001, the inking was put off due to the massacre of the royal family in June 2001 and the ensuing political turmoil.

In between, the South Asian Association for Regional Cooperation countries proposed a SAARC investment cooperation agreement and Nepal started to go slow on the bilateral agreement with India. Though talk on the agreement resumed in 2003, and in the following year, when the then Nepalese Prime Minister Sher Bahadur Deuba visited New Delhi at the invitation of Prime Minister Manmohan Singh, both sides agreed to speed up the agreement, but the king's coup the next year put paid to that. Now, however, Indian investors once again feel the need for such an agreement with the Maoists poised to join the government soon.

The agreement aims to safeguard investors from anti-investor measures taken by the host country, like forcible nationalisation and forced closures. The need for the agreement was surely felt in 2005 when the royal regime in Nepal disconnected the telephone services of United Telecom Limited, a joint venture between India's Mahanagar Telephone Nigam Limited, Videsh Sanchar Nigam Limited and Telecommunications Consultants India Limited and Nepalese company Nepal Venture Private Limited, that became the first Private telephone service provider in the kingdom.

Nepal has also asked for Indian help to establish a special economic zone in Birgunj in southern Nepal, where India has a consulate and the proposal has been receive favourably by New Delhi. The government also wants the cooperation of the Indian authorities to crack down on illegal border trade. With the two countries sharing an 1800 km open border, smuggling is rampant and amounts to over double the volume of legal trade. Nepali vanaspati ghee manufactures are also hoping that New Delhi will double the quota presently allocated to them. There is optimism both in the government and private sector in Nepal following the Indian gesture of waiving four percent additional customs duty on select goods imported from Nepal, taking the tally of such exempted items to 111. The waivar came after Nepal's Prime Minister Girija Prasad Koirala visited New Delhi in 2006, when he made the request. The bilateral trade talks in Kathmandu were followed by the SAARC ministers meet to discuss SAFTA on February 26 where the agenda included the sensitive list, non-tariff barriers and dispute settlement mechanism.

Since restoration of peace and stability in the Himalayan kingdom is in the interest of both the countries, Indo-Nepal relations should be peaceful and friendly. We need to move ahead with will and imagination, sensitivity and confidence.

NEPAL'S NEW PRIME MINISTER PRACHANDA'S VISIT TO CHINA AND ITS REPERCUSSIONS

Within a weak of taking office Nepal's new first Maoist Prime Minister Pushpa Kamal Dahal 'Prachanda' made China his first international destination attending the closing ceremony of the Olympics in Beijing on August 24, 2008. Prachand is the first Nepalese leader in the history of Nepal to make Beijing his first stop and not New Delhi. However, the Maoist Minister for Law and Justice, Dev Gurung said "Prachand's visit to China cannot be regarded as directed against India. The Maoist Government wants to follow the policy of "equi-distance" from India and China."

In his first address to the Nation, Nepal's Prime Minister said on 22 August 2008. "Nepal's bilateral ties with other countries including our neighbours would be based on the five principles of coexistence, the Panchsheel." During the China visit the Nepal Prime Minister met both Chinese President Hu Jintao and Prime Minister Wen Jiabao. Hu was reported as saying that China and Nepal are "good neighbours, good friends and good partners". Hu noted that "the two countries have established a good neighbourly partnership and enjoyed friendship generation upon generation."

Hu added, "This fully demonstrates the great attention Nepal attaches to relations with China and its profound friendship with the Chinese people. We highly appreciate that." Clearly, Prachanda is building up China as a hedge against India, much in the manner of all of India's other neighbours. Which, in its own way, is not cause for alarm in New Delhi, except for what it might bring in its wake, in terms of greater Chinese access into Nepal. China has also promised a lot of assistance to Nepal, which widens its choices, from being dependent on India, a dependence that has ramifications in its domestic politics. On the other hand, Beijing was never a supporter of the Maoists, and in fact, during the jan andolan, it had taken the side of the now deposed monarchy. Even now, China remains worried about Tibetan protesters continuing their protests in Nepal.

China showed her readiness to continue to provide help in Nepal's economic and social development and promote the long-term and stable development of the partnership.

Prachanda said he considers China as a reliable friend and expects more help from it to achieve peace and promote economic development in Nepal. He said the government is willing to cement cooperation with China and elevate bilateral ties to a new high.

Hu thanked Nepal for adhering to the One-China policy and firmly supporting China on the Tibet issue.

FOREIGN AFFAIRS MINISTER VISIT TO INDIA

Foreign Affairs Minister Upendra Yadav came to India for a four day visit on August 29, 2008 to attend the foreign ministers meeting of BIMSTEC to finalise an anti-terror agreement. During the visit he met Pranab Mukherjee.

NEPAL'S PM PRACHAND'S VISIT TO NEW DELHI

On 15 September 2008, the new Maoist Prime Minister of Nepal arrived on his first political visit to India. Prachanda downplayed his visit to China saying it was only for the Olympic's closing ceremony. Prachand found the relations with India were 'crucial and vital' and 'cannot be compared with China.' He said, "Due to our specific cultural, historical proximity and tradition of economic inter dependence, relations with India are crucial and vital and cannot be compared with China."

Prachand assured that his country soil would not be used for action against any country. India's fear is Pakistan's ISI using

Nepal as a base to hit India. Prachand said we are in between India and China, we should benefit from this.

India and Nepal decided to take preventive measures for the protection of barrages on the Gandak and other rivers under the existing bilateral arrangements in the wake of the Kosi disaster. Both the sides discussed the problem of inundation in the border areas, damage caused by the Kosi river and agreed to take up prevention on the basis of bilateral consultation.

With India and Nepal agreeing to check recurrence of flood in the Kosi river, the Joint Commission on Water Resources, which last met in 2004, now met again in Kathmandu on September 29-30 to discuss various issue.

Sustaining the special bilateral relationship is the single most important outcome from the visit of Prachand. Making the case for an equal relationship with India, Prachand asked for review and revision of the treaty. "Nepal has now become a republic after big political changes, therefore the 1950 treaty needs to be reviewed." What change he wants is still not explained by Prachand. Recognising the urgency of bringing bilateral ties up to speed, India readily agreed on this.

The India and Nepal Treaty covers much wider ground from Bhutan Treaty. Kathmandu has benefited immensely from this unique agreement with New Delhi that allows Nepal citizens to work in India including in the elite civil services. Neither country has such arrangement with any other.

India assured Prachand to start afresh with the new Nepal. New Delhi and Kathmandu must now act quickly to modernise the unique bilateral relationship. Popular expectations in both countries are high. India and Nepal, during their Prime Minister-level talks held in New Delhi, had emphasised on the importance of peaceful, political, democratic transformation of historic significance in Nepal. The two prime ministers had agreed to review, adjust and update the 1950 Treaty of Peace and Friendship and other agreements, while giving due recognition to special features of bilateral relationship.

The PM Prachand had raised the issue of updating and revising the Indo-Nepal friendship treaty of 1950.

Prachand said India and Nepal needed to address the issue of security collectively. "We understand the security concerns of India and we are also very concerned about our own security."

Indian industry is concerned over security and labour unrest in Nepal in view of the office of the Dabur group's Nepal Office being stormed by a group of Maoists in August, 2008.

Addressing the India-Nepal Parliamentary Friendship Forum, Prime Minister Prachanda said,

> "No two countries in the world possibly enjoyed the kind of "sweet relations" that India and Nepal have traditionally and historically had. These bonds have to be strengthened through a "fresh start."

He reminded that the two countries were linked through "thousands of small links that cannot be broken", but there was need for a "new dynamism" in the relationship that could be given by focussing "not on the small things, but looking at the big picture."

During the New Delhi visit Prachanda talked about Nepal's need for rail link in Tarai region and power project in Nepal and in these he wanted India to help and hoped that "Nepal ties with India cannot be broken but need to be strengthened through a new dynamism and a new conceptual framework. Both the countries want to give a fresh impetus to bilateral ties in trade and commerce, water management and curbing crime and drug running along the border.

Maintaining that Nepal wished to grow and prosper along with India, Prachanda said business was an engine of growth, and that it would ensure peace and stability in his country through rapid progress in economic development.

In this connection, he invited Indian corporate houses to set up plants in Nepal where he said special economic zones could come up to "accelerate the process of inclusive economic development".

During the visit of Prachand, Delhi was not too perturbed about his earlier declaration in April 2008 that Nepali Gorkhas should not be allowed to join the Indian Army.

There are, after all, almost 40,000 Nepali Gorkhas gainfully employed in the Indian Army and paramilitary. Nepal has more to lose than us."

In fact, the representation of "Indian domicile Gorkhas" in the Army's seven Gorkha Rifles (1st, 3rd, 4th, 5th, 8th, 9th and

11th)—each of which has five to six battalions (around 800 soldiers) — has been steadily going up over the years.

"Earlier, almost 90% of the soldiers in Gorkha Rifles used to hail from Nepal. But now, just about 60% come from Nepal, with the rest coming from Dehradun, Darjeeling, Dharamsala and other places. For instance, the Rais and Limbus in 11th GR come both from eastern Nepal as well as Darjeeling.

Right since the 'official' agreement on recruitment of Nepali Gorkhas in the Indian Army in 1949, the two countries have had strong military ties The relationship became even stronger when the Maoist insurgency began gaining ground in Nepal around a decade ago, with India then seeing it as "a common security challenge."

DEALING WITH A NEW NEPAL

The official state visit of Prachanda as the first elected Prime Minister of the Republic of Nepal marks the beginning of India's engagement with a new Nepal. To make this engagement constructive and mutually advantageous, India has to grasp the degree and depth of the radical transformation that Nepal has gone through in the last couple of years. The former Kingdom has witnessed the spread of political consciousness at the grass roots, upsurge of socio-economic aspirations and the unprecedented rise of people's power. Its 240-year-old Monarchy has been pushed into the dustbin of history and the hitherto marginalised and oppressed social groups have entered the mainstream political dynamics as major stakeholders. India can no longer pursue its vital strategic and economic interests in this radically transformed Nepal on the basis of its old colonial policy mindset and bureaucratised traditional tools of diplomacy.

It may not be very difficult for India to respond positively to the issues that Mr. Prachanda may put on the table during his visit. The question of review and revision of treaties (Kosi and the 1950 Treaty) is not a big deal. It is for the Maoists to precisely identify the areas where they want revisions as India has already shown its readiness to engage on this issue. Once the Maoists' proposals are formulated and backed by a national consensus in Nepal, their acceptability or otherwise may be sorted out through diplomatic channels.

The Maoists would like to have India's creative responses to the four areas of their principal concerns namely; political stability of the coalition regime, culmination of the peace process through security sector reforms, timely conclusion of the Constitution drafting and implementing the vision of "economic revolution" in a decade. The policy document released this week in Kathmandu highlights all these concerns. In these areas, India has no basic conflict of interests. Peace and political stability in Nepal are in India's genuine interests and Indian diplomacy and security agencies must be seen to be convincingly distanced from the discordant voices raised within Nepal questioning the stability of the Maoist-led government.

India has always provided generous assistance to Nepal for economic development. A Rs. 100 crore package offered in the immediate post-Jan Andolan-II phase has not been fully utilised. The Maoist promise of 10,000 MW of hydropower generation in a decade is a win-win proposal for India as well. A vibrant Nepali economy will reduce the outflow of migrant labour into India.

The vast convergence of interests between India and the new Nepal has always been obvious. What is needed on both sides is a creative political approach towards each other, free from ideological obsessions and past prejudices. India can easily afford to go more than half way to assure the Maoist leadership that it wishes new Nepal well.

A sour point with Maoists in Nepal has been the 1950 Indo-Nepal Treaty of Peace and Friendship. They believe that the treaty is skewed in India's favour. Dahal, who continues to head the party, raised the issue during his meeting with Manmohan Singh and has received assurance from New Delhi that the treaty would be reviewed. Dahal assured that Nepal was conscious of India's security interests. Now, it is for the Nepal government to identify contentious aspects of the treaty so that it can be reworked to the satisfaction of both parties. India and Bhutan had renegotiated their 1949 treaty last year after Thimpu sought changes that included more freedom in areas of foreign policy and defence. A similar approach would help New Delhi and Kathmandu clear misconceptions in both countries and take bilateral ties to a level that reflect the aspirations of the present time.

There is every reason for New Nepal, as Dahal described the republic, to build on its historic ties with India. Unlike in the past, it is a relationship between two republics that share common ideals like secularism and democracy. The political mainstream in Nepal, including the Maoists, has acknowledged the positive contribution of India towards that country's political transformation. The Indian experience in building a liberal democracy and a vibrant economy could serve as a lesson for Nepal. Kathmandu should see India's huge market with significant private capital as a plus. Nepal will need capital and expertise to rebuild its war-ravaged economy and could ask for Indian help. There is talk of building large-scale hydroelectric projects in Nepal. The presence of an energy-hungry economy next door should provide the impetus to begin work on that, of course after careful study of the region's fragile ecology. The assurance that Kathmandu will take measures to facilitate Indian private and public sector investments in Nepal is a step in the right direction.

Anti-India rhetoric may attract a small section of the Nepalese population, but Indo-Nepal ties go back a long way. Apart from its cultural roots and sentimental value, it makes economic sense for the two neighbours to foster friendly relations, including free trade. Hopefully, Dahal's visit will strengthen this sentiment.

Recently during a meeting in September 2008, with Nepal's defence minister Ram Bahadur Thapa, China's minister for defence Liang Guanglie announced a military aid of NRS 100 million (over $ 1.3 million) for Nepal. It is the first military aid received by the new Maoist led government of the Himalayan republic.

India is closely watching the Prachand's and Ram Bahadur Thapa's visit to China. China was the only neighbourhood country to supply arms to the Nepal army during King Gyanendra's regime. During King Gyanendra's government, India took serious umbrage at the royal government going on an arms buying spree and paying the Chinese manufactures hard cash while ignoring the mounting dues to India for the supply of arms at a high subsidy.

Nepal would give priority to strengthen relations with India and China, according to the government's programmes and policies for 2008-09. Unveiling the document, President Ram Baran Yadav said: "Friendship with India and Nepal would be given special priority."

Within 48 hours of Indian Water Resources Minister Pawan Kumar Bansal visiting Nepal to inspect the repaired embankment of the Kosi river that had created havoc in both countries last year, India gave Nepal NRs. 131.6 million (about $1.6 million) to fight floods.

The assistance comes after a decision by the India-Nepal Sub-Committee on Embankment Construction and Joint Committee on Inundation and Flood Management.

India has been providing assistance to Nepal for strengthening and extending the embankments along the Kamla, Dalbakeya and Bagmati rivers. With the present assistance, the total grant assistance for embankment construction along these rivers during 2009 stands at NRs.449.10 million.

India has also committed an additional grant assistance of NRs. 109.9 million for flood protection work along the Tri-juga, Lakhandehi, Sunsari and Kankai rivers.

India-Nepal relations have been badly mismanaged on both sides. The time has come to make a break with the past and explore new beginnings. Suspicion and mistrust grew and became a massive impediment to good relations between the two countries.

Nepal for its part is very conscious of being a land-locked country and would like to maintain and add to the numerous overland transit points, and to secure an outlet to the sea through India. It also dreams of generating large revenues from the export of electricity to India from a number of hydro-electric projects on the rivers of the Ganga system. At the same time, there is also some worry about large projects in the Himalayas and about an excessive dependence on India as the sole buyer of electricity.

The fact is that there is in Nepal a deep ambivalence about India, which many in India tend to misinterpret as anti-Indianism. On the one hand, Nepal sees the value of closer political and economic relations with India; on the other, there is a wariness about excessive closeness. There are visceral anxieties about Indian largeness and the unequal relationship that this might imply.

A "peaceful, stable and prosperous" Nepal is in India's interest.

India and Bhutan—A Cordial and Harmonious Relationship

Bhutan is a small landlocked neighbouring country of about 46,500 sq. km. bordered on the south and east by Tibet and India, on the west and south by India and between two big countries India and China. The southern border of Bhutan with India was established under a treaty with Britain in the 19th century. Bhutan is strategic ally important to India. The Sikkim-Nepal-Bhutan triangle was ignored by India being subjected to benign negligence. But now India realised its importance. Bhutan could keep a check on Chinese influence as a buffer state along the Himalayan corridor. Bhutan has a special relationship with India. Bhutan has realised this fact that the topography and geo-politics of this sub-continent demands the security and progress of the kingdom stands related to cordial relations with India.

King Wangchuk always said that "India is not only our close neighbour but our genuine friend also." The Indo-Bhutan relations are deep, friendly, co-operative satisfactory and healthy. Speaking in New Delhi in 1968, King Dorji Wangchuk said,

> "The ties that bind our two countries is a matter of history. Our spiritual heritage which we consider to be our greatest treasure stems from the teachings of the great son of India, Lord Gautam Buddha. The bonds of understanding and

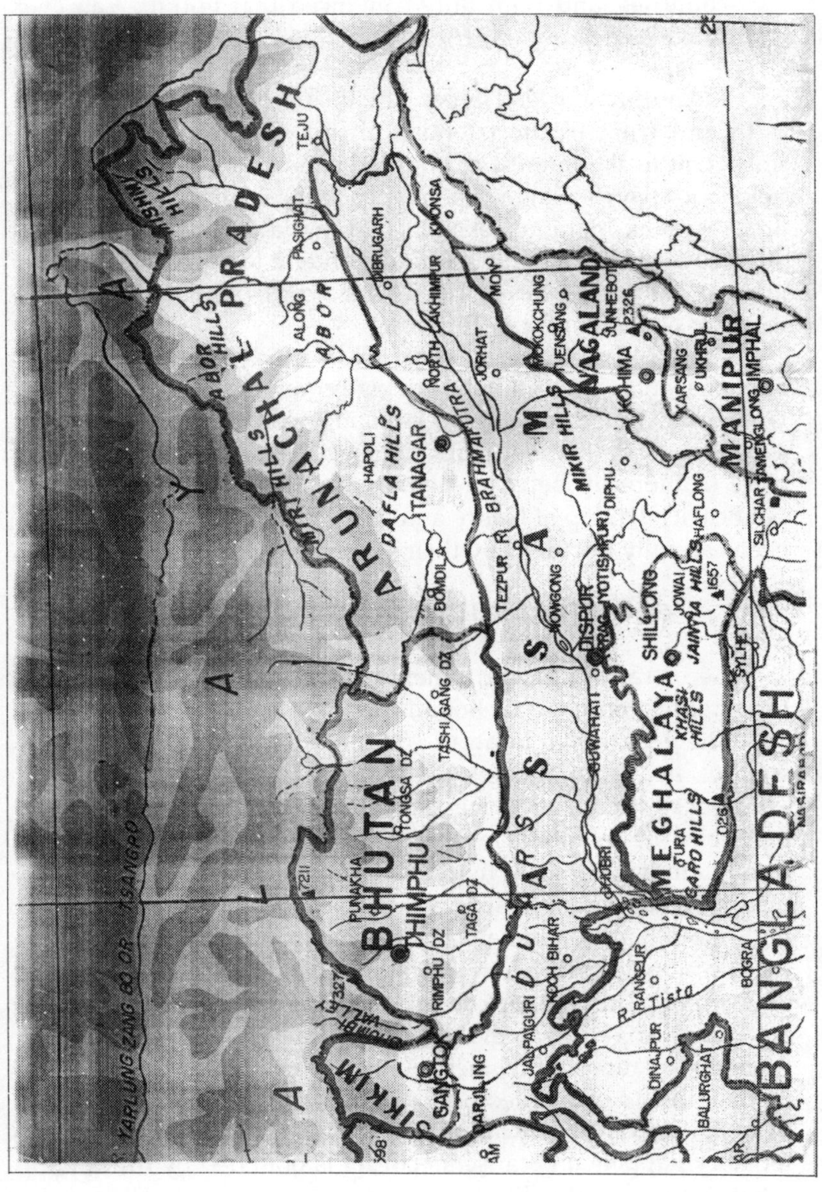
YARLUNG ZANG BO OR TSANGPO
ARUNACHAL PRADESH
MISHMI HILLS
ABOR HILLS
DAFLA HILLS
TEJU
PASIGHAT
ALONG
DIBRUGARH
KHONSA
ITANAGAR
HAPOLI
BOMDILA
NORTH LAKHIMPUR
JORHAT
MON
MOKOKCHUNG
TUENSANG
NAGALAND
KOHIMA
MANIPUR
IMPHAL
UKHRUL
KARSANG
ASSAM
BRAHMAPUTRA R.
TEZPUR
NOWGONG
DISPUR
DIPHU
MIKIR HILLS
HAFLONG
SILCHAR
MEGHALAYA
SHILLONG
JOWAI
KHASI HILLS
JAINTIA HILLS
GARO HILLS
TURA
DHUBRI
BHUTAN
THIMPHU
PUNAKHA
TONGSA DZ
TASHI GANG DZ
TAGA DZ
RIMPHU DZ
SIKKIM
GANGTOK
DARJILING
JALPAIGURI
KOCH BIHAR
DUARS
RANGPUR
R. Tista
DINAJPUR
BALURGHAT
BOGRA
SYLHET
BANGLADESH

> friendship have been further consolidated as a result of the growing economic and technical co-operation between two countries, and I am fully convinced that nothing can ever shake or destroy our friendship."

India-Bhutan friendship is a model friendship with complete faith and trust in the friendship. Indo-Bhutan friendship is important to the interest of both the countries. Bhutan is such a neighbour who is playing an independent role in the international arena with harmonious relations with India. It is not a satellite or ally country of India, it has an independent identity in the world affairs. The Indo-Bhutan ties in the words of the then Prime minister of Bhutan Dana Teshering.

"The Indo-Bhutanese ties are a model in international relations today. Though India is a big power and Bhutan is a small landlocked Kingdom, yet we go along well. What can be more satisfying than this model relationship." An era of the uniquely close relationship between Bhutan and India started under the political leadership of Nehru and Jigme Dorji Wangchuk. This has been carefully nurtured by their successors.

GEO-STRATEGIC LOCATION OF BHUTAN

Geo-strategic location includes the size, location, climate topography and national boundaries

The geographic location and landlocked nature of Bhutan isolates her from the rest of the world. Because Bhutan is landlocked and sandwiched between two Asian giants, it maintains its relations and contacts with the rest of the world through Indian territory. Inaccessibility is one of the characteristic feature of the country. Geographical factors such as thick forest, high mountains, extreme cold all make it inaccessible from the east, west and north. There are no railways, roads are only mode of transport. The climatic conditions are causes of thin population also. Bhutan geo-strategic location influences its political and economic relations with other countries. The interference of China in Tibet in 50's compelled Bhutan to change its traditional policy of isolation. The infiltration of Tibetan refugees into Bhutan territory happened because its border is bounded by the land of Tibet. Consequently Bhutan's trade relations with Tibet were disrupted. The small geographical size of Bhutan gives it small population, and militarily weak status incapable of defending itself. As a small power it has to depend on India for its economic and industrial development and defence needs. Inadequate human and natural resources, compels Bhutan to invite labour and trained administrators from India. The geo-strategic location also pushed it to follow the path of non-alignment in its foreign policy. A small country like Bhutan can achieve progress and security only through such a policy. The membership of SAARC and Commonwealth by Bhutan was due to its geo-strategic location.

THE INDO-BHUTAN FRIENDSHIP TREATY OF 1949

Soon after independence, Nehru assured all neighbouring countries that his government was bound by the obligations of the treaty and agreements of former British India. Thus Bhutan sent its delegation to India on April 23, 1948 headed by Raja Sonam T. Dorji. The purpose of his visit was to ask for revision of the Anglo-Bhutanese Treaty of 1865, and to discuss their relations with a new independent India. The negotiations resulted into a treaty of friendship signed on August 8, 1949, Under Article II, Bhutan agreed to be guided by the Government of India in its external relations. And India assured that it will not interfere in the internal administration of Bhutan. According to Article III of this treaty, Government of India increased the compensation grant to a consolidated amount of Rs. Five lakh annually. Article IV established the principles of equality in the bilateral relationship between Bhutan and India. In support of this principle, the Government of India agreed to give back the area of Dewangiri hill strip, an area of thirty two square miles to Bhutan (Bhutan had renamed it as Deothang) which was annexed in 1865. Article V of this treaty established free trade and commerce between India and Bhutan.

By this treaty, Bhutan as sovereign state entered into a special relationship with India. The treaty institutionalized the formal relationship between Bhutan and India. The treaty conceded the independent and sovereign status of Bhutan and played a vital role in promoting and fostering friendly relations with India. Though Bhutan was not happy with second part of article II which restricted Bhutan from extending her relations beyond India. The treaty of 1949 had played a significant role in the formulation of the foreign policy of Bhutan. From India's point of view to strengthen friendship with Bhutan was important in view of her key position on the Indian border. From the defence point, India benefits from this security arrangement. As an ally of India, Bhutan provides a natural barrier to protect the Himalayan frontier of India.

INDIA PARTNERSHIP IN BHUTAN'S DEVELOPMENT

In 1961, Bhutan formally ended her isolation and planned to modernize herself through rapid socio-economic development with generous financial and technical assistance from India. The team of India Planning Commission visited Bhutan in 1961 and drafted its first five year plan (1961-66) which was totally funded by India. Since then India is deeply involved in the process of planned socio-economic development of Bhutan. India has emerged as the main development partner of Bhutan laying roads and building schools, hospitals and airports under project Dantek. India gave her financial and technical assistance in building Phuntsholing-Thimphu national highway which links the capital of Bhutan with India. The Border Road Organisation (BRO) is playing an active role in developing roads. Both are engaged in water resources development. The two governments are working together to harness the mighty potential of Bhutan's perennial rivers. The Indian engineers have constructed and operate Chukkha Hydel project which not only has brought power to western Bhutan but exports surplus power to India also, a boon to India. Revenue from the sale of power of this 336 MW Indo-Bhutan friendship project now constitutes nearly 30 percent of Bhutani annual income, as India is purchasing electricity from Bhutan. On November 25, 1990 the two governments signed a Memorandum to begin Project on Tala Hydro-electric Project (1000 MW) and the Wangchu Reservoir Scheme (600 MW) popularly known as Chukkha II and Chukkha III. Also an Memorandum was signed for the 1520 MW Sankosh Multipurpose Project which will also irrigate half a million hectares in West Bengal. The Tala project is entirely funded by India. One of the most critical areas of cooperation is Human Resource Development (HRD), the training of personnel for running hydel projects, constructing and maintaining roads and bridges, managing enterprises. This HRD will help in the functioning and further development of the state and society of Bhutan. The Indian military Training Team is training Royal Bhutanese Army after a joint defence agreement was signed in 1965. Both perform joint patrolling operations along the border. Power and agriculture are other fields of cooperation. Bhutan purchases nearly all its goods and services from professional managers to unskilled labourers from India. Ninety percent of Bhutan's trade is with India. Bhutan economy is based on agriculture and animal husbandry. The mountainous terrain, heavy forest and non-availability of infra-structure has made its economy dependent.

There are many facets of Indo-Bhutan economic cooperation which mainly emerge in water, electricity resources and HRD. Bhutan has a hydro power potential of 20,000 MW which it is keen to harness with Indian assistance. During King Wangchuk visit to India in 2005, the two sides talked in detail on Punatsangchuu hydel project which will have an estimated generation capacity of 870 MW. It has been identified for implementation under the 10th five year plan of India.

India took a significant step in strengthening ties with Bhutan when on July 28, 2006, she signed with her north-eastern neighbour three agreements in the areas of hydro-electricity, power and trade. India is looking forward using the immense hydel power potential of Bhutan as New Delhi is actively engaged in building a series of hydel power dams in Bhutan. India is also keen to purchase more than five thousand MW of hydel power—the cheapest mode of power generation from Bhutan in the next 10 to 15 years.

India is also going to set-up Bhutan's first railway network. The technical studies for the West Bengal-Bhutan railway network are at an advanced stage. Once completed, the project will go a long way in meeting developmental aspirations of a country that measures its wealth in terms of gross national happiness. During the visit India and Bhutan signed two agreements-one for long-term cooperation in the field of hydel power and another protocol document for the purchase of power generated by the 1,020 MW Tala Hydel Project.

INDIA-BHUTAN: POLITICAL AND STRATEGIC RELATIONS

After the independence of India, it was important from India's point of view to strengthen Bhutan's friendship in view of her key position on her border. India treated Bhutan as her equal thought it is a very small country. The Treaty of Friendship of August 8, 1949 gave an opportunity to play as an independent and sovereign state while the principles of Panchsheel incorporated by Nehru in India's foreign policy which served as the guiding force in its relations with her neighbouring states.

India is the only country in the SAARC region which has substantial trade relations with Bhutan. More than 90% of Bhutan's external trade is with India.

Giving importance to India the King of Bhutan Jigme Dorji Wangchuk paid a visit to India first time in 1954 to make an assessment of India's attitude and policies towards his country. In the following year in 1955, he invited the Indian delegation to Para in Bhutan led by R. K. Nehru, then Foreign Secretary. Next year in 1956 the king once again came India on a pilgrimage. In 1958, the Indian Prime Minister Jawahar Lal Nehru visited Bhutan. During his visit he expressed the spirit of the new relationship:

> "Some may think that since India is a great and powerful country and Bhutan a small one, the former might wish to exercise pressure on Bhutan. It is, therefore, essential that I make it clear to you that our only wish is that you should remain an independent country, choosing your own way of life and taking the path of progress according to your own will. At the same time we two should live with mutual goodwill. We are member of the same Himalayan family and should live as friendly neighbours helping each other. Freedom of both Bhutan and India should be safeguarded so that none from outside can harm it."

The height of the friendship was tributed in the words of Zakir Hussain, President of India during the visit of king in New Delhi in 1968. He told the king that the Government of India expected the "Bhutanese people will came to regard India as a second home away from home."

"In response king commented that there was "no

misunderstanding, no dispute, no argument between two countries." During the Indo-Pak war of 1965, Bhutan was the only neighbouring country which extended its "full support to India and assured every possible help."

CHINA FACTOR AND INDO-BHUTAN STRATEGIC RELATIONS

Unlike China, India in 1946 recognised Bhutan as an independent state and stated that it could not be equated to the princely state of the Indian territory. After 1947, India was the logical successor to Britain position in Bhutan, India again treated Bhutan a separate independent nation by excluding it from India's legislative and executive jurisdiction. China on the other hand claimed its suzerainty over Bhutan by publishing maps and topographical sketches in which nearly 300 Sq. miles of Bhutanese territory in the north and north east was demonstrated as Chinese land. In 1954, Bhutan was termed as a "lost Chinese territory by China and said, "Bhutan is wrongfully held by imperialist India." The Sino-Bhutan boundary was sanified by customs and usages.

China found the Indo-Bhutan Treaty of 1949 as an encroachment upon its suzerainty over Bhutan. It was also against the clause which empower India to interfere in external matters of Bhutan. That was why when Bhutan sent its protest against a Chinese map through Indian Ambassador, China did not recognise the Indian envoy right to negotiate on Bhutan border on behalf of the Bhutanese. China wanted to talk directly and bilaterally "The Chinese ecrge that Bhutan, in enlight ended self interest may now by pass India and start direct negotiation." But the King declared at a press conference in Calcutta on January 30, 1961 that Bhutan did not want to negotiate directly with China. He further said "We do not want to be either friends or enemies of China."

The China's motives were to bring a rift between India and Bhutan and in doing so, as China thought, it could secure the sympathy of Bhutan for China. During Chou-en-Lai's visit to India in April 1960, a suggestion from the King Dorji Wangchuk that he should be associated with the talk with the Chinese leaders over the border dispute was turned down by India.

ANNEXATION OF TIBET BY CHINA AND INDO-BHUTAN RELATIONS

The China military activities in Tibet, its occupation by China in 1951, Eastern Tibet revolt against China in 1954-55, and the Chinese suppression of the Tibetan revolt in 1959—all these activities created serious apprehensions in Bhutan. Tibet and Bhutan shares the same cultural and religious background. When Bhutan Prime Minister Jigme Paldan Dorji visited India in 1959, he "sought a written guarantee of Indian support in the event of Chinese attack on Bhutan."

After Tibetan revolt in 1959, many Tibetan refugees infiltrated into Bhutanese territory. Soon Bhutan closed its borders with Tibet in 1960 to prevent the flow of refugees from Tibet. Before that, Bhutan had imposed a ban on trade with Tibet and China, which gave a severe blow to the Bhutanese economy, because Tibet was a good market for Bhutan's surplus rice. These developments compelled Bhutan to maintain friendly relations with India. Nehru, protecting friendship, made a statement in the Lok Sabha on August 28, 1959 that "The protection of the borders and territorial integrity of Bhutan is the responsibility of India and that India would consider any aggression on Bhutan as an aggression on India."

THE SINO-INDIA WAR OF 1962 AND ITS IMPLICATIONS FOR INDO-BHUTAN RELATIONS

The Sino-India war of 1962, on the one hand aggravated Bhutan's sense of insecurity and suspicions about China. On the other hand, the defeated and weakened India had shaken Bhutan's confidence in India's capability to defend and protect Bhutan, if China repeated its Tibetan exercise in Bhutan or against Chinese attack. This insecurity of Bhutan led her to soften her attitude towards China. The Nepali foreign policy model of "equal friendship with India and China" was also suggested by the one group to follow. But Royal government of Bhutan again opted the way of closer links with India.

The Chinese policy of instruction and expansion of the Chinese boundary on the southern slopes of the Himalayas were motivated of taking over the Gateway of India. It was also oriented to test the special relationship of India and Bhutan. China wanted to pressurise Bhutan to establish independent relations with China. As militarily Bhutan was very weak, India introduced the Indian Military Training Team (IMTRAT) in Bhutan, whose headquarter is situated in Ha Valley, adjacent to Chumbi Valley in the high mountain passes.

In 1966, China started heavy concentration of Chinese troops along the Tibetan-Bhutanese border. Chinese intrusion was also taking place in the Doklan area in Bhutanese territory and southern part of Chumbi Valley. India protested to China on behalf of Bhutan and urged China to withdraw its troops from Bhutanese territory.

INDO-BHUTAN RELATIONS IN THE PERIOD OF KING JIGME SINGYE WANGCHUCK

After the death of his father, addressing his first press conference on August 20, 1972. King observed:

> "Our foreign policy will continue to develop friendship, understanding and cooperation with all countries and specially with our neighbour."

He added,

> "The treaty is working well and India had been helping us a lot to accelerate the pace of economic development set forth by my father. We are receiving technical and financial assistance from India or through India."

During this period the Royal Government of Bhutan according to Treaty of 1949, accepted India's advice on its three issues of foreign policy:

- Not to internalise the question of rights of landlocked countries in the United Nation General Assembly.
- Not to open its country to European nations either for economic trade or tourism.
- Bhutan recognised Bangladesh as sovereign and independent state on advice of Indian government.

During the coronation ceremony of King Wangchuk in June 1974, Bhutan invited about 150 foreign countries to attend it. Representatives from United States of America, Britain, France,

China, Soviet Union, Canada, Switzerland, Australia and New Zealand attended the function.

It was for the first time, Bhutan had opened its doors to the outside world. But India did not allow her to open diplomatic office in Bonn, London, New York and Paris to issue visas to encourage tourism in the country. India granted her permission to resume trade with Tibet.

At this time India made some changes in her stands and decided to encourage Bhutan to develop links with the outside world. Therefore India sponsored Bhutan's name for the Colombo plan of 1962. India also sponsored Bhutan's name for membership of the Universal Postal Union in 1969 and the United Nation in 1971 and in 1973 for the Non-Aligned Movement.

MERGER OF SIKKIM IN 1974 AND INDO-BHUTAN RELATIONS

Sikkim, situated on the western border of Bhutan was merged by India into the Indian Union in 1974. Bhutan did not like this act of India describing it as a loss of cultural identity of a neighbour, Himalayan Kingdom. Bhutan again got frightened. But Bhutan's position is different. It was not a protectorate of India as Sikkim was, In spite of this Bhutan is a sovereign and independent state which has a separate national identity of it.

In 1979 Bhutan took a small step forward running an independent foreign policy at Havana non-aligned summit on the Cambodia issue. India wanted to keep the Kampuchean seat vacant, while Bhutan voted to allow it to be occupied by the ousted Pol Pot government. It was contrary to Indian state and important in the context of the Indo-Bhutan Treaty of 1949. Bhutan enjoyed the excellent relations with India during Janata Government and Indira Gandhi regime. After desiring by Bhutan to hold bilateral talks with China, India allowed it. The first direct talks was held between the twos at Beijing in 1984. Since then they are having border talks.

In 1980s, while Bhutan and India shared common standings on Afghanistan issue against United States policy, Bhutan also followed independence in taking decisions related foreign policy. Bhutan actively participated in South Asian Regional Cooperation since its inception in 1981 onwards. In 1983, it established diplomatic relations with Nepal and in 1985 with Denmark, Sweden, Switzerland, Netherlands and ECC. It was clear now that both Bhutan and India taking liberal interpretation of Article II of the 1949 Treaty.

The exchange of visit between New Delhi and Thimpu strengthened the relations more, On February 1, 1985, King of Bhutan visited New Delhi and appreciated the understanding and mutual cooperation between the two countries. On the assassination of Prime Minister Indira Gandhi, Bhutan mourned for 21 days.

On his visit to Bhutan in September 1985, Prime Minister Rajiv Gandhi stated, "Our relationship shows that when there is true respect and understanding, difference of size do not come in the way of equality. It will be India's endeavour to build further on the excellent foundation that have been laid."

King Wangchuk also showed the spirit of friendship when he said, "We have succeeded in demonstrating to the world that an enlightened and farsighted leadership can make it possible for a large country like India and a small neighbour like Bhutan to co-exist in perfect harmony, trust and cooperation."

On the visit of President R. Venkatraman in October 1988, the King Wangchuk said that the friendship and cooperation between the two countries has continued to flourish and grown with passing generation."

In July 1990, when Indian Energy and Civil Aviation Minister Mohammed Arif Khan visited Bhutan, the King of Bhutan expressed his full confidence and complete satisfaction with Indo-Nepal relations. The Chief Minister of West Bengal, Jyoti Basu also invited by Bhutan to discuss the issue of Nepali immigrants. Jyoti Basu assured Bhutan for not using the territory of West Bengal for any agitation against Bhutan. The Government of India also warned Nepalese settlers in India for not joining any anti-Bhutan activity. During his visit to India in January 1993, analysing the Indo-Bhutan relations, the King said,

> "These relations are unique and based on complete trust, understanding and friendship. This friendship is a fine model for a troubled region like South Asia, as these relations were managed successfully for the last fifty years."

On many regional and international issues, India and Bhutan has different views and opinions. It is clear that Bhutan does not consider itself bound by Article II of the Treaty of 1949, which made India responsible for the external affairs to compel Bhutan to follow a similar path.

Though India and Bhutan both are the members of United Nations, NAM and SAARC, But at the NAM summit in Havana in 1979, Bhutan supported the Pol Pot regime of Cambodia, while India opposed it. Also in the United Nations, the stand taken by Bhutan was different from that of India on the rights of land locked states. Unlike India, Bhutan signed the Nuclear Non-Proliferation Treaty (NPT) in 1985 and also supported Pakistan's proposal that South Asia should be a nuclear-free zone.

PROBLEM OF NEPALESE IMMIGRANTS

The problem of Nepalese immigrants is the mutual problem of India, Bhutan and Nepal. The Nepalese started coming to Bhutan soon after the Treaty of Sinchula in 1865, and settled down in South-West Bhutan. The number of migrants increased alarmingly with time and now it is more than two lakhs. The Citizenship Act of 1985 gives the citizenship to those Nepalese who are domiciled in Bhutan since 1958, or his/her parents should have been citizens of Bhutan. This led the serious resentment among the Nepalese which presently resulted into the activities of murder, rape, burning villages and terrorism.

In order to prevent terrorist activities, Bhutan is constantly engaged in talks with Nepal and India. India is treating this problem as Bhutan's internal affair, which should be solved bilaterally.

THE PROBLEM OF ULFA MILITANTS IN BHUTAN

The security and integrity of Bhutan were severely threatened by United Liberation Front of Assam (ULFA) in 90s, the 720 kilometer long Indo-Bhutan border and the geo-strategic location and mountainous terrain gives an immense opportunity for infiltration. Bhutan's southern border touches the north-east regions of India, where Bodo and ULFA are working. And the north east is just 20 kilometer away from Bhutan border is suitable for arms smuggling from Nepal, China and Tibet, which had created a new "Gun Culture" in the region. In the beginning of 1990, many Assamese militants and terrorists of ULFA and NDFB (National Democratic Front of Bodoland) took shelter in Bhutan which were working for various similar organisation like BLTF (Bodo Liberation Tigers Force) and KLO (Kamatpuri Liberation Organisation). In order to prevent terrorist activities along with the border, the King had meeting with the Chief Minister of Assam and West Bengal. During his visit in March 1996, the King of Bhutan indicated for a mutual extradition agreement to deal with the problem of cross border terrorism and organised crime. But all these attempts could not control the cross-border infiltration and Bhutan had become a sanctuary for ULFA and Bodo militants.

The Bhutanese Foreign Minister Jigme Thinley said in an interview on July 24, 1998, "However the issue of ULFA and Bodo insurgents is a domestic problem of India, but it had spilled over to Bhutan and is considered as a threat to the security and sovereignty of Bhutan since the armed people entered our land and have forcibly occupied our areas.

The Government of India proposed to initiate a joint Indo-Bhutan Army (JIBA) operation to drive out these militants from Bhutan. But Royal Government of Bhutan (RGB) did not respond to it and decided to take action on its own. The Bhutan's National Assembly, Tshongdu, passed a Four Point Action in 2000 to flush out insurgents from Bhutan territory.

- Cut-off food supply to the militants.
- Punish those groups helping insurgents by invoking National Security Act.
- Pursue dialogue with the militants to make them leave peacefully.
- If all efforts fail, military action will be taken.

King Wangchuk during his visit to India in September 2003, showed its great concern over the presence of nine ULFA, eight NDFB and four KLO camps running on Bhutan's soil. He said, "Bhutan is fully committed to the understanding between India and Bhutan, as close friends and allies. We will not allow our territories to be used by anyone for carrying out activities that are harmful to each other's national interest."

A military action known as Operation Flush Out (Operation All Clear) was taken by RGB as a last resort on December 31, 2003. All the militants and infiltrators were flushed out from Bhutan. It was a great success and achievement of a small country like Bhutan.

KING WANGCHUK VISIT TO INDIA IN 2005

King Wangchuk five days state visit to India in January 2005 as Republic day chief guest for the second time had strategic importance to India. These issues prompted King's visit:

- China's road building ventures in Bhutan.
- Requisition by Pakistan Prime Minister to open their embassy in Thimpu.
- Operation All Clear.
- Indian assistance for Bhutan's Ninth Plan.
- Punatsangchhu Hydro-electric Project.

On 25th January, the Prime Minister and King signed on an Memorandum of Understanding (MoU), that a study shall be done on the extension of railway network in the border area of West Bengal and Bhutan.

KING WANGCHUK VISIT TO INDIA 2006

Prime Minister Manmohan Singh had a talk with the visiting Bhutanese King on July 29, 2006 in New Delhi. The talks assume significance in view of China's increasing interest in Bhutan in particular and the region in general. Earlier in July 2006, China connected its mainland with Tibet through a Lhasa-Beijing train—a US$ 4 billion engineering marvel which has a huge strategic importance for India. Also China has been showing keen interest to set-up direct diplomatic relations with Bhutan—a country which traditionally had no diplomatic ties with any nation other than India.

But the destinies of the two nations are inextricably intertwined. The statesmen and leaders of our two countries have realized the truth of inter dependence. Being a small and landlocked country, Bhutan's foreign policy is operating on the basic principles and objectives of peace, non-aggression, mutual respect, cooperation, non-alignment and faith in United Nations. To achieve these goals, Bhutan believes in internal development, extension of diplomatic and economic relations with other countries and active involvement with non-controversial regional issues.

Some issues and steps taken by Bhutan are posing threat to India. Bhutan's King is following "nationalistic policies." Nepali language is removed from the curricular and government introduced a "One nation, One people" policy. Nepalese are forced to flee.

Recently India asked to Bhutan for access to a road to connect Tawang-home of Tibetan Buddhist monastry as it today takes more than 48 hours to drive to Tawang. But Bhutan has refused access to this route.

BIRTH OF DEMOCRACY IN SHANGRI-LA

It is good for democratic India that this tiny state has gone to adopt democracy. King Wangchuk handed over throne to his son in 2007. This democratisation of Bhutan will improve the relations between the two democracies. In December 2005 King Jigme Singye Wangchuk said he will abdicate in 2008. In December 2006 King had abdicated his throne in favour of his son. Mock elections were staged for people in April 2007. The year 2007 also marked the 100th year of the Wangchuck dynasty in 2006. On December 31, 2007 People voted in first ever democratic elections. "This is perhaps the world's only peaceful transition in people's rule." Khesar Namgyal ordained a new constitution ushering in constitutional monarchy in Buddhist kingdom.

INDIA TO TAP BHUTAN FOR MORE POWER

India has committed a financial support of nearly Rs 9,300 crore for Bhutan's hydro-power development over the next 12 years and is aiming to import up to 10,000 MW of power from the Druk country by 2020, up from earlier estimates of 5,000 MW.

CONCLUSIONS

Neither India nor Bhutan can take each other for granted Mutual respect for each other's interests is the secret of their stable friendship. The cornerstone of this mutuality of interests, of course, is a shared strategic perception. Both the countries have a major stake in the security, stability and prosperity of the other.

Indo-Bhutanese bilateral relations have acquired many dimensions in today's international scenario. The problems faced by both the countries are common whether it is poverty, health, illiteracy, sustainable development, migration or terrorism. And the solutions lie in the cooperative attitude and political will of the leaders.

The peace and progress of Bhutan will depend on the peace and progress of India, which can take both the countries to the greater heights of peace, progress, and prosperity. Though India's foreign policy interests have a global dimension, the starting point has to be sound relations with our immediate neighbours to that is linked our security, our prestige, our economic well-being.

"Over the years, India and Bhutan have established and strengthened a mutually beneficial relationship. Since the time of Pandit Jawahar Lal Nehru and Jigme Dorji Wangchuk, we have shown to the world that an enlightened and far-sighted leadership can make it possible for a large and powerful country like India to co-exist with a small neighbour like Bhutan in perfect harmony, understanding and friendship."

Bhutan is a friend on whom India can rely at time of need. And this friendship have cemented with the frequent visits of the political leaders. Their visit have contributed enormously in understanding Bhutan's special needs and problems.

Bhutan is not alone in suffering from ethnicity linked conflict, but India's stand is clear: it has not allowed and will not allow the Indian soil to be used for activities directed against Bhutan. Further it has taken every possible care to ensure the free movement between India and Bhutan. Mechanism have been set-up to ensure effective cooperation between the security forces on the two sides of the border. This cooperation takes place within the framework of Friendship Treaty of 1949, which is now replaced with a new Indo-Bhutan Friendship Treaty of 2007. When the King of Bhutan visited India in February 2007, the Treaty was signed between King and Pranab Mukherjee, Indian External Affair Minister. It will give a new height to Indo-Bhutan old and trusted friendship.

India-Myanmar Partnership: Need for Widening and Deepening

Myanmar earlier known as Burma is an ASEAN country with which India shares land and maritime borders. Myanmar is considered a natural "land bridge between South and South-East Asian regions." India and Myanmar represent two important areas of the world, South and South-East Asia respectively, as well as the non-aligned and SAARC world. Geographically, Myanmar has a long land border (1643 km.) with India. The five Indian states—Arunachal Pradesh, Nagaland, Manipur, Mizoram and Assam are situated along Indo-Myanmar border. In terms of maritime distance Myanmar is nearer to India. The Andaman and Nicobar Islands are situated just 50 km away from Myanmar and 90 km from Indonesia. Physical proximity has remained a critical factor in shaping India's relations with Myanmar from the time immemorial.

Historically too, India and Myanmar had a common colonial past. Till 1973 Myanmar was a part of India and on 1 April 1937, Myanmar was separated from India and made a separate state. Myanmar got its independence on 4 January 1948. Myanmar remained a province of the British Indian Empire till 1937, since when it was directly ruled from London. Inspired by the Indian freedom movement, Myanmarese leaders led their national

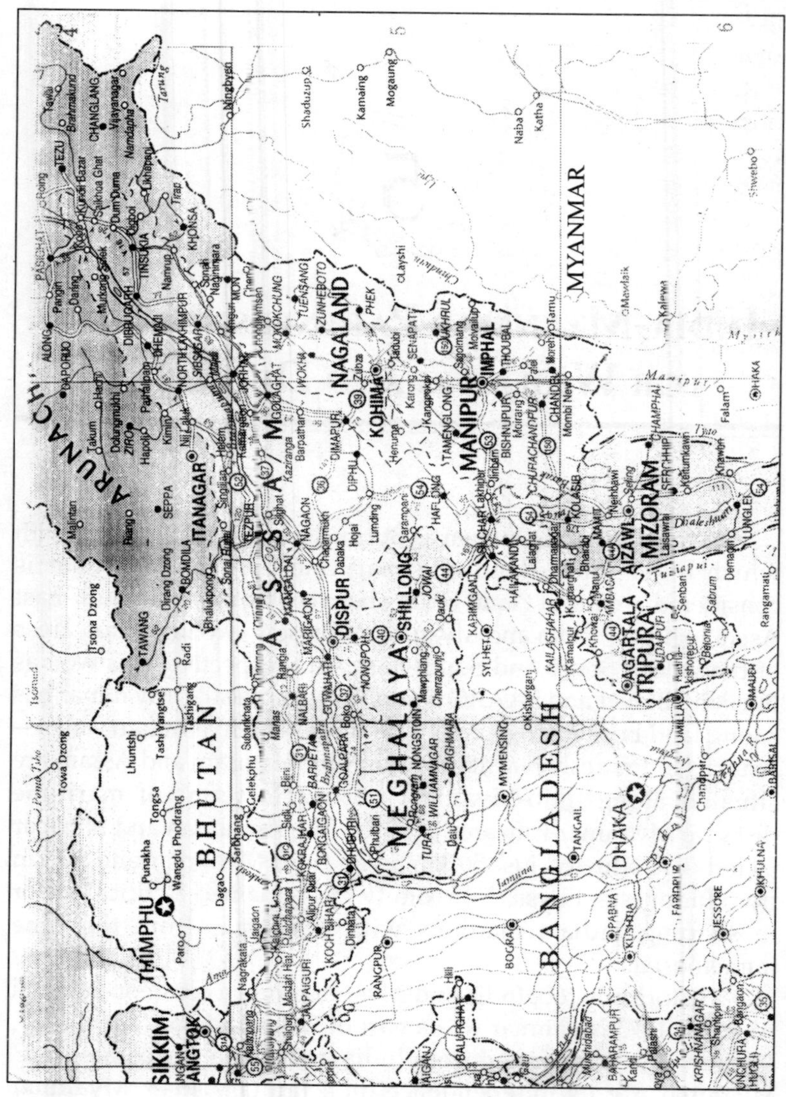
BHUTAN
BANGLADESH
MYANMAR
MEGHALAYA
NAGALAND
MANIPUR
MIZORAM
TRIPURA
SIKKIM
THIMPHU
DHAKA
ITANAGAR
DISPUR
SHILLONG
KOHIMA
IMPHAL
AIZAWL
AGARTALA
GANGTOK

movement on the Indian lines to secure independence in 1948. Culturally also Myanmar is close to India. Buddhism is the dominant religion of Myanmar which binds them together. India also shares a common membership with Myanmar in BIMST-EC established as a sub-regional group for the economic development of the sub-region. For India, sub-regional arrangements offer the most practical strategy of dealing with the ASEAN. Myanmar or Burma has an oppressive military regime that is singularly responsible for isolating the country from the rest of the world. As a result it is perhaps one of the poorest and most backward countries the South-East Asian region.

The size and population of neighbours, play an important role in shaping the foreign policy. India and China's size and population are the reasons of fear and anxiety to the Myanmar. This fear was reflected in the November 8, 1947 speech of U Nu:

> "Burma's total population, compared to her immediate neighbours east and west, is a mere handful. This is a hard world, a cruel world. Even if all of us are perfectly united still the preservation of our independence will be no easy task."

Myanmar as a small nation always 'mistrust' bigger 'India'. The then Myanmarese Minister of Commerce and Industry's statement also reflected this:

> "Small nations always mistrust bigger ones, especially those close by. For years past, every Burman has mistrusted China, whether under Mao or Chiang. They also mistrust India; for that matter also mistrust Soviet Russia and even America."

But it was also true that the greater fear of China made Myanmar to think in terms of cooperating with India. In the same speech U Kyaw further added that, "We are entering into closer relations with India, Pakistan and Indonesia and are trying to find a formula for peaceful co-existence in this part of our world."

Myanmar in beginning was also apprehensive about the ambitious attitude of India when wanted to become a leader of Asian movement. The Myanmar's fear was not baseless. Nehru had a broad vision of South Asia Federation of Afghanistan,

Burma, India and Iran. Nehru wrote in his book 'The Discovery of India' that India will develop as the centre of economic and political activity in the Indian Ocean area. But after Independence India did not follow the policy of interference with her any neighbours.

INDIA AND MYANMAR RELATIONS BEFORE 1947

India and Myanmar had a long historical bindings. The political connections of Myanmar with India was started in the middle of the 18th century during the Bayinnaung's empire of the Toungoo Dynasty. It was during his time that Manipur was attacked and subdued. He also sent a mission to Mughal India. The Mons, who overthrown the Bayinnaug's empire were known as Tailangs. The term was probably derived from Telangana in South India. There were many Indians from this region came to Burma. The Mons were later on suppressed by Alaungpaya (1752-60) of the Konebaug dynasty which lasted till the Britishers came.

The other group in Burma, the Arakanese, also had connections with India. When the Arakanese king was ousted by the Burmese in 1404, he fled into Bengal and served with king of Gaur later on in 1430.

As early as 1944, Sardar K.M. Pannikar had focused on the strategic significance of Burma to India by saying:

> "The defence of Burma in fact is the defence of India and it is India's primary concern no less than Burma's to see that its frontiers remain inviolate. In fact, no responsibility be considered too heavy for India when it comes to the question of defending Burma."

PROBLEM OF INDIAN NATIONALS IN MYANMAR

The issue of the rights of the Indian nationals, who had been living in Myanmar since first century, became an irritant in Indo-Myanmar relations in late fifties and early sixties. The Indian immigration to Myanmar was date back to first century, but the real beginning was started from the year 1826, when British annexed of lower Burma to the British Indian empire. Indian immigration led to the political and economic consequences on the Myanmar economy and politics. By 1852, the Tamil Nadu Chettyars started their banking business money-lending in Myanmar. By 1871 there were 1,31,000 Indians in Myanmar. The Annual Report on the administration of Burma for the year 1884-85 revealed the fact.

The poor financial condition of the country due to constant war of Myanmar kings with the British, gave an opportunity to Indians to come over Myanmar. That was why the Chettyars involved into money lending business. Besides this the Indians were also employed in the rice mills as labours. Thus the Indian population was risen sharply from 420, 800 in 1891 to 1,017,825 in 1931.

This flow of Indians in Myanmar caused the violent break out of anti-Indian rioting in Rangoon in 1930. Even the demand of separation of Burma from India was raised which was ultimately given effect to in 1937 under the Government of India Act 1935. The anti-India feeling was further increased against the Indian's marriages with Burmese girls which resulted into half caste children. In 1938 the anti-Muslim riot broke out in Myanmar as they were more against a Muslim marriage with a Burmese Buddhist girl. The off springs of this marriage were called the Zerbadis. A book written by a Muslim containing highly critical remarks against Buddha was also the reason for the riot.

Besides religious gap, there was a cultural gap also. The Indians did not assimilate easily into the political and social life of the country.

To control the problem of immigration the government of Myanmar concluded an agreement with the Governor General of India in July 1941. The Agreement provided for passports, visas, permits, penalties for unlawful stay in Myanmar, a literary test, registration of Indian residents in Myanmar, etc. Only those Indians who were in Myanmar on July 15, 1941 were entitled to remain in the country indefinitely.

The Indians called the agreement as dishonourable. With certain changes the Government of Burma passed an emergency Act in June 1947 in the matter of Indian immigration. This made the possession of visa passport or a permit compulsory for all foreigners. The Indian flow of immigrants to Burma was on rise during 1948, 1949 and 1950 which was 33,399,15,160 and 17,023 respectively.

After independence of Burma, India took bold steps to control infiltrations. Indian Deputy Minister of Foreign Affairs Dr. B.V. Keskar said on March 8, 1949 that:

> "We have encouraged Indians who have settled down in various countries to take up the nationality of and to merge themselves with the people of those countries and their interest."

Following this policy India wanted that Indians with property in Burma should permitted to return back to Burma after independence of Burma. Though the action was not wrong in principle, but Burma did not like to have a large population including Indians into their country. Inspite of the Myanmarese hostile attitude and the difficulties caused by the insurgents, the Indians did not like to leave Myanmar. Dr. Keskar reported in the Parliament on August 28, 1951 that "very few Indians who are even in the insurgent areas have expressed a desire to come back to India." This situation created the uneasiness in the relations.

Pandit Nehru was against the idea of dual citizenships. Though Nehru had good relations with Myanmar, but he did not want to give China an issue as an excuse for intervention. After the independence, the Indian Constitution and the Union of Burma Citizenship Act 1948 made clear that Indians who acquired the Myanmar citizenship were required to renounce their Indian nationality. In September 1947, the Myanmar Government brought an end of discrimination in citizenship and employment between natural born Myanmarese and naturalized Myanmarese of Indian origin. U Nu, the Prime Minister of Myanmar assured the Indians who had acquired Myanmar citizenship that they would be treated equally with the Myanmar people.

According to the constitutional provision on citizenship, granting of Myanmar citizenship to the Indians would be automatic (naturalised). For those who did not like to elect Myanmar citizenship, they had to register themselves as Indian citizens under the Registration of Foreigners Regulation.

These provisions created a group of stateless persons. The many people residing in Myanmar could not be able to decide their nationality. There was no provision in the Indian Citizenship Act of 1955 to treat the Indians living in other countries as Indian citizens so the problem of stateless people was arised, neither they were Myanmarese citizens nor they were Indian.

The problem of stateless persons became more severe when the Burma Citizenship Act of 1948 empowered the Government to cancel any citizenship certificate within a year of granting if the courts found a person to be disloyal to Union of Burma. And under the amendment of 1958, citizenship could be revoked even without court inquiry. These all provisions were very disturbing to the Indians who had become Myanmar citizens.

The fact was that the Indians were never liked by Myanmarese people. The Indians were discriminated in matters of postings and promotions. The Sikhs were treated as "bearded Burmans."

In the field of education also, the Indians faced the medium problem of Burmese. The Myanmar government was in favour of use of their language at the primary level only and secondary level it should be Burmese so the Indians established an Indian High School.

Being a small country to control large scale flow of funds the Myanmar Government on October 4, 1949 ordered to produce foreigner's registration certificate compulsory for remittance money orders. As most of the Indians did not register themselves as foreigners, they were unable to remit money. The problem was increased when only income tax payers were allowed to remit abroad and that too only upto Rs. 30 per month to only to dependents included only a wife and children and no more. This irritated the Indians, as this excluded even the parents, brothers and sisters.

Nehru took these issues as "petty" and "minor matters". In 1948, the Myanmar government passed the Land Nationalization Act which provided the compensation for nationalized lands and prohibition of selling nationalized land. From this act the Chettyars were very much dissatisfied with the compensation as they had invested a lot in agriculture and in urban property. On the request of Chettyars, an Indian delegation visited Myanmar in June 1950. But the delegation had to return to India without a settlement. The Chettyar's case made relations sour between India and Myanmar. In 1958, the Government of Myanmar agreed to pay Rs. 2500 in cash to every landowner and the rest of the amount in bonds with three percent interest annually.

When Ne Win came to power in 1962, he tried to limit the hold of the money lending on the peasants. He brought a new Money Lenders Act which permitted only Burmese nationals to lend money which marred Indo-Myanmar friendship. The Chettyar's attitude was mainly responsible for this. But no doubt that Chettyars on the Indo-Myanmar relations were very considerable. They formed a powerful groups.

Besides the Chettyars, the Indian employees also faced various difficulties. A high proportion of Indians were employed in Myanmar in the forest, civil, police, medical, contractorship, etc. In 1947, the Government of Myanmar had notified that unless the Indians became Myanmarese nationals, their jobs would be fortified. Consequently 1000 Indians returned to India by February 1949.

The situation got worsened during the Myanmar government servants went on strike in February 1949. The Government of Myanmar dismissed about 1900 Indians till May 1949 when they failed to return to their work. In the meantime, the civil war in Myanmar was at its height which disrupted the Myanmar economy with the result many Indians were thrown out of employment. The Myanmarization of civil and government service further compelled Indians to flee away from Myanmar. The Government of India attitude towards this was very cold. Nehru was considering this as "petty matters".

In February 1963, Ne Win government had announced the policy of bank nationalisation. The Indian banks in Myanmar like SBI, PNB, BOB were not allowed under Myanmar laws to make remittances to India. The Myanmarese authorities denied an appeal of Indian Finance Minister, Morarji Desai to allow the affected Indian employees to come to India with all their savings and assets. Despite this, the nationalized banks were given compensation in 1966, while the nationalisation was done in 1963.

The Ne Win military government had also nationalized the export-import trade, rice and tobacco industries, travel agencies, newspapers and other businesses except the Indian sweepers. Though these nationalizaton schemes were non-discriminatory but the Indians were the worst affected as they were in the large number in Myanmar. For the solution of all these problems, the External Affairs Minister Sardar Swarn Singh paid a goodwill visit to Myanmar in September 1964. But the visit could not resulted in any solution.

After this visit, General Ne Win visited India in February 1965 and convinced Indian government about the non-discriminatory nationalization schemes. On September 22, 1964, Swaran Singh admitted that the "Burmese government's measures were entirely non-discriminatory, but it had created human problems". The Indian government had given greater importance to the 'policy of friendship' with Myanmar than the legitimate claims of the Indian citizens in Myanmar. The Prime Minister Lal Bahadur Shastri disclosed in Parliament that "while there maybe some hitches, our relationship with Myanmar is exceeding by good at the present moment." Shastri visited Rangoon in December 1965 for further smooth relations and general Ne Win assured Shastri that" the resident foreigners who could play a useful role in the new social order that Myanmar is building would be given facilities to enable them to live and to work in Myanmar as citizens." This caused the External Affairs Minister M.C. Chagla saying in his meeting with the Myanmar leaders in January 1967 that "there are no outstanding questions left between India and Myanmar." But the problem of compensation for nationalized properties persisted. The fact was that our relations with this close neighbour were soured by its treatment of Indians, living and working in that country.

Thus the question of Indians in Myanmar brought the two countries into a conflict. Frequently the question of Indians in Myanmar figured in the Parliament, especially after 1962. The Indian External Affairs Ministry in its Annual Report for 1964-65 said that "the presence of nearly half a million persons of Indian origin in Myanmar has on occasion tended to be a disturbing factor in the friendly relations between the two countries." This soft attitude of India was criticised as the policy of appeasement and as a "week kneed" and as a "soft pedal attitude."

But the attitude of India was not wrong. Myanmar had the sovereign right of passing non-discriminatory legislation. It was on the way to achieve 'Burmese way to Socialism', India was also achieving concept of welfare state through Socialism. Myanmar was not hostile to India only. So how could India interfere in its policy of nationalization.

THE MYANMARESE IN INDIA

The most of the Myanmarese in India were concentrated in the Andaman (about 5000) before the Andaman island became a part of India. After independence the problem of Myanmarese was arised. Some of them had criminal charges. They had the fear of retaliation by the Myanmar government. The Myanmarese nationals who wanted to stay permanently in the Andaman were allowed to do so after taking resident permits. In 1967 an agreement was signed between India and Myanmar over the repatriation of 2000 Myanmarese from the Andaman island to Myanmar. The Indian government was quite sympathetic towards those Myanmarese who wanted to stay in India only, but the Government of India pointed out to Rangoon that it would not be possible to undertake the additional burden.

India-Myanmar relations were close during the first Prime Minister of independent Myanmar U Nu (1948-62) who considered Mahatma Gandhi his political Guru. India played a pivotal role in making Burma politically and militarily strong in the early years of its independence. Independent Burma was facing early teething problems. The assassination of Aung San, commander of the Burmese forces, was followed by revolts by the Burmese Communist Party (BCP) and the Karens—the minority ethnic group. India was very much concerned with this as emergence of Communist China which sharing common borders with India and Burma was also a subject of concern for India. So India took initiative in providing military and economic aid to Burma along with Commonwealth nations. The Commonwealth nations offered a loan of six million pounds in June 1950.

A coup in March 1962 by general Ne Win and his long military rule until 1988 maintained a low profile relationship between India and Burma. The Ne Win regime had no regard for democratic institutions. He followed a policy of isolation from the rest of the world and withdrawal from international forums such as the United Nations, the British Commonwealth and the Non-Aligned Movement (NAM).

Even though the bilateral relations between India and Myanmar were very low. Prime Minister Indira Gandhi and Rajiv Gandhi paid official visits to Rangoon in 1967 and 1987 respectively. India showed her interests in a purposeful partnership with a strategically potential neighbour. Rajiv Gandhi made a fine gesture when he advocated Myanmar's entry into SAARC. But Myanmar was cool to this proposal as it had set its sights on the membership of ASEAN.

On September 18, 1988, the military junta seized power after the exit of Ne Win following the brutal suppression of the students and others were protesting against the repressive military regime of Ne Win. The military junta under the banner of state Law and Order Restoration Council (SLORC) had ruled Myanmar.

India adopted a hard line attitude towards the military government in Myanmar. India was one of the first countries who denounced Junta's repression of pro-democracy activities in 1988. The Indian Embassy in Yangon offered shelter and support to Myanmarese students but also encouraged activist students to cross over the boundaries. The then Foreign Minister P.V. Narasimha Rao issued "strict instructions" not to turn back genuine refugees from Myanmar. In May 1990 elections the National League for Democracy (NLD) under the leadership of Aung San Suu Kyi won the election. The victory of democracy was a solace for India.

India pro-democratic attitude and reservation about the suppression of democracy made Yangon to declare that India was making undue interference in the internal affairs of its "next door neighbour." Even Myanmar was feared of Indian military intervention on behalf of the Myanmar's democratic movement.

CHINA'S PROXIMITY WITH MYANMAR

After Myanmar achieved freedom in 1948, its foreign relations were dominated by the government's desire to establish and maintain real political and economic independence. Initial pro-western orientation and British Commonwealth ties did not prevent the country from being the first non-Communist state to recognize Communist China in 1950. Thereafter China occupied an overriding importance in its foreign policy. She made and developed good relations with this increasingly powerful neighbour.

This attitude of India produced a low profile relationship between New Delhi and Yangon and India's pro-democratic power's support pushed Yangon towards Beijing. China grabbed the opportunity and gave its full support to military regimes.

In October 1989 and in November 1994, Yangon and Beijing concluded two arms deals and China supplied a large quantity of military equipments for the re-organization of its armed forces.

China was giving help to military regime of Myanmar in a big way. China had become a potential ally. China provided Burma fighter planes, patrol boats, tanks and ammunition in addition to sophisticated communication equipment. China also extended its help in developing infrastructure, including the construction of roads from Yunnan frontier to Rangoon as well as upgrading Burma's ports. Today Myanmar has come up a big consumer market for Chinese goods.

In early 1990s Myanmar started the program of upgrading its naval forces with the help of Chinese assistance. China also wanted to secure access to Bay of Bengal and Indian Ocean through Myanmar "to keep vigil over the Indian naval activities in the Indian Ocean," as the commander of the Chinese People's Liberation Army Navy (PLAN) said in his visit to Chittagong port in 1986 that "Indian Ocean is not India's Ocean."

INDIA-MYANMAR FRIENDSHIP GESTURE

Both India and Myanmar are following the policy of non-alignment since independence. In the words of U Nu, "Burma is pledged to the policy of positive neutrality and non-alignment with any bloc." But it is true that both in their national interests were not truly non-aligned but having the cordial relations with both the blocs as they were economically underdeveloped.

Indian policy of non-alignment was also adopted by the Myanmar. Like India, Myanmar was also in a need of foreign aid from all quarters for the development of the nation. In 1952 Myanmar had launched an aim of converting Myanmar into a Happy Land (Pyidawtha) as a Welfare State. So Myanmar wanted to pursue an independent foreign policy to fulfill her national needs.

Both India and Myanmar followed a policy of non-alignment since independence. Where India was not aligned with any major group of power, Myanmar also under U Nu leadership followed the policy of positive neutrality and non-alignment with any bloc. Then Myanmarese foreign minister U Tin Tut said that "Burma has no desire to be entangled in any alignment of world powers."

But both could not followed strictly non-alignment policy. Both the countries had to fall back upon the United Kingdom for sheer necessity. India, for instance needed British arms assistance for its industrialisation and trade and commerce. India's membership of British Commonwealth and its past history of British colonialism also made her pro-British.

Though Myanmar was not a member of the British Commonwealth, it did not stop her from becoming pro-western. Britain was a good ally of Myanmar. The Prime Minister U Nu strongly defended the Anglo-Burmese Treaty for defence during his reign, which was strongly criticised by the Burmese Commonists. The U Nu government was sharing the power with the Communists which pursued the government "to secure political and economic relations with Soviet Russia in the same way as they were having these relations with Britain and the United States" under the "15 point programme."

KUNMING INITIATIVE (1999)

Through the Kunming Initiative (1999) (in Yunnan province), China took an initiative to establish a forum for Regional Economic Cooperation among the four countries—China, India, Bangladesh and Myanmar. The basic objective of the Kunming Initiative was "to strengthen regional economic cooperation and cultural exchange among the sub-regional states." The region is very rich in terms of bio-diversity, energy potential and human resources. There is tremendous scope for trade and services, software, banking, insurance, education, health and human resources. The economic rational for this sub-regional plan is that India could develop its north eastern region as well as equally underdeveloped economy of Myanmar with China's Yunnan province which is rich in resources and is fast emerging as an industrial hub. China also took interest in the economic development of Myanmar. It offered Myanmar a 50 million yuan interest free loan in 1991. Sino-Myanmar trade was reached in 1992 to $1.5 billion from a very few in 1980s.

SINO-MYANMAR BORDER AND ITS EFFECTS ON INDO-MYANMAR RELATIONS

Myanmar like India has a common border with China in the north. The tri-junction where the three countries India, China and Myanmar meet is an undemarcaded boundary. China claims that this disputed triangle belonged to China as far back as the Tang dynasty in the 7th century. China considers the 250,000 square mile of territory disputed. Communist China showed the large area of Kachin, Shan and Wa states of Myanmar in the Chinese communist publications in 1951 as belonging to China.

This border dispute brought Myanmar closer to India, as both were facing the Chinese threat on the border issue. The Chinese government considered that the tri-junction lay not at the Talu Pass but at the Diphu Pass, five miles further south. Myanmar did not accept Diphu Pass as the correct boundary.

In the direction of securing Myanmar's security, the Sino-Burma Boundary Treaty took place on 28 January, 1960. China accepted the McMahon Line only in the case of Myanmar. Early in 1961 the Government of Myanmar and Communist China completed the negotiation of frontier treaty, which settled out standing border question and concluded an economic and technical co-operation and payments agreement.

This Sino-Burma Boundary agreement made the Indian position more embarrassing. The question was raised by Myanmar that if Pakistan can settle their boundary question's with China, why is it that the Indian government can not negotiate and settle its boundary question with the China. China tried to demonstrate "India's rigid attitude" for not solving the Sino-India border dispute.

This attitude of Myanmar was objectionable as Myanmar did not realize that the Sino-Indian dispute was different in nature from the Sino-Myanmar border dispute. However during the Sino-India conflict in 1962, Myanmar played a neutral role—a stand which definitely favoured china.

INDO-MYANMAR BORDER PROBLEM

Before independence, Myanmar was a part of British India. In the past, there was many parts of India—Manipur, Assam,

Naga and Mizo hills occupied by Myanmar and it withdrew its occupation with the time. By the Treaty of Tandabo (1826), the Myanmar withdrew from Manipur which they had occupied since 1821. Two years later, a Boundary Commission fixed the frontiers where it now is and the Manipuris withdrew to the west of Ninghce in 1834.

The Naga and the Mizo Hills boundaries were fixed in the 1870s. The southern point of this frontier was the tri-junction between India, Myanmar and Pakistan. The northern point was the tri-junction between India, Myanmar and China on the 17,349 feet high peak. North of the peak, the frontier was along the crest of the mountain which decided the tributaries of the Brahmaputra from those of the Irawaddhy. The south of the boundary cut across the Valleys of the Nataleik.

Further south in the Mizo Hills the border lies for some distances along the rivers the Tuisa, Tyao and Boinu—all the tributaries of the Kaladan which drained the eastern Mizo Hills into the Bay of Bengal through Myanmar.

NATURE OF THE BOUNDARY PROBLEM

After independence a Report of the Sub-Committee on North-East Frontier (Assam) was submitted to the Constituent Assembly in 1948-49 indicated that the Tirap Frontier Tract, the Lakhimpur Frontier Tract and the Naga Tribal areas included considerable areas of virtually unadministered. The Committee suggested the extension of the administration gradually upto Myanmar Frontier whatever the legal status of the area may be under the Government of India Act.

The report raised the hopes of Myanmar to gain control over large parts of these undemarcated areas. The Indian policy was also to gain control of all undemarcated areas upto Myanmar border.

As Myanmar was pre-occupied with the civil war, after two years in 1951, an editorial was published in July 1951, Nation that "there were areas where the boundaries between Assam and Myanmar had never been demarcated at all and India is determined to adopt a forward policy."

In 1960s, the Kachins of Myanmar, the Nagas and Mizos of India raised the demands of independent states. The government of India was fully aware of the aspirations of the minorities. As the Naga tribes were also living on the Myanmar side of the border. So India did not enforce the passport rules for the hill tribes of these border lands. The hill tribes of Myanmar border lands were allowed to enter into 25 miles in India without any passport from the land border.

The negotiations for the settlement of Myanmar-Pakistan border began in 1953 and the dispute was solved in 1964. The existing Indo-Myanmar boundary is same as it was in 1885 when the British conquered Upper Myanmar and ended the Myanmar independence.

After solving the border problem with China, Myanmar now turned its attention towards Indo-Myanmar border. Nehru and U Nu had taken a joint tour of Indo-Myanmar border in 1953. In 1962 they also had a preliminary survey of the border. His successor Ne Win was engulfed with serious domestic problems. So no negotiations took place between the two nations. This led to the unrest in the tribal hill people which converted into separatists elements.

Explaining the provisional position of the Boundary in the north, M.C. Chagla said in the Parliament:

> "The position with regard to the tri-junction is this. As far ourselves and China are concerned, we have shown the boundary upto a particular point-that is $5^1/_2$ miles further north. On that there is a dispute between ourselves and China in the sense that China claims these $5^1/_2$ miles and we also claim the $5^1/_2$ miles. But there is no dispute as far as Myanmar and ourselves are concerned."

We had to persuade Myanmar to agree to the India's claim of $5^1/_2$ miles because there was already the Sino-Myanmar agreement. Myanmar agreed to this that it was the issue between China and India to settle and they had no concern with this.

The Agreement also dealt with the establishment of the Joint Boundary Commission for the task of planning and carrying out demarcation of the boundary with the preparation of boundary maps and with drafting of a boundary treaty. Subsequently a Joint Boundary Commission was established in 1967 and during the period from 1967 to 1971, the Commission met ten times for the demarcation of the boundary. The actual physical demarcation was started on December 1, 1968 and completed before 1974.

In February, 1967, an Indian delegation went to Yangon to discuss the question of delimiting and demarcating the boundary. As a result of it, a Boundary Agreement was signed on March 10, 1967. The agreement incorporated the description of the traditional boundary according to the existing alignment. Clearing the term existing alignment, M.C. Chagla said, "Existing alignment means that the boundary is already accepted. That is the existing alignment. All that was done was to formalise it."

Article 1 of the agreement described the alignment as:

> "Following the watershed between the Patkoi Bum to Peak Shawshan bum; thence along the watershed between the Irawaddy and the Brahmaputra river systems to its northern extremity, the exact location of which northern extremity will remain provisional pending its final determination."

India first took the question of delimiting and demarcating the boundary with Myanmar during the visit of External Affairs Minister M.C. Chagla to Myanmar in January 1967. Though the Indo-Myanmar border had no border dispute at government level. There was only border demarcation and delimiting problems. And these were the problems of 'mutual interest.

Under the Indo-Myanmar Border Agreement of March 10, 1967, field work started on November 16, 1968. The demarcation of the first 240 miles in the middle sector was completed in 1973-74. Both the countries were so cautious about the solution of the border problems that they made an adjustment in the case of the Light House on the Table Island in the Bay of Bengal.

INDIA-MYANMAR ECONOMIC TIES IN POST-COLD WAR YEARS

The trade relations, which had been established between two during colonial period continued even after independence as both were under developed economy.

After the independence of Myanmar, India was interested in giving economic and military aid to Myanmar to suppress the communist there, as the insurgency in Myanmar could adversely affected the Myanmar trade and commerce and could encourage the spread of communism in Myanmar and through it to India. But this help accepted discreetly by Myanmar, as U Nu did not want to give an opportunity to his rebels to discredit U Nu for selling Myanmar to India.

India also followed the policy of non-interference during the Burma-Karen conflict. India took an active part in the London Commonwealth Prime Minister's conference in April 1949, where a decision was taken to help Myanmar with a loan of six million pound, to which India contributed one million pond.

Myanmar was so much conscious about her sovereignty that it was suspicious about the Colombo plan of 1950. Later on, however, it entered the plan in 1952. The Burmese fear was that "linking our interest with India will impose on us some of the burdens of the Commonwealth."

Following the Commonwealth loan and India's aid, India and Myanmar signed a commercial trade agreement on September 29, 1951 tenable for five years. This trade agreement of 1951 was a general revival of trade between India and Myanmar. Indeed the trade agreement was a step towards greater friendship and cooperation. With this the Burmese suspicion of India seemed to subside, while India was soft towards this friendly neighbour.

India's relations with Myanmar in the post-cold war years are quite cordial. Under the "Look East" diplomacy, India extended its financial and economic privileges to Myanmar. Rajiv Gandhi as a Prime Minister visited Myanmar in 1987. In January 1994, the Government of India and Myanmar did a border trade agreement in order to exchange goods produced locally by people living along 25 kilometers both sides of the border. Accordingly the first trade route between the two countries was opened in April 1995 at Morch in Manipur and Tamu in Myanmar. To boost this border trade, the Government of India has agreed to provide better communication system in Morch and sanctioned necessary funds to the north-east states. At present, two-way trade between India and Myanmar stands at $922 million, of which $780 million constitutes Indian imports from Myanmar and a large chunk of this is rajmah.

The two sides are also reported to have agreed on converting the existing Moreh (Manipur)-Tamu (Myanmar) border trade point into a regular trading route. Another regular trade route through Mizoram will also be added shortly.

SHIFT IN INDIA'S MYANMAR POLICY

The Chinese strategic incursions into Myanmar and its growing interests in Asian South East countries as well as its membership of ASEAN—all these developments have warned India to look and re-think about its foreign policy towards South East nations especially towards Myanmar, its immediate eastern neighbour.

Today India had shed the policy of initial boycott of the military junta and establishment of democracy in Myanmar. Now India is a partner in the development of Myanmar. India had successfully completed the 135 kilometer Kalemyo-Kalewa-Tamu road link which connects Manipur with Myanmar.

India was very much concerned with the growing friendly gestures of Beijing towards Yangon on its eastern border. Its eastern immediate neighbour was more pro-Beijing rather than pro-New Delhi. Besides this, Myanmar-India north eastern border had become a safe passage for smuggling Chinese arms and ammunition, drugs and human trafficking. These were largely attributed to security disturbances in the north-east states of India.

In March 1993, the Indian Foreign Secretary J.N. Dixit paid an official visit to Yangon to enhance "constructive engagement." Before Dixit's visit, the Director General of the Myanmar Foreign Ministry U Aye also came to Delhi. During these visits, both were agreed to manage common border against smuggling, drug trafficking and insurgency.

There was a shift in India's attitude towards Myanmarese 14,000 refugees. India announced in April 1993 that all refugees who were elsewhere in Myanmar to return back to India government run border camps. This Indian stand was in sharp contrast to its previous stand in 1989 when the then External Affairs Minister P.V. Narasimha Rao gave "strict instructions" not to turn back any Myanmarese refugees. On the Kashmir issue, Myanmar again supportive to India, she is in the favour of peace and tranquility in the Valley. Myanmar has good relations with both the conflicting countries. It does not wish to see India and Pakistan go to war again over Kashmir. Once foreign minister U Win Aung said,

"The only hope for the people of Kashmir is the peaceful

resolution of the crisis and we know that this cannot be achieved without the active participation of parties to the conflict. We hope that peace and tranquility will reign in the Valley of Kashmir."

Myanmar is still not member of SAARC, but in ASEAN, Myanmar played a positive role in integrating India with ASEAN. Myanmar with Cambodia, Laos, Vietnam and Singapore extended its support to India's demand of Full Dialogue Partner (FDP) to summit level which was finally conceded by ASEAN summit in November 2001.

Myanmar also enthusiastically joined the sub-regional grouping of BIMST-EC for economic cooperation. In response of India's friendly gesture, Myanmar also pursued a "supportive policy" with India in the area of border management in countering terrorism, drug trafficking and smuggling.

Today Myanmar is against all forms of terrorism. It does not want to use its soil for terrorist activities against neighbouring countries. Once the foreign minister of Myanmar U Win Aung said in an interview that "We will never allow terrorism in any guise to use our territory as a spring board for attacks against any neighbouring countries. We will with all might and resources curb and deter terrorism"

Myanmar also shares India's stand on the nuclear non-proliferation issue. Myanmar gave a good signal by permitting India in November 2002, after a long period of 23 years, to open diplomatic consulate in Mandalay. Thus India joined the exclusive club of China and Bangladesh which were the only one to have consulate in Mandalay. Myanmar, in response, also re-established its own consulate in Kolkata in 2002.

Mekong Ganga Project is an another example of India-Myanmar cooperation to counter China's growing influence in the region. Myanmar is one of the poorest countries in the world, despite its vast natural resources after decades of mismanagement by successive military government.

Basic infrastructure in Myanmar continued to decay. Frustration at soaring prices for basic goods is now turned into protests. The pro-democracy movement and opposition is urging ruling Junta to focus on improving the crumbling economy and solving the economic problems of the people. Unfortunately,

India has not yet evolved a comprehensive policy towards Myanmar.

MEKONG GANGA COOPERATION (MGC)

In November, 2000 India signed along with Myanmar, Cambodia, Laos, Thailand and Vietnam the Vientiane Declaration at Laos. Named as Mekong Ganga Cooperation (MGC), this new six nation sub-regional forum seeks to promote tourism, human resources, culture and transportation among the Mekong countries. It is the grouping of nations from Ganga to Mekong. The basic thrust of the MGC is to undertake economic development of the Mekong region by developing the infrastructure facilities. Road construction, linking the north-east and MGC country, Myanmar will get the benefit from this.

Myanmar has emerged as the Sino-Indian strategic signpost on either side of the Malacca divide. China's strategic interests in the Indian Ocean and its growing closeness as arms supplier to Bangladesh and Sri Lanka has made Myanmar an strategically important for India. China wants an access to the Indian Ocean through its south western province of Yunan, Myanmar and Bangladesh as part of its "encirclement" under "Look West" policy. The Chinese involvement in the development of Myanmar roads and ports and installation of defence surveillance facilities on Myanmar's islands near the Andaman is well known.

Recently in September 2008, Myanmar Government has signed a MoU with the Indian Government. The Myanmar Government has signed a Memorandum of Understanding (MoU) with the Indian Government for taking up Detailed Project Reports (DPRs) and execution of two major hydro power projects on its soil on Chindwin River. Under the agreement, the Department of Hydropower Implementation (DHPI) with the help of NHPC, will develop the 1200 MW Tamathi hydro power project and the 600 MW Shwzaye hydro power project. Both the parties would form a joint venture company to execute the projects. Similarly, credit line agreement between Exim Bank of India and Myanmar Foreign Trade Bank for $64 million has been agreed for financing three major transmission lines to be executed by Power Grid Corporation.

INDIA-MYANMAR TOWARDS MORE MILITARY ENGAGEMENTS

Vice-Admiral Soe Thane of Myanmar visited India from April 1 to April 5, 2007 with a seven member delegation. Earlier the defence minister Pranab Mukherjee as well as the three Service Chiefs have visited Myanmar over the last couple of years to bolster bilateral ties.

Indian and Myanmarese armies are conducting "coordinated operations" along the Indo-Myanmar 1,643 km border to flush out terror outfits like ULFA and UNLF. India has accepted Myanmar's request for military hardware and software in return for the military junta's full cooperation in flushing out Indian insurgent groups operating from its soil.

As part of bilateral agreements, India has already started the process of transferring equipments like 105 mm light artillery guns and T-55 tanks being phased out of the Indian Army, apart from two Islander surveillance aircraft.

India has promised more military aid and training to Myanmar as part of its policy to counter strategic inroads being made into Myanmar by China and Pakistan, as well as to get its military junta's continuing support in flushing out Indian insurgent groups operating from its soil.

India transferred four naval islanders aircraft to Myanmar at "friendship prices" recently. In fact, plans are afoot to give Myanmar even more Islanders, bought from UK in the late-1970s, since the Indian Navy is phasing them out due to its Rs 726-crore acquisition of 11 new Dornier-228s for medium-range maritime reconnaissance and patrolling. Moreover apart from technical support and training, the transfer of 105mm light artillery guns, T-55 tanks, naval gun-boats, mortars, grenade-launchers, rifles and other small arms to Myanmar is already underway.

With India shrugging aside western concerns about supplying military equipments to Myanmar due to realpolitik reasons, the level of bilateral military engagement and cooperative mechanisms has also been bolstered. After the visits by the Army and IAF chiefs and defence secretary, Navy Chief Admiral Suresh Mehta left for Myanmar on May 16, 2007 for a five-day visit to discuss military ties.

Over the past few years, the Navy has been actively pursuing a policy to build "bridges of friendship" with maritime countries to enhance security in Indian Ocean Region (IOR). This of course, will also help counter China's "string of pearls" strategy to expand its arc of influence in IOR. India also remains concerned about the large number of camps of Indian insurgent groups in Myanmar, the only ASEAN country with which it shares land and maritime borders.

With the upswing in military ties, the Indian and Myanmarese armies are now conducting "coordinated operations" along their 1,643 km land border to flush out outfits like United Liberation Front of Asom, United National Liberation Front, People's Liberation Army and Kannglei Yawol Kanna Lup, which have set-up bases in the thick jungles there.

Several top military leaders from Myanmar like Navy chief Vice-Admiral Soe Thane and quarter-master general Lt-Gen Thiha Thura Tin Aung Myint, have visited India in recent days. A team from Myanmar is also stated to be trained at the Army's counter-insurgency and jungle warfare school at Vairengte in Mizoram.

China has been the principal source of arms supplies to the Myanmar security forces, followed by India, Serbia, Russia, Ukraine and other countries. During and after the protests also, in January 2007, External Affairs Minister Pranab Mukherjee promised to give a favourable response to the Myanmar Government's request for military police and security equipments. India supplied military and security equipments, ammunitions and expertise including non-lethal arms to Myanmar. These direct and indirect transfers of arms were confirmed by United States and Australia media. In April 2007, it was reported that Indian and Myanmar security forces were "conducting joint military operations along the 1643 kilometer long Indo-Myanmar border to neutralize insurgent groups." India has not reported to the UN any arms transfers to Myanmar. Myanmar military co-operation with the Indian Governments in dealing with the insurgent groups was linked with an Indian offer to supply military hardware such as tanks, aircraft, artillery guns, radar, small arms and advanced light helicopters. The EU published a report in July 2007 outlining in detail about the potential transfer of attack helicopter to Myanmar from India that contains components, technology and ammunitions.

JOINT EFFORTS TO CURB TERRORISM

To help keep tabs on the movements of North-East insurgents and Pakistan based terrorists and smugglers, Myanmar has agreed to set-up a 'police liason post' at the border.

The post, to be set-up by both the countries, will provide a platform of daily interaction and joint interrogation of persons arrested for drugs or arms smuggling and for insurgency related activities. India and Myanmar had agreed on the joint interrogation exercise in 2005, but it did not make much headway in the absence of a proper mechanism.

The setting up of the 'police liason post' could be a step towards a joint operation against terrorists a reality in due course. Although Myanmar has so far not agreed to launch a crackdown against insurgents on its side the way Bhutan did against ULFA in 2003, the agreement on the 'Police liason post' would at least help in joint sharing of information at the field and national levels. The decision on the liason post was taken during a meeting home minister Shivraj Patil had with his Myanmar counterpart, Major-General Moung Oo in December, 2006. The agreement is significant as it comes in the wake of reports that Pakistan based terrorist group LeT is trying to set-up base in Manipur, which borders Myanmar. Official believe that liason at the police post would help check this new trend which had earlier been restricted to Bangladesh.

On December 19, three Manipuri youths suspected to be Lashkar-e-Taiba cadres were arrested by the police in Delhi. Security agencies believe that the Lashkar operatives have been using Myanmarese soil to train cadres recruited from Manipur.

Besides agreeing to set-up the 'police liason post', Myanmar also agreed to release 17 Indians currently lodged in various jails in the country at the earliest. Among other issues, both sides also discussed matters related to drug trafficking and effective border management. While Myanmar agreed to cooperate on security issues, India, on its part, assured the neighbour of all possible assistance in the field of training and capacity building of its home ministry officials.

MYANMAR OPERATION AGAINST MILITANTS

Myanmar is now quite India-friendly. The Myanmar Government has launched an operation against militants in November 2007 after visiting India's Home Secretary to Myanmar. Myanmar is interested in flushing out militants of the north eastern region of India from Myanmar. The banned ULFA, it is claimed, had shifted some camps deep inside Myanmar from thickly forested areas of Arunachal Pradesh in the wake of growing pressure from the security forces. The Assam Rifles has been particularly going after the ULFA's main strike force the 28th battalion, which is reported to have its headquarter in Myanmar.

MYANMAR PREFERS CHINA OVER INDIA FOR GAS EXPORTS

India attempts to enter into energy tie ups with Myanmar to achieve energy security got a set back when Myanmar turned down a proposal to export gas to India and instead decided to business with China. Myanmar wants to export gas from discoveries made in offshore block A-1 and potential reserves in Block A-3 to China. ONGC Videsh Ltd and GAIL have 30 percent stake in A-1 and A-3 blocks. GAIL in 2006 proposed a 1,573 km pipeline from Myanmar through Mizoram, Assam and West Bengal to Gaya in Bihar to transport gas from A-1 and A-3.

In 2007, China National Petroleum Corporation (CNPC) was awarded three deep sea blocks by Myanmar off its western Rakhine coast, adjacent to the Indian border. With the acquisition of these three blocks, Chinese oil companies now have production contracts in six blocks off the Myanmar coast. The other three are with China National Offshore Oil Corporation (CNOOC). Besides these, Chinese companies have contracts in five on shore blocks.

China has reportedly told Myanmar it will lay a 900 km pipeline in country to transport the offshore gas to the Myanmar-China border. The distance from the gas fields to the India-Myanmar border is about 290 km, making it the more economical export option, but Myanmar's military leadership preferred to go with China. India is concerned over the rise in tempo of China's acquisition of oil and gas assets in Myanmar as this could affect Indian plans to exploit Myanmar's energy reserves.

India lost out to China on Myanmar gas blocks as Yangon ready to hand two blocks to Petro China. The offer to Petro China would end GAIL's dream to bring piped gas through the north-east. The proposed Rs. 8500 crore Myanmar India LPG gas pipeline is now shelved. Myanmar in December 2007 called for bids for selling 3.5 million tons per annum of LNG from Daewoo's A-land A-3 blocks. India's bidding for selling gas through a pipeline was found unsatisfactory by Myanmar.

Similarly recently the Myanmar government has signed a MoU with Petro China, ignoring India's bid, for selling all gas from Blocks A-1 and A-3 where GAIL holds 10 percent and ONGC Videsh 20 percent equity.

The gas is to be wheeled through a 2,300 kilometer pipeline for an annual transit fee of $130 million a year for 30 years. This has cast shadows over GAIL's plan to bring gas through a pipeline via north-east.

It is sad that Myanmar has got the feeling that the Indian Government do not have very serious interest in the energy sector of Myanmar. On the other hand China's support to Myanmar Government against protest movements in the UN Security Council has provided it an opportunity to exploit Myanmar's oil and gas.

In 2006 India has assured investment in developing the Sittwe Port and extended a $20 million credit for restoration of Thanlyin Refinery. India was also sided with Yangon on an unsuccessful United States attempt to pass a United Nation censure motion against the military regime, while China also opposed the United States move in United Nations that has provided the Chinese firms a preferential treatment in award of blocks and gas. China's Petro China recently in 2007 secured exploration rights for off shore blocks AD-1, AD-6 and AD-8 taking the Chinese tally to six offshore and five onshore blocks.

VISIT DIPLOMACY AND INDIA-MYANMAR RELATIONS

General Maung Aye Visit to New Delhi

In November 2000, General Maung Aye, Vice Chairman of the Myanmar's State Peace and Development Council and the second most powerful leader in Yangon's military Junta visited New Delhi. This was the first exchange at the higher political level since Prime Minister Rajiv Gandhi visited Yangon in 1987. During the visit, the two countries agreed to step up bilateral cooperation by establishing cross border transport and communication infrastructure to improve trade and business ties. Also India extended a $15 million credit loan to Myanmar for the purchase of industrial and electrical equipment from India.

Jaswant Singh Visit to Myanmar

Following General Aye's visit, Jaswant Singh, India's External Affairs Minister visited Myanmar in 2000. During this visit, the Myanmar's construction minister Saw Tun and Jaswant Singh opened the 160 kilometer Indo-Myanmar Friendship Road linking the north east India border town of Morch in Manipur with Kalewa on the Chindwin River in Myanmar. Jaswant Singh also inaugurated the Myanmar-India Friendship Centre for Remote Sensing and Data Processing "which was developed with Indian technical expertise to help Myanmar regarding weather forecasting, determination of forest cover and other land use delineations, ground water survey and other areas.

Jaswant Singh again Visited to Myanmar

On April 6,2002 Jaswant Singh again visited Myanmar and inaugurated a trilateral highway project linking Thailand and Myanmar with India. This highway from Morch in India and Moe Sot in Thailand through Bagan in Myanmar is under construction and will enhance trade, investment and tourism among these three countries.

Than Shwe Visit to India

Chief Army Staff Than Shwe, which have the status of President in Myanmar, paid a six-day state visit to India from October 24 to October 29, 2004. This was the first visit of Myanmar President to India during the last 24 years. The bilateral dialogue was held between two heads of state after a gap of 17 years. From this point of view General Than visit was very important. There was eight ministers in the delegation. All of them had separate meetings with their Indian counterparts.

The two heads talked on ULFA activities conducting from the land of Myanmar. Both had decided the cultural exchange program for 2004-06 for strengthening the mutual relations. Two other agreements were signed on Tamanthi hydro-electric project of Myanmar and on non-traditional security.

President Kalam Visit to Myanmar

In March, 2006 President Kalam visited to Myanmar in which bilateral issues were discussed. The agreements were signed on:

- MoU on Myanmar-India gas pipeline. The natural gas found in Asakan could brought to India via a gas pipeline through Mizoram. India is exploring gas in the two blocs of Asakan. When Bangladesh rejected the project of laying pipeline through Myanmar-Bangladesh-India, India was now interested in laying it through Mizoram.
- Myanmar would get the space information through two Indian satellites on concessional rates.
- India declared a 30 lac dollar aid for the project of ocean survey, 1 crore dollar to Kaladan multi-model transport project and 13 lac dollar to establish a remote sensing center at Yangon.
- India also proposed finance aid of two crore dollar for agriculture and water needs. India expressed its will to develop an IT park in Mandalay.

Defence Secretary Visit to Myanmar

Negotiations for the proposed "arms for military co-operation swap" were conducted during a September 21, 2006, visit to Myanmar by India's Defence Secretary Shekhar Dutt. During his two-day trip, he held discussions with the Vice Senior General Maung Aye, and other senior Myanmar military officers, focussing on New Delhi providing Yangon T-55 main battle tanks, which the Indian Army was retiring, armoured personal carriers, 105 mm light artillery guns, mortars and the locally designed advanced light helicopter at a 'special' price.

Air Chief Marshal Visit to Myanmar

On November 22, 2006, that Air Chief Marshal S.P. Tyagi made a three-day visit to Myanmar to discuss several arms offers made almost two years ago by his predecessor, Air Chief Marshal

S. Krishnaswamy. These included a comprehensive fighter aircraft upgrade programme and the sale of Hindustan Aeronautics Limited (HAL) built advanced light helicopters, Bharat Electronics (BEL) radars, airborne radio equipment and surveillance electronics.

Pranab Mukherjee's Visit to Yangon

Pranab Mukherjee visited Yangon on 23 January 2007. Mukharjee's contention that north-eastern insurgent groups were using sanctuaries on the Myanmarese side of the border to engage in anti-India activities. While the Myanmar had an opinion that lack of infrastructure was hindering his troops from extending full cooperation to India. Mukherjee offered to help with cost of infrastructure development in the densely forested and inhospitable terrain.

North eastern insurgent groups—ULFA, Khap-lang faction of National Socialist Council of Nagaland and secessionist outfits from Manipur, have set taken shelter here and procure arms from Myanmar's ethnic rebel groups like Karens and Kachins to attack Indian targets. Pleased with the outcome, Mukherjee, told reporters that Burmese authorities were "very receptive and responsive" to India's concerns.

On the other hand the wish list of the chief of Myanmarese army, General Thura Shwe Man who visited New Delhi in December 2006, consisted of 35 MM field guns, helicopters, mortars, submarine detecting SONARs, Islander aircraft and spares for MIG fighters.

Coinciding with a renewed bid by Western countries to isolate Myanmar because of the denial of democracy to its citizens by the ruling military leadership, the twin understandings underline India's desire for a deeper engagement with its only neighbour.

Besides, there were understanding on completing fencing of Myanmar's border with Nagaland as well as swift negotiation of Bilateral Investment Protection Agreement and Mutual Avoidance of Double Taxation—two agreements which will be crucial for Indian companies, particularly public sector energy majors like ONGC, keen to make investments here.

India and Myanmar agreed to India's proposal to

institutionalize cooperation between the armies of the two countries for operations against ULFA and other insurgent groups in the North-East.

The understanding was reached at a meeting where India's foreign minister Pranab Mukharjee also agreed to Myanmar's pending request for supply of military equipment.

During the visit, while Myanmar has been cooperating with India's drive against insurgency in the north-east and has even taken action on the basis of information provided by New Delhi, it has not been enough to prevent insurgent from crossing over to Myanmar.

Home Secretary Duggal Visit to Yangon, 13-17 February 2007

A fresh demand for a Bhutan army type operation against ULFA and other north-eastern insurgent groups was made to Myanmar during the visit of Union Home Secretary V.K. Duggal to Yangon. Issues like drug trafficking and effective border management also figured high on the agenda. Myanmar, however, does not accept presence of insurgents in its territory engaged in anti-India operations. The northern states have been voicing concern over this issue, pointing out the importance of Myanmar as the gateway to East Asian countries.

Discussions on border management and fencing would assume significance in the backdrop of reports of smuggling of Chinese grenades and counterfeit Indian currency through the Myanmar's border.

Home Secretary Level Talks-2008

India and Myanmar expressed a desire to strengthen security cooperation and also to work towards realizing the benefits of various infrastructure projects besides enhancing economic cooperation between the two countries by turning the border into a symbol of peace and prosperity. Both sides agreed to work closely to achieve these objectives.

They also discussed various institutional mechanisms to strengthen security cooperation during the 14th home security-level talks between the two countries that concluded in New Delhi on March 10, 2008.

General Maung Aye Visit to India

During the four day visits of General Maung Aye, India and Myanmar signed on three Agreements on 2 April, 2008 :

- Rs. 546 crore Kaladan multi-modal project which will be completed in 60 months to enhance the connectivity between the two countries especially with the north eastern states . The project is fully funded by the Government of India and to be executed by the Inland Waterways Authority of India. The selective dredging of the Kaladan river over a 225 kilometer stretch would allow to and fro links between Mizoram and other north east states.
- Development of the Sittwe port in Myanmar would give a brand new access to the Bay of Bengal and reduce transportation cost. The route of project will be—Kolkata to Sittwe by sea 539 km, Sittwe to Setpyitpyin through inland water 225 kilometer, Setpyitpyin to border by road 62 km.
- The handling point will be Hinawngbu (Mobul) in Mizoram and Myeikw in Myanmar.
- Another agreement on intelligence sharing was also signed, details of which are not opened.

Maung Aye, in his talks with the Vice-President, welcomed Indian investment in hydrocarbons, IT, long-term contract farming—essentially for pulses. During his meeting with President Pratibha Patil, both the leaders noted with satisfaction the growing cooperation at the regional and multilateral level, especially keeping in mind India's Look East Policy.

Maung Aye thanked India for its assistance for cross-border infrastructure projects, construction of roads, lines of credit and establishment of IT Centre at Yangon. Cooperation in security matters on the India-Myanmar border was also discussed.

As Myanmar having a space program, the general ranked number two in the Myanmar's Junta also visited Banglore's ISRO—India's premier space agency. India's known capacity in space launches of its own and foreign satellites has been a object of admiration and sometimes envy in its neighbourhood. Improved ties between India and Myanmar led the Junta to take up what is a fascination for the Junta—a presence in outer space with India.

KALADAN PROJECT

The Rs. 545.85 crore Kaladan multi-modal transport project is India's first significant investment in Myanmar. In the words of Jairam Ramesh, Minister of State for Commerce "We now look at Myanmar as an investment opportunity." No doubt it is a strategic engagement of India. Myanmar is just 25 minutes away from the Andamans. The Kaladan project will establish an Indian beach head at the historic port of Sittwe. From there, a 225 kilometer waterway will be developed till Kaletwa and a 180 kilometer road onwards to the Indian border. The project is expected to be completed in five years. The strategic and commercial benefits to India are considerable. The project will provide an access to Mizoram and to other north eastern states to Myanmar as well as an oyster to the sea by passing Bangladesh.

The more important strategic point that India will make to the world is that it is not going to abandon Myanmar to the tender mercies of the Chinese. It is vitally important for India to protect this particular flank from the pervasive Chinese influence on India's periphery. Just as in Tibet, where Han Chinese have been imposed on the local population, Indian strategists have, over the years, noticed with concern that Myanmar too is succumbing rapidly to the Han Chinese presence. "East of the river Irrawaddy is completely Chinese populated," India believes it's important that it provides a credible and rewarding alternative to the Myanmarese. The project will help India get a foothold in a country where China has already established itself.

MYANMAR MILITARY JUNTA AND INDIAN FOREIGN POLICY

The recent protests in Myanmar in October 2007 by Buddhist monks and thousands of people in typical Gandhian style using the weapon of non-violent against the excesses of the military junta kept India non-interfering in its internal developments. India a former champion of democracy in Myanmar has been conspicuously silent on the developments there.

In the 1980s New Delhi steadfastly stood by the Burmese people's democratic struggle: in the true spirit of the fraternal friendship between Jawaharlal Nehru and Burma's legendary hero Aung San steeled in the flames of their respective struggles for freedom from alien rule. Our late PM Rajiv Gandhi boldly extended full support to the non-violent movement for democracy launched by Aung San's daughter, Suu Kyi. This policy continued till the International Understanding was conferred on Suu.

Today with the 'pragmatists' running the South Block, the Government of India has not only taken a u-turn in its Burma policy, it is going out of its way to woo the military junta there for the purpose of containing the North-East insurgency in the one hand and countering Chinese influence on the other. On both counts it has not recorded any form of success.

India has officially called for a "broad-based process of national reconciliation and political reform" in the words of minister of external affairs Pranab Mukherjee. However, New Delhi has also made it explicit that it will not interfere in the internal affairs of Myanmar.

India's muted response against a military government in a neighbouring country which has a dubious human rights record is not befitting of its credentials as the world's largest democracy and a rising great power. Paradoxically, this puts India on the same side as the world's largest authoritarian state, China. It behoves India to depart itself from its current position on Myanmar and respond proactively for moral and strategic reasons.

India, which was highly critical of the military coup in Myanmar in 1988 became more vocal after the dismissal of the 1990 election results, and led the international condemnation against the junta at the UN. India also opened its borders to political refugees from Myanmar. In 1993, India even awarded the prestigious Jawaharlal Nehru Award for International Understanding to Aung San Suu Kyi, who had been placed under house arrest by the junta since 1988.

However, India slowly began to reverse its policy towards Myanmar as New Delhi calculated that its moralistic approach to Myanmar was not only ineffective in promoting democracy there but also adversely affected India's national security interests. In 1992, during the visit of the vice foreign minister of Myanmar, U Baswe, India reassured Myanmar that it would not interfere in its internal affairs. In 1993, Indian foreign secretary J.N. Dixit visited Yangon and signed several bilateral accords to promote commercial ties. Since then, India has also sold military hardware to Myanmar. India extended a warm welcome to General Than Shwe in 2004, who was the first head of Myanmar to visit India in 25 years.

India began engaging the military junta for four primary reasons. First, India wanted Myanmar to take military action against rebel groups that were based and trained in Myanmar and were active in several insurgencies in north-eastern India. Second, constructive engagement with Myanmar was crucial for the success of New Delhi's "Look East" policy. Myanmar's geographic location as the "land bridge" between India and South East Asia made close ties with Yangon necessary. Third, India is interested in Myanmar's huge natural gas reserves to fuel its rapidly growing economy. Finally, India's condemnation of the junta between 1988 and 1992 only led to an increase in Chinese influence in Myanmar. India's economic and security stakes are too high to allow a coercive policy against Myanmar.

Faced with similar student demonstrations against the communist government in Beijing and the crackdown in Tiananmen in 1989, China was sympathetic to the junta. China's economic military engagement with the military junta soon became essential to the regime's survival. Beijing is also interested in Yangon's vast energy resources. China is further seeking access through the Irrawaddy river into the Bay of Bengal/Indian Ocean region.

In spite of competing with Beijing, New Delhi has not been able to achieve its goals in Myanmar. The junta has duly taken limited military actions against the north-eastern rebel groups based in Myanmar.

The developments in Myanmar have the potential of upsetting India's security calculations in the northeast, besides delaying its attempt for a firmer foothold in the hydrocarbon sector. Other initiatives that could take a back seat if the situation worsens are an unprecedented breakthrough in getting an alternate terrestrial route to the northeast via Myanmar and bilateral and multilateral negotiations to promote trade and commerce.

Criticising India's Myanmar policy it is said that this is not right that crisis is purely an internal affair and of no concern to India. In a globalised world of increased inter-dependence, we cannot live in isolation from one another. What happens in one country has the potential to affect all.

In a region which has transformed itself—socially, economically and politically, Myanmar stands out as a shameful anachronism. Its government belongs in the darker chapters of 20th century history, not in the dynamic and vibrant world of 21st century Asia. The Burmese people needs hope of peace and prosperity. They deserve nothing less.

Many within India, not speak of the Western government and Burmese dissidents, are appalled at the extreme realpolitik that defines India's Burma policy. To be sure, New Delhi must not allow expediency to silence its reservation about the generals' conduct. A free, democratic India cannot simply eliminate political values from the conduct of its external relations. The least India can do is insist on a more credible roadmap for democracy that allows the full participation of Suu Kyi.

The restoration of democracy which the ruling junta has denied it from 1962 and more pronouncedly for almost 20 years not must be an issue of worry for India. The pro-democracy protests by Buddhist monks and ordinary people and their arrest clears that the military junta of Myanmar happens to be one of the most repressive and cruel regimes in the world. Junta's refusal to hand over power to Aung San Suu Kyi despite her party landslide victory in the countrywide elections in 1990, was a greater affront to democracy. Even today she is under house arrest not with standing the world wide condemnation of her persisting detention passionate plea that "India should look to winning the heart of the Burmese people".

While the world and UN are expecting us "to do more" on Myanmar using its influence as the world's largest democracy to put pressure on the regime, India implicitly supporting the Myanmar's military junta by supplying arms, and oil dealing with the military regime in Yangon.

India's stand on Myanmar is that it has to be appropriately resolved by its own people and government through their own efforts of dialogue and consultations. During an interview in Bangkok, Pranab Mukherjee stuck to India's line that it did not interfere in internal developments in any country. India believes that instability in Myanmar would be far more dangerous to the region. Besides India is not overly enamoured of outside interventions to settle internal issues.

India does not want sanctions in Myanmar. But keeping bilateral relations intact, the government has agreed to work on the Myanmar military regime with UN for national reconciliation and dialogue. India also joined the UN secretary general's Group of Friends, a group of 14 countries including India, China, Japan, ASEAN and the P-5, to be able to exert influence on Myanmar while working out ways to help the country emerge from its isolation and poverty.

CONCLUSIONS

Just 70 years ago Burma was an integral part of India. Nearly 20 lakh people from other provinces lived and worked in Burma; two-thirds of the population of Rangoon (as it was then know) comprised migrants from India; Karen and Kachin contingents added muscle to the Indian army; Burma rice was a staple and the Burma cheroot an indulgence. From the pagoda that once graced Calcutta's Eden Gardens (adjoining the cricket ground) and King Thibaw's palace of exile in Ratnagiri to Sarat Chandra Chatterjee's novels, Burma was etched in the Indian consciousness.

The separation of Burma from India in 1937, the expulsion of nearly four lakh Indians in 1963 and the military regime's self-imposed isolation from the world may have contributed to Burma's receding mind share in India. Actually, the eclipse was part of a larger process of the physical and mental truncation of India.

India and Myanmar got independence almost at the same time. And before independence, both of them supported each other's nationalist movement against British imperialism. However after independence, both the nations followed the policy of non-alignment but it was not a true policy of non-alignment. Both of them had to depend on the west for economic and military aid. No doubt the policy paid a rich dividend to both the countries. In the mid fifties, the west began to understand the policy and non-aligned nations as honest brokers in the East-West confrontation.

After becoming independent, Myanmar followed the principles of non-alignment and peaceful coexistence which were similar to the foreign policy principles of India. Thus the journey of friendly and cooperative relations between the twos was started. The historical, cultural and economic links further provided the impetus to more close relations. In 1949, China's emergence as a communist power had developed fear in the Myanmarese. But Myanmar felt that the equidistance with both India and China would be the best policy. However with time, Myanmar realised the importance of good relations with India and today both are having highly friendly cooperative relations and there exists no dispute between them.

Initially India and Myanmar had some differences over the issue of demarcation of borders. Today these differences stand mostly resolved and nearly 1000 miles of Indo-Myanmar border stands demarcated. Both the sides are committed to settle and demarcate through negotiation the remaining areas still form the undemarcated borders between the two states.

Naga and Mizo rebels of India have, at times, made use of Burmese territories for organising anti-national and unlawful activities in NEFA and other Eastern states of India. The existence of thick and dense forests and a terrain which hinders access, has been exploited by these rebels for carrying out hostile acts. The Governments of India and Myanmar have always agreed upon the need to check the operation of rebels in these areas and have in the past collaborated to prevent the rebels from undertaking hostile activities. With the emergence of Bangladesh as a sovereign independent state and due to the effective steps taken by the Government of India, the rebel problem has ceased to be a big problem. India and Myanmar are today bound by an agreement under which Myanmar has accepted the responsibility to help India in liquidating the rebel bases in border areas. This has definitely helped the process of development of cooperative and friendly relations between India and Myanmar.

The geographical portion of Myanmar between India and China always compelled Myanmar a small nation to good relations with both the countries. Myanmar was always in search of place with its two big neighbours, as it knew very well that she was a sandwich between two big countries as a neighbour—China in the north and India in the west.

China's emergence as a communist nation also produced some fear in the mind of Myanmar. Initially Myanmar led a border problem with China. This led Myanmar to have close association with India, so that in the event of any border conflict with China, India could give support to Myanmar.

The trade and commerce between the two countries raised with time. Because of the climate of friendship between the twos, the issues of people of Indian origin, citizenship immigration and land nationalization were sorted out. India did not favour the idea of double nationality, but the Government of India encouraged the people of Indian origin to adopt Myanmar nationality.

Though the issue of land nationalization during U Nu period had created an misunderstanding between the twos. India was not against the nationalization but it wanted an adequate compensation should be paid to affected Indians. So until 1967, the problem of compensation for nationalized properties persisted in spite of the India's declaration that there were "no outstanding questions" between the two nations. India adopted the policy of appeasement for the sake of peace and friendship between India and Myanmar. To some extent it was true that there was a feeling in certain sections of Indian public opinion that the Government of India was paying a very high price for Myanmar goodwill towards India.

Where the defeat of India in 1962 Sino-India war made neighbours doubtful to India's military capability, the India's victory in Indo-Pak war of 1965 convinced the small neighbours of India's power. From 1967, the understanding between the two countries brought them closer to each other. In 1967, a Border Agreement was signed between India and Myanmar for the delimitation and demarcation of their boundaries. The border problem between India and Myanmar was peacefully settled. One important feature of the Border Agreement was that the Myanmar was ready to show in the map the northern tip of the boundary five miles north of the Diphu pass. It was the victory of India. This shift in Myanmar's attitude towards India greatly affected the Indo-Myanmar trade and commerce.

Since 1998, India has extended more than $100 million in credit to the Burmese regime, including for upgrading the Rangoon-Mandalay railway line. In addition, it has contributed

$27 million to the building of the 160-kilometre Tamu-Kalewa highway in Sagaing Division.

India has also emerged as Myanmar's second largest market after Thailand, absorbing 25 per cent of the country's total exports, and it hopes to double bi-lateral trade to $1 billion per annum in the next few years. India is also providing training to Myanmar's armed forces and helping it build border infrastructure. As a part of its energy strategy, it also plans to buy natural gas from Myanmar. This would benefit the military regime millions of dollars annually.

Presently, there exists no major problem between India and Myanmar and this makes it possible for us to predict that Indo-Myanmar relations are bound to develop more friendship and cooperation in the years to come. Both the countries now fully realise the importance of their bilateral relations. A.B. Vajpayee once well observed, "We have historic and cultural ties of long-standing with Myanmar which is a bridge between South and South East Asia." India and Myanmar won their freedoms almost simultaneously and both of them are among the founder members of the non-aligned group. During the freedom struggle our paths converged at many points and it is not surprising that the national leadership of the two countries developed more or less the same world veiw as well as the same commitment to Asian solidarity. During the 38 years of their bilateral relations, both have been successful in keeping the relations friendly and cooperative. Both have developed a mature understanding of each other and are presently cooperating towards the achievement of a new international economic order. Burma has expressed its readiness to rejoin the Non-Aligned Movement (NAM). It withdrew from NAM when Cuba became the 'chairman of the Non-aligned. Myanmar felt that under a committed country like Cuba, NAM can neither fulfil the desired objectives nor play an effective role in world politics. Now, when India is the chairman of NAM, Myanmar has expressed its willingness to rejoin the movement.

It is indeed a healthy and welcome thinking and would surely give new strength not only to the non-aligned movement but also to the bilateral relations between India and Myanmar. However, the China factor, the desire of Myanmar to develop more cooperative relations with ASEAN and the Indo-Myanmarese differences over the Kampuchean issue and

Afghanistan crisis need careful handling by India. The strong cultural and historical links with Myanmar must be used to meet this need. The new President of Myanmar, USan Uh and Prime Minister Maung Maung Kha, were fully awarded to the need of maintaining good neighbourly and friendly relations with India. So was Rajiv Gandhi and the Government of India. Prime Minister Rajiv Gandhi's 1987 visit to Myanmar had strengthened the process of development of increased economic trade and technological cooperation between the two countries. It has encouraged Myanmar, to think in favour of rejoining the NAM. This visit has further developed friendship and cooperation between India and Myanmar.

India is now interested in developing physical connectivity and infrastructure in its bordering neighboring states as well. India is now realized that infrastructure development of the north east region has emerged as the single largest hurdle to not merely development of the region but the region's carrying capacity for India's foreign policy. India's relations with Myanmar and important transit and trade agreements with Bangladesh, China and Myanmar is now in sync with development of the north east. That was why the PM Manmohan Singh gave a special package to North East states.

The north-east, which has 99 km of its borders with other countries, shares its longest international border with Myanmar. If we are connected to South East Asia it is through Myanmar, not just through the North East. Thé north east is a bridgehead for India and for South East Asia Myanmar is the bridge.

India has 'multi-dimensional' interests in this country. India's interests in Myanmar are rooted in energy, security keeping insurgents in check and countering China's overpowering influence on India's doorstep.

Myanmar is also important for India to extend its power into south east Asia, politically and militarily. These interests have kept India and China engaged in Myanmar which is a threat for India's security. India already lost the competition for energy resources in Myanmar to China. Further more China has established naval facilities on Myanmar's Coco Island, putting India's security at some risk.

Myanmar was always regarded as the buffer zone between India and an expansionist China. But India abdicated its responsibilities and allowed Beijing to become the dominant influence in Burma. Today, China lurks over India from Pakistan, Tibet, Nepal and Burma. Its shadow has encroached into the Bay of Bengal and the Andaman islands.

The current political developments in Myanmar present India with an opportunity to craft a new strategy to meet both its moral and strategic goals. For India, the upsurge in Burma is an opportunity to turn the clock back. But before that happens, Burma must return to our mental map. India needs Burma more than Burma needs it.

Myanmar, Bangladesh, Nepal, Bhutan all are India's long-term strategic objectives. That is why for the first time, the Ministry of External Affairs (MEA) is now deeply involved in the north east, taking forward its new mantra of bringing India's foreign policy to its borders. Foreign minister Pranab Mukherjee took a first comprehensive group of minister's meeting on developing infrastructure and physical connectivity in north-east.

It means India's foreign policy on countries like Bangladesh and Myanmar are dictated by these premises rather than anything else. It is a signal statement of Indian foreign policy that will not only affect India's Look East initiatives, but also its neighbourhood policies. India's Look East policy will not pay dividends without a coherent line on Myanmar.

India's top priority is the transit facilities through Bangladesh and Myanmar. The Ministry of External Affairs is involved in re-crafting India's Bangladesh policy which resulted into starting of Dhaka-Kolkata raillink.

The Kaladan multi-modal transport project is a move to ensure cross-border rail link. Myanmar has shown considerable interest similarly in a corridor connecting China with India through Myanmar.

India with technology and Myanmar with energy can be beneficial to each other. While differences are there opportunities for economic cooperation and exchange exist at many level.

India has gained a natural gateway to the east through the territory of Myanmar to reach into the heart of the ASEAN group.

India's buzzwords for Myanmar are peace, stability and reconciliation.

India-Bangladesh Relations—Big Neighbour-Small Neighbour Syndrome

Bangladesh is a difficult eastern neighbour of India, but important in India's diplomatic calculus. Geographically, Bangladesh has a strategic location—a bridge between developed ASEAN and developing South Asia. The liberation of Bangladesh and its coming on the world map as a free and sovereign nation is a result of India's efforts. But despite of the multi-cultural and multi religious personality of India and the cultural affinity of the two Bengals, the relations between these two neighbours are eroding day by day. Small issues were magnified to create a gulf between the two countries. It moved from an anti-Pakistani posture to an anti-Indian one. Though the climate of negotiations are warm, but both the governments could not taken any substantive decision on important issues plaguing bilateral relations. Bangladesh is also not finding herself in India's "Look East" policy skipping its giant neighbour. Mutual distrust is growing. India does not want to ignore crucial problems and is keen on addressing them. India wants peaceful existence with its eastern neighbour.

From the point of view of security and strategic, India-Bangladesh relations occupy a seminal importance. The strategic

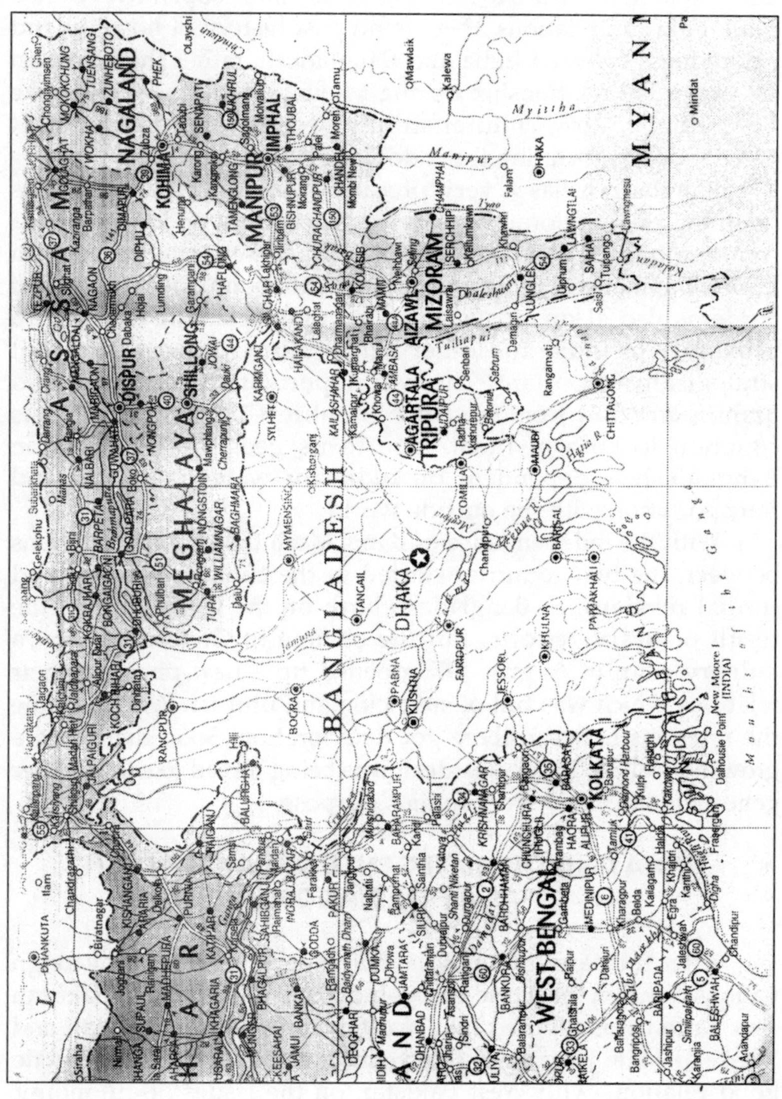
BANGLADESH
DHAKA
MEGHALAYA
NAGALAND
MANIPUR
MIZORAM
TRIPURA
WEST BENGAL
KOLKATA
SHILLONG
KOHIMA
IMPHAL
AIZAWL
AGARTALA
DISPUR
CHITTAGONG
SYLHET
MYMENSINGH
TANGAIL
COMILLA
KHULNA
JESSORE
BARISAL
FARIDPUR
PABNA
KUSHTIA
BOGRA
RANGPUR

location of Bangladesh and India's geo-strategic necessities demand both countries to remain friendly and cooperative. Unlike India-Pakistan relations, there is no past history of hostility and hateredness between India and Bangladesh, rather they have an era of cordial relationship during Mujib period. The factors like geography, history, cultural affinity, security and development perception are dictating the Indo-Bangladesh relations.

Bangladesh has a very precarious strategic location. It is bounded by India on three sides— North, East and West with a common border. The Chittgong Hill Tracts separate Bangladesh from Myanmar and India's Tripura and Mizoram. The China-Tibet border is also 90 km far away in north of Bangladesh. Bangladesh proximity to India and other neighbouring powers makes it strategically important. The two important rivers Ganga and Brahmputra flow from these two countries. The Bay of Bengal is common to both of them. Due to its geographical location Bangladesh is dependent on India for water resources and transportation with the outside world.

With the independence of Bangladesh the bilateral relations between the two countries started in the climate of warm and cordial relations, as Bangladesh birth on the world map is the result of India's efforts. But the change of Government by a military coup in August 1975 opened up a new phase in their relations which was full of suspicion and untrust. With the time the relations between them got deterioration. Soon there was a growing feeling that Bangladesh was being forced to sacrifice her genuine interests to serve India's purpose.

INDIA AND THE EMERGENCE OF BANGLADESH AS A FREE NATION

After the partition of India, two independent and sovereign nations came on the world map—India and Pakistan. But Pakistan as a nation was divided into two territories—East Pakistan and West Pakistan. Ever since the creation, the East Pakistan has no good relations with West Pakistan on the issues of autonomy, language and culture. It led to the birth of Awami League—a political party committed to secure the rights of the people of East Pakistan who often liked to call themselves East Bengal. The East Pakistan in 1970 launched a civil disobedience movement for securing their legitimate rights against the dictatorship of General Yahya Khan. Awami League after securing a clear majority in March 1970 elections gave rise to a revolution which gave birth to a free and sovereign nation.

During the period of protest and allegation, the refugees from East Pakistan started to flee from East Pakistan and entered into India in a large number. This put a big burden on Indian economy and de-formed the demographic character of bordering states. The Government of India demanded the Government of Pakistan to take back the refugees. On the other hand Pakistan was blaming India in creating the trouble and unrest in East Pakistan. It began charging India of interfering with the internal affairs of Pakistan. The Prime Minister Indira Gandhi and external affairs minister Swaran Singh under took world tours to secure world public opinion for the political settlement of East Pakistan crisis, but India's efforts could not succeed. On 15th June, 1971, Indira Gandhi declared in Rajya Sabha that "we will have to go through hell to meet the challenge posed by the developments in East Pakistan.

India started providing help to Mukti Bahini for securing their rights and liberation. The Indian army formed a joint command with Mukti Bahini and both jointly fought against the Pakistan Army. Ultimately a successful military operation succeeded in getting liberation of Bangladesh on 16 December, 1971.

India played a leading role in the liberation of Bangladesh. Indian Army's sacrifices made possible securing people the freedom and rights. India was the first country who recognised Bangladesh on 16 December, 1971.

INDIA-BANGLADESH RELATIONS-MUJIB ERA (1972-75)

On 16 December 1971, India granted recognition to Bangladesh as a free, independent and sovereign state. The first Chancellery of Bangladesh was formally opened on December 9, 1971. While recognising Bangladesh as an independent state, Indira Gandhi, Prime Minister of India, laid the foundation of India-Bangladesh friendship. She said—

"In future, the Government and people of India and

Bangladesh who share common ideals and sacrifices, would forge a relationship based on principles of mutual respect for each other's sovereignty, territorial integrity, non-interference in internal affairs, equality and mutual benefit".

The Mujib regime can be called the golden period of India-Bangladesh relations. Many bold steps were taken towards a close relationship. The geographical location of Bangladesh, India's crucial role in the independence of Bangladesh, the ideological affinity between the Awami League and the Indian National Congress spirit of nationalism, unity in the principles of democracy, socialism and secularism, believe in parliamentary system of government, faith in the policies of non-alignment, peaceful co-existence, anti-colonialism, anti-racialism and anti-imperialism and mutual understanding among the leadership of the two countries-all these factors gave good support in the beginning of warm, cooperative and friendly bilateral relations between the two countries.

Emergence of Bangladesh as an independent state on her eastern border was a great source of satisfaction for India, as relations between India and Pakistan since 1947 were not friendly. Re-emergence of Bangladesh appeared to Indian leadership as a defeat of two nation theory and a victory of Indian foreign policy. Besides this, emergence of Bangladesh was seemed as an 'economic bridge' between Indian heartland and isolated states of north-east India. Opportunities were opened for transit connection through Bangladesh inland and air between eastern region and India.

After returning from Pakistan Jail, Sheikh Mujib, during his brief stop over at New Delhi on January 10, 1972, he paid his tribute to India and her people for her historic role in the liberation of Bangladesh. He observed that the people of his country would never forget the sacrifices made by their Indian brothers for making it possible for them to achieve liberation. While welcoming Mujib, Indira Gandhi hoped that since the culture and economy of their countries were complimentary, the scope for economic, cultural and technological cooperation was great.

Just after the surrender of the Pakistani army, India provided substantial help to restore the shattered economy of Bangladesh. Technical experts, construction materials, food grains, fund were sent to Bangladesh until June 1972. India topped the list of donors, which aid percentage of 36 percent out of 67 percent of the total disbursed aid.

On 5th January, 1972 the Foreign Minister of Bangladesh, Abdul Samad Azad visited India for strengthening the relations with India. An agreement was signed to help Bangladesh for its economic reconstruction. India agreed to provide Bangladesh goods and services upto 25 crores in the shape of aid and grants. A loan of 25 million was also given to Bangladesh to meet its foreign exchange requirements which was to be repaid by Bangladesh in 15 equal yearly installments after five years.

On January 22, 1972, India's special emissary D.P. Dhar visited Bangladesh to discuss the issues of withdrawal of Indian troops from Bangladesh and trial of Pakistani Prisoners of War (POW). Bangladesh Finance Minister Tajuddin Ahmed visited India on February 2, 1972 to talk for increasing Indo-Bangladesh economic cooperation. India agreed to give five million tonnes of food.

MUJIB'S VISIT TO INDIA 1972

From 6 to 8 February 1972, Sheikh Mujibur Rehman, the Prime Minister of Bangladesh visited India. Both the leaders agreed that India would withdraw all its troops from Bangladesh by March 25, 1972. Both expressed their determination to promote cooperation between Government and people with a vision of lasting peace, amity and good neighbourliness. India gave two aeroplanes to Bangladesh Viman on loan for initiating the country's internal airline. The Indian troops were finally withdrawn till March 13, 1972, 12 days in advance of the pre-fix date. It proved that India had no desire of occupying Bangla territory.

INDIRA GANDHI'S VISIT TO DHAKA

In March 1972, Indira Gandhi paid a return visit to Dhaka. The main achievements of this visit resulted into a treaty of Peace Friendship and Cooperation between the two countries. A number of agreements were signed to strengthen the bilateral ties. This was decided that the ministers of defence, commerce, cultural, etc., will meet bi-annually to strengthen cooperation. A Joint Rivers Commission (JRC) was established for studying and surveying the shared rivers and formulating joint projects for flood control and irrigation facilities.

- For the revival of trade between the border areas of the two countries, a Trade and Transit Agreement was done.
- A understanding was reached on exchange of informations, regarding technological and scientific research for industrial development and utilisation of future space research for communication purposes.
- Agreed to strengthen cultural relations.

INDO-BANGLADESH TREATY OF PEACE, FRIENDSHIP AND COOPERATION

During the Dhaka visit of Indira Gandhi, a 25 years Treaty of Peace, Friendship and Cooperation was signed by the two leaders. The Treaty, with 12 Articles and a Preamble, was designed to maintain good neighbourly relations, to transform the borders into a border of peace and friendship, to uphold non-alignment and peaceful co-existence, to promote and strengthen the existing relations of friendship and cooperation, to maintain peaceful settlement of disputes and to safeguard peace, stability and security.

Article 1: Provided steps for securing the above objectives declared in the Preamble.

Article 2: Condemned colonialism and racialism.

Articles 3 and 4: Reaffirmed their faith in non-alignment and peaceful co-existence.

Article 5: Mutual cooperation in the fields of scientific, technical, trade, transport and communication.

Articles 6 and 7: Suggested for joint studies and actions in flood control, hydro-electric power, irrigation and river management.

Articles 8 and 9: No military alliance against each other and shall not allow their territory for any act, which is a threat to the security of the other.

Article 10: Refrain themselves from giving any assistance to any third party taking part in an armed conflict against the other party.

Articles 11 and 12: Stated that treaty was for 25 years and was a renewable by mutual agreement.

Like the 1971 Indo-Soviet Treaty of Peace, Friendship and Cooperation, this Treaty was also for bilateral close relations.

INDO-BANGLADESH COOPERATION IN POST-TREATY ERA

After the Treaty both the countries entered into many bilateral agreements for implementing the articles of Treaty. Border trade for people residing within 15 km of the borders was started. It was beneficial for daily wagers. The Treaty also allowed goods of special interest upto 50 crores on a balanced basis. On July 5, 1973 a new three years Trade Agreement was signed by both the countries in which the limit was extended till 30.5 crores. In 1975 Bangladesh agreed to export fish worth Rs. 3.5 crores to India. Further a protocol for exchange programme in the fields of culture, education, information and sports was signed on September 27, 1974.

In the fields of atomic energy, space research, and training, cooperation was promoted by signing agreements in 1972, 1973 and 1974. Bangladesh had given its support to India on peaceful nuclear explosion and found it a matter of pride for developing countries.

During the May 1974 Summit meeting, four Joint Ventures was declared :

- A Cement Plant at Chatak in Bangladesh, limestone supplied from Meghalaya.
- A Clinker Plant in Meghalaya for supplying Clinker to Bangladesh.
- A Fertilizer Plant in Bangladesh for supply of urea to India.
- A Sponge Iron Plant in Bangladesh supplying iron ore from India.

A Joint Commission on Jute was another achievement of the summit. On August 27, 1973 a treaty was signed for exchanging information on atomic research and literature between the two countries.

BORDER AGREEMENT, 1974

As Bangladesh and India are having border dispute, a Border Agreement of May 19, 1974 was a step towards demarcating it. Under this agreement India retained Berubari enclave and in exchange Bangladesh received Dahagram and Angarpota enclaves. With the least disturbance to the population, the border demarcation was done. The fixation of midstream boundaries along Muhuri and Fenny rivers was also done by the agreement.

The visit diplomacy strengthened the relations more. In 1972 President of Bangladesh Abu Sayeed Chawdhary came on a 10 day visit to India. In 1974, President V.V. Giri paid a return visit to Dhaka. In 1973 foreign minister of Bangladesh visited India and in return external affairs minister Swaran Singh went to Dhaka in 1974.

India and Bangladesh during this period had a similar perspectives on international issues also whether it was the policy of non-alignment or Panchsheel. On the Kashmir issue Bangladesh had given its full support to India and welcomed the Simla Agreement.

India tried whole heartedly for getting international recognition to Bangladesh. India gave full support to the August 9, 1972 application made by Bangladesh for getting the membership of the UN. The Chinese veto prevented Bangladesh from getting success in it.

START OF DIFFERENCES

Though the period of Mujib was a period of closer and warm relations, but the seeds of future discord were planted in this period also. The anti-India propagandists started pointing the India-Bangladesh as unequal partnership. It was said that the policies of Bangladesh towards India were failed to protect the national interests of the country as India was putting Bangladesh under her dominance. And ultimately Mujib's friendship with India was a factor led to the August 1975 coup against Mujib's regime.

Initially the differences started on the issue of shifting of arms and ammunition to India. As the Pak army surrendered to the joint command of India and Bangladesh, Bangladesh had legitimate claim to certain share of those arms. Denial of share had been bitterly felt by the poorly equipped Bangladesh army. An another factor of raising Jatiya Rakhkhi Bahini (Para Military Force) by the Awami League contributed to the overthrow of Awami League Government. As Bangladesh had not gone to an institutional army but Mujib Government went for a ceremonial army in the form of Rakhkhi Bahini but the Rakhkhi Bahini factor created much frustration in the rank and file of the Bangladesh army which gave impression of Indian army's vulnerability in Bangladesh.

POST-MUJIB ERA

These two factors were mainly responsible for the coup of 1975 against Mujib Government. After the murder of Sheikh Mujib on August 15, 1975 Bangladesh came under political instability. The political power gained by army and Bangladesh cease by military regime under General Zia-ur-Rahman till May 30, 1981, when he was assassinated by army. Lt. Gen. H.M. Ershad brought Bangladesh under military dictatorship in 1981.

Since then India-Bangladesh relations have passed through a process of many ups and down, suspicions and irritants and re-building the bridges of understanding. The post-Mujib regimes started to look upon India as a "hegemon", "big bull", "giant power". The democratic India and a military regime of Bangladesh began a new hostility.

After Mujib, Zia-ur-Rahman regime fostered anti-Indianism. To mute Indian influence in the sub-continent, president Zia forged closer strategic links with Pakistan and China. Border disputes were reported in 1976. President Zia was assassinated in May 1981. General Ershad reimposed military rule in Bangladesh. During the Ershad regime, some of unresolved issues such as the Chakma refugees, Tin Bigha and sharing of the Ganga water contributed irritation in the India-Bangladesh relations.

Sheikh Hasina being daughter of Sheikh Mujib, Father of Nation was pro-India. She was obliged India's military and moral support to the liberation of Bangladesh. The Ganga water sharing agreement of 1996 was a big achievement of its foreign policy. But the illegal migrants and fundamentalist terrorist training camps were the main issues irritating the relations.

Begum Khaleda Zia was anti-India and it was reflected in her attitude, speeches and policies. She charged India with pushing back non-Bangladeshis when India's Home Ministry had launched "Operation Push Back" and described it as an "unfriendly act" and "Indian hegemonism". Even Khaleda Zia visited to China and sought the Chinese intervention in curbing India's "strategic hegemony".

IRRITANTS IN INDO-BANGLADESH RELATIONS

Along with the time, the relations between these two friendly countries have become unfriendly. The following factors are responsible for this:

1. The poverty of Bangladesh.
2. The anti-India propaganda of Bangladesh.
3. The role of Pakistan.
4. The rise of fundamentalism and terrorism in Bangladesh.

Soon after the liberation of Bangladesh, Chinese premier Chou-en-Lai said, "Bangladesh would prove to be a milestone round India's neck." It has proved truth. Henry Kissinger also called Bangladesh an international basket case casting doubts about the viability of the country.

The boundary demarcation, insurgencies, drug and human trafficking, illegal migration, cross border terrorism are the main security problems between the twos. A number of outstanding issues have contributed to a strain and unfriendliness in Indo-Bangladesh relations.

The first unresolved issue causing strains in Indo-Bangladesh relations is border dispute involving Tin Bigha and South Talpathi, barbed wire fencing along the common border, demarcation of the maritime boundary. Among these issues the Tin Bigha issue has been resolved amicably. It was transferred to Bangladesh in June 1992 on a perpetual lease but India would continue to have its sovereignty over this 178 × 85 metre corridor.

Demarcation of maritime boundary is of vital importance to the exploitation of petroleum in the sea-bed.

With time, the relations between these two countries have become unfriendly on these issues:

I. Border dispute-New Moore Island
II. Chakma Problem
III. Illegal Migrants
IV. Farakka
V. River's water dispute
VI. Trade Imbalance
VII. Myanmar-Bangladesh-India gas pipeline.
VIII. Terrorism and religious fundamentalism.
IX. China factor.

I. Border Dispute

India with concern of her security started barbed fencing of the 4095 km porous border. Bangladesh says that India's fencing of the border is a violation of the 1975 border guide lines. Bangladesh has claimed that India's move to fence the border between the countries with barbed wire, has sparked frontier tensions. It was a violation of 1975 land-boundary guideline. Under it India can erect fence 150 yards from the border. India proposed to erect the barricade within 150 yards (about 200 meters) of the zero line.

Bangladesh argues erection of the fence within 150 yards of the zero line violates the 1975 Boundary Agreement between the two countries, which stipulated that no barricade can be set-up by either country within this distance of the border. There was a bloody exchanges between Bangladesh Rifles (BDR) and Indian Army and BSF. Unarmed civilians erecting fences are fired upon. Militants from the North East set-up businesses in Dhaka and camps in the border districts demanding that New Delhi, negotiate with them sovereignty over Indian territory.

However the question of fencing of the 4095 km long border between the two countries still remains unresolved with Bangladesh resisting the move contending that the fencing has "a defensive structure" attached to it.

India wants to conduct border fencing to the level of zero line due to topographical reasons.

India-Bangladesh border is 4095 km long in which 1/3 area is covered with rivers rest out of 3200 km., only half has been covered with fencing. On the boundary there are 64 BSF battalions are deported. The work of surveillance can only achieved better through fencing and high speed boats. Bangladesh has still not given the permission for these boats.

New Moore Island

The New Moore island or the South Talpatty as Bangladesh calls it—1.5 sq. km. in area was first owned by India in 1970. The island was important for securing sea food, mineral resources and natural gas. The island lies at a distance of barely 5.2 km from the nearest Indian landmass and 7.6 Km. from the nearest landmass of Bangladesh. Both Britain and USA naval maps show New Moore as an Indian island. Suddenly in 1978 for the first time, Bangladesh questioned the Indian ownership over the island. In December 1978 Dhaka presented to India a US satellite map showing India, Bangladesh and the river Hariabhanga. On the basis of this map, Bangladesh staked its claim on the island as a mutually accepted river boundary, but India was not agreed upon this and claimed its ownership of the island. In 1981 both sides were agreed for the peaceful settlement of this issue on the basis of mutual trust and benefit. But it is still an issue in Indo-Bangladesh relations. India's claim on this island is based upon three factors:

- India owns the island since its birth in 1970
- Island is closer to India (5.2 km.)
- The main channel of the Hariabhanga and the estuary flows along the eastern side of the island.

Dhaka claim is based on :

- It is 7.6 km. from Bangladesh landmass.
- On the basis of US satellite map, Bangladesh finds Hariabhanga river as boundary between India and Bangladesh.
- Thus New Moore lies on the Bangladesh side.

II. The Chakma Problem

The Chakma tribe belongs to the Buddhist tribe and residing in the Chittagong Hill Tracts (CHT). When Bangladesh passed a bill in January, 1974 declaring herself a 'uni-cultural' and 'unilingual' nation, the Chakmas demanded 'self government'. Reflecting this demand, the Mujib government encouraged the Muslim landless cultivators to settle in the CHT areas. Fearing with the reduction of their numbers and dominance of Buddhism, the Chakmas formed a party Jan Janghati Samiti (JSS) and set-up a Santi Vahini as a military front to fight the security forces of Bangladesh. Instead of addressing their socio-economic, cultural and settlement problems, the Bangladesh government contributed repression of Chakmas. This ultimately forced them to make into the north-eastern states of India, which alerted the Indian Government on illegal infiltration of Bangla refugees.

The Dhaka government agreed to provide physical security including giving 5000 taka to each Chakma to facilitate their return to the Bangladesh. But they were scared to come back. In 1997 the Bangladesh Government announced a package of Rs. 15000 to each Chakma family for construction of houses, free ration for six months, education to children. The meeting between Tripura government and Bangladesh officials ultimately assured the Chakmas to return back in 1997. It was in pursuance of these efforts, the process of Chakmas repatriation also began and the Chakma problem was solved.

III. Bangladesh Migrants

The Bangladesh migrants came into India after March 25, 1971 and permitted to stay as Indira Gandhi-Mujib Agreement of 1972. Neither the Indira-Mujib pact nor the Assam Accord of 1985 between Rajiv Gandhi and AASU leaders held out any promise of citizenship on the post 1971 entrants. In the extremely porous 4095 Km. border that India shares with Bangladesh, West Bengal alone covers 2,216 Km. Bangladesh-India boundary is soft and they crossed the border in search of work. Almost all of them are economic refugees. Though rural West-Bengal and the North East region are as poor or only relatively better off than its eastern neighbour. Yet pressure on land in Bangladesh and better job opportunities in India have prompted millions from Bangladesh to migrate in India. Since 1971, when Bangladesh was born, India is unable to prevent this illegal migration—five million each in Assam and West Bengal and the rest in Bihar, UP, Delhi and Maharashtra. Since a majority of them are Muslims, the issue acquires political and communal. This migrant issue upsets India's demography and socio-economic balance and poses a security challenge as never before.

Bangladesh migrants have moved into various parts of India, Assam, West Bengal, Bihar, Tripura and from Punjab to Bombay, Nagaland to Orissa. The Pakistan's ISI use them in smuggling of arms and narcotics and in urban India they are the cheapest labour available. These Bangladeshis have so much mingled out in bordering states that it is difficult to differentiate them from locals. They have changed the demography of bordering states with predominantly Muslim population in Assam. AASU had started an agitation against them. But infiltration of migrants from Bangladesh is still continued.

It is difficult to know exactly the figure of Bangladeshi migrants living in India. In a recent Indian documentary called 'The Bangla Crescent ISI Infiltration the number of Bangladesh immigrants an estimate, it is about 1.50 crore, out of which there are 80 lacs in Bengal, 50 lac in Assam, 3.75 lac in Tripura, 4 lac in Delhi and about 80 thousand in Nagaland and Mizoram. Infact it has been estimated that illegal Bangladeshi migrants are in a position to influence the outcome in 3.2% of the total Assembly seats (40 out of 120) in Assam and 18% (52 out of 294) in West Bengal. This heavy influx has been creating pressure on land and employment resulting in clashes between the immigrants and the local people. This has created strains on bilateral ties and turned bloody border incidents.

External Affairs Minister K. Natwar Singh on his visit to Dhaka in August, 2005 showed India's concerns regarding illegal migration from Bangladesh front. Bangladesh foreign secretary did not agree that there is any illegal migration from Bangladesh. During this visit both the countries agreed to setup coordinated border patrolling and finalise an extradition treaty.

IV. Farakka Dispute

Bangladesh has inherited the problem of Farakka by Pakistan. In 1957 the Government of India decided to construct a barrage at Farakka across the Ganga to save Calcutta port from silting as a result of the slow flow of Ganga. Pakistan was against these construction. But India started the construction in 1975. The talks between India and Pakistan could not solve the issue.

In 1971 with Bangladesh's existence, the Farakka issue now

became the issue between India and Bangladesh. The two countries agreed to resolve the issue through mutual negotiations. In 1972 both the countries established a Joint Rivers Commission (JRC) aiming to secure equitable utilisation of common river's water between twos.

Farakka is a major problem between the two countries. The problem started in 1972 when India decided to build a barrage across the Ganga below Farakka so that Calcutta port could be operational by flushing the Hoogly river with the water from the Ganga during the lean season in which the flow of Ganga comes down. The Farakka Agreement was signed in 1977 but it failed to safeguard the interest of India. As Bangladesh wanted to augment the flow of Ganga during lean season by using water stored in reservoir, constructed in Nepal Himalayas. Thus Bangladesh wanted to involve Nepal in negotiations over Farakka. India wanted to settle the problem bilaterally.

The 1977 Agreement was expired in 1982 as it was for a period of five years. Since then the Indo-Bangladesh Joint Rivers Commission (JRC) is studying the feasibility of all possible alternatives which can lead to the augmentation of the Ganga flow during the lean season. In 1982 the JRC reached on an ad-hoc agreement on the sharing of Teesta waters in the ratio of 39 : 36 percent between India and Bangladesh and leaves 25 percent water as unaccounted water flow. Similarly an agreement has been reached to study the economic, technical and implementability aspects of all the proposals for augmenting the flow of Ganga below Farakka. Bangladesh seems ready for Brahmputra-Ganga link canal proposed by India while India is ready on Bangladesh proposal for water storage in Nepal Himalaya.

Farakka issue continues to be the major problem of Indo-Bangladesh relations.

Indo-Bangladesh Ganga Water Accord 1985

The Bangladesh President H.M. Ershad and Indian P.M. Rajiv Gandhi reached on an agreement in 1985 on sharing of Ganga water the next three years. It was agreed that the joint study would identify alternatives for the sharing of the water resources common to both countries to the mutual benefit.

Ganga Water Sharing Agreement 1996

Ganga water sharing agreement signed between New Delhi and Dhaka on December 12, 1996 for 30 years during the visit of Sheikh Hasina to India. It was a landmark in Indo-Bangladesh relations.

V. River's Water Dispute

The sharing of river water is the most persistent problem between India and Bangladesh. Bangladesh being the lower riparian, is indued to perceive that India, as the upper riparian has been constructing barrages in almost all the major rivers and thus depriving Bangladesh from her due share of river waters in the dry season. The issue of augmenting and regulating of water flows is another issue in sharing of water. India wants to construct a 200 mile long 'link canal' connecting Brahmaputra with the Ganga near Farakka, while Bangladesh has proposed the building of reservoirs on the tributaries of Ganga in Nepal. Bangladesh has rejected the link canal proposal, while India is against reservoirs.

Bangladesh and India has many common rivers. Ganga and Brahmaputra are the major ones and others are Teesta, Khowai, Gumti, Muhuni, Manu, Dharla, Dudhkumar, Kushiyara and Mahananda. The problem with these rivers will come up as soon as India will start construction of barrages over them.

After Bangladesh birth in 1971, a Joint Rivers Commission (JRC) was established in 1972 to formulate schemes for equitable utilisation of common eastern river's waters between India and Bangladesh. The water dispute are the issues of the flow of Ganga, construction of water reservoir in the Himalayas, Brahmputra-Ganga link canal, Teesta river water, etc.

- India wants to increase the water flow of Ganga during the lean season to save the Calcutta port from silting.
- Bangladesh wants to augment the flow of Ganga during lean season by using water stored in reservoir in Nepal-Himalayas. India is against involving Nepal.
- India advocates the construction of Brhamputra-Ganga link canal for augmenting the flow of Ganga.
- Dhaka is also against the plan of interlinking of rivers.

The Joint Rivers Commission (JRC) had many round of talks but no amicable solutions.

VI. Trade Scenario Between India and Bangladesh

Bangladesh is a small country and steadily it has established a credible record of sustained growth. It has a large domestic market of about 140 million and an abundant and cheap source of human resources. Bangladesh provides a market of 1.5 billion people which is 1/5th of the global population out of which 450 million are the strong middle class. India's treaty of SAFTA (1 July, 2006) with Bangladesh has opened a new market for India. But today there is a trade imbalance between the two countries, inspite of this fact that India and Bangladesh have a bilateral trade agreement since 1980.

India's Ten Major Imports from Bangladesh

Inorganic chemicals, paper yarn, vegetables, textile fibres, fish and crustaceans, fertilizers, cotton, raw hides and skin, plastics and plastic articles, soap, washing preparations fruits, nuts, apparel and clothing accessories.

This trade imbalance between twos is a major complain of Bangladesh. The Bangladesh Prime Minister Khaleda Zia during her visit to India on 28th March, 2006 contended that being the larger of the two countries, India should allow unilateral concessions by permitting duty-free access to exports from Bangladesh to correct the trade imbalance with Dhaka. The ever growing trade gaps between India and Bangladesh is a matter of considerable concern for Bangladesh. There was differences on Double Taxation Avoidance Treaty and Investment Protection Treaty also, both of which fell through after Dhaka presented some amendments to the drafts. To explore trade concessions, India has asked Bangladesh to provide a specific list of products for India to consider with an open mind.

VII. Myanmar-Bangladesh-India Gas Pipeline

India and Bangladesh are agreed on a one billion dollar tri-nation gas pipeline project that would allow New Delhi to bring natural gas from Myanmar. Under the project, India will build a 290 Km. pipeline through Bangladesh to connect offshore gas fields in Myanmar to West Bengal.

Dhaka still sees the pipeline as a political tool than an economic boon. It would be for the benefit of both the countries. New Delhi wants to remove the road blocks hindering the

Trade with Bangladesh

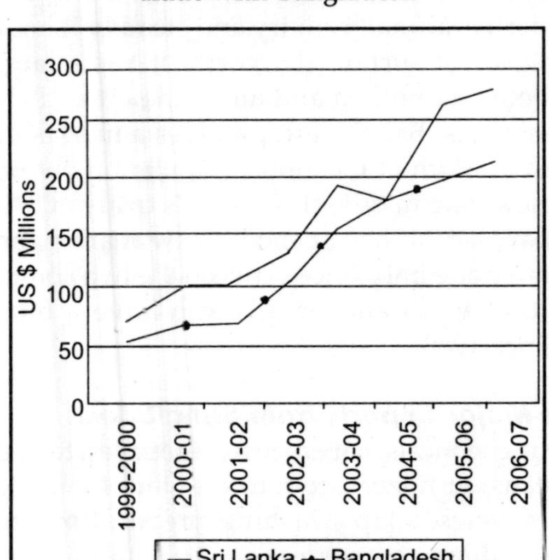

Opportunities

- Natural Gas Exploration and industries based on it like Electricity, Fertilizer and Petrochemicals.
- Engineering consultancy in Infrastructure (power, telecommunications, ports, roads and railways;
- Information Technology (Data Processing and Software Development)

Problems

- Poor infrastructure, corruption, uncertain law and order situation, inadequate commercial laws and courts, and policy instability (i.e., policies altered when anew government comes to power).
- Investors in infrastructure and natural resource sectors, including power, mineral resources and telecommunications must seek approval from the corresponding government ministries. They have to face lengthy and corrupt bureaucratic procedures.

On the Trade front:

- In Bangladesh, slow pace of liberalization, tariff reduction and increase in the scope and levels of para-tariffs to protect domestic consumer goods industry.
- Non-tariff barriers by India, protection to domestic textiles and apparel industry.
- Constraints on imports by the land border by both countries.
- Congestion, delays, bribes, etc. at customs. Consequently Illegal trade between the two countries amounts to 3/4 of regular trade.

Myanmar-Bangladesh-India gas pipeline which needs political consideration of Bangladesh leadership.

VIII. Terrorism and Religious Extremism

From the beginning, Bangladesh is aiding and abetting insurgencies in the north eastern states. Apart from the Pakistan ISI, Bangladesh intelligence agencies were also behind the insurgency in the north-eastern states. In 1996, Bangladesh Prime Minister Sheikh Hasina had acknowledged the existence of camps for training and providing logistical support to insurgents on Bangladesh soil.

Bangladesh in recent past has come out as a religious fundamentalist country. A large number of madrassas have come up on both sides of the border, which are working as the factory for producing Islamic militancy.

The two Bangladesh based Islamic extremist outfit—HUJI (Harkat-ul-Jihad-al-Islami) and Asif Reza Commando Force were behind the Varanasi blast (2006) and January 22, 2002 attack on the American Centre in Kolkata. These two outfits are linked with JeM., LeT, Al-Qaida and LSI. The HUJI established in 1992, aims to establish Islamic rule in Bangladesh and reportedly maintains six camps in the hills of Chittagong. It was assigned the task of recruiting Bangladeshi and Indian Muslims to fight in Kashmir under the command of the Harkat-ul-Mujahideen. Its activities frequently cross over to India for terrorist activities. ISI is using Bangladesh to foment terror in India. The Islamic terrorists from Bangladesh have chosen a route through eastern India to enter into different countries. Terrorist camps operating in Bangladesh is a contentious issue. Delhi had earlier supplied Dhaka with a list of 172 terrorist camps, together with documentary evidence of how terrorists are being trained in camps in Bangladesh to foment violence in India. But Bangladesh has taken no action.

India has a dcep and high concern for Bangladesh emergence as an exporter of global terrorism. India does not want to allow Bangladesh soil to be used for anti-Indian activities. The 4096 Km. eastern border with Bangladesh is porous and India could not allow Bangladesh as a launch pad for terror attacks on India.

The extremist and militant activities of Bangladesh along the border is the subject of worry for India. India has asked Bangladesh to destroy 172 camps run by North-Eastern insurgents in its territory and to apprehend 103 militants including top ULFA leaders based in Bangladesh. The list of 103 militants included ULFA chairman Arabinda Rajkhowa, its general secretary Anup Chetia, and top leaders of insurgent groups like both factions of the NSCN, NDFB, ATTF, NLFT, KYKL, PLA, HNLC and ANVC. The BSF provided the Bangladesh Rifles (BDR) with lists of the rebel camps and militants and sought strong action against Indian insurgents operating from Bangladesh. According to BSF 10 page press note, "most insurgent outfits in the North-East are acquiring sophisticated weapons from Thailand with the active connivance of Bangladesh intelligence agencies. Bangladesh has provided all possible help in terms of shelter and training." The note provided specific details on how Bangladesh intelligence was coordinating its activities with the Pakistani ISI.

The mushrooming illegal madrassas is another point of dispute. The IB report has identified 208 madrassas and 458 mosques in ten districts on the Indo-Nepal and Indo-Bangla borders. Although the report admits that all the "recognised" madrassas function under the State Madrassa Board, there are several illegal ones, which are suspected to have come up too close to the border.

IX. China Factor

The Bangladesh perception was based on that that India is a source of threat to its security. Being India-locked and a small country, Bangladesh is very sensitive to its security and development. The threat perception is rooted in the Bangladesh psyche of intolerance of India's predominating role in the sub-continent and beyond it. This is why India and Bangladesh have wide differ differences on NPT and Nuclear Weapon Free Zone. Bangladesh is against India's nuclearization. It finds it against the security climate of South Asia. Instead of it wants to declare the South Asia region as a nuclear weapon free zone.

For the security purpose, today Bangladesh has more cordial relations with Pakistan and China, two hostile countries of India. And with friendship of these twos, Bangladesh wants to control the India factor and to contain the influence of India. After the assassination of Sheikh Mujib, China made a shift in its Bangladesh policy by adopting a soft and sympathetic attitude to Bangladesh. President Zia for minimizing the Indian influence, tried to cultivate the Chinese friendship to counterweight India's hegemony. His visit to China in 1977 marked the beginning of a "New Chapter" in Bangladesh-China relationship. From then onwards China is supplying arms and ammunition to Bangladesh.

VISIT DIPLOMACY TOWARDS CORDIAL RELATIONS

In August, 2005 first external affairs minister K. Natwar Singh and Foreign Secretary Shyam Saran went to Bangladesh. After that Manmohan Singh went on a three day trip to Bangladesh. While Delhi wants to improve relations it also wants its security concerns addressed.

PRIME MINISTER KHALEDA ZIA'S INDIA VISIT

Prime Minister Khaleda Zia's visit to India in March 2006 was important as the bilateral relations were very low between the two nations in 2005. The two nations were engaged in a virtual war of words. The Bangladesh Rifles (BDR) and Border Security Force (BSF) had encounters in which some BSF jawans were killed. This was resulted into the heated exchanges, and India demanded the postponement of the SAARC summit scheduled in Dhaka in January, 2005. This was followed by the news of terrorist charges along the Indo-Bangla border and emergence of Bangladesh as a religious fundamentalist country. The situation was worsened more when accused in the Delhi (October 2005) and Varanasi bomb blasts having Bangladesh links that put a question mark over the security situation. To mend fences between the two countries, Prime Minister Manmohan Singh invited Khaleda to India for bilateral talks. So this visit was aimed at clearing the air and having the frost between the neighbours. Terror, trade and security were the main bilateral issues to talk.

This was her first visit to India. Both the leaders were agreed on that they were the victims of terrorism and to combat it both should jointly handle it. Both the nations have given their consent on building Sealdah-Devpura rail. Bangladesh pressed on to put Bangladesh goods import tax free to end the trade imbalance with putting more Indian investment in Bangladesh. The two agreements were signed during the visit-one is on increasing bilateral trade and second is concerned with controlling and stopping illegal smuggling of narcotics. While addressing on the joint meeting of FICCI, ASSOCHAM AND CII, she called the Indian industrials to invest in Bangladesh as it has plenty of cheap labour.

But the visit did not achieve a major breakthrough. On religious extremism and terrorism, Khaleda Zia assured India that she would not allow Bangladesh soil to be used for anti-India activities. On the gas pipeline, Bangladesh still is not agreed and India seems to agree to adopt a flexible stance on trade to keep up the pressure on Dhaka to curb terror. But the two agreed to working closer on "security, trade and sharing of water" is the success of the visit.

During the Visit

- The two nations are agreed to set-up coordinated border patrolling.
- The two are also agreed to sign the extradition treaty.
- Free trade agreement has done.
- The Indo-Bangla joint ministerial team headed by union water resource minister Saifuddin Soz and his Bangladeshi counterpart Hafizuddin on 15th Sept, 2006 visited the disputed areas on the border in South Tripura-Muhuricher along the Muhuri Sabroom. They also visited the border areas in Sabroom where Bangladesh Rifles have been opposing the construction of pump houses along the Feni river for the past few years.

MENON VISIT TO DHAKA

Foreign Secretary Shiv Shankar Menon travelled to Bangladesh from June 25, 2007 for a visit during which the entire range of bilateral ties, including issues related to operation of north-east insurgents out of that country and illegal immigration, are discussed, Menon, is visit was for foreign office consultations with his counterpart Touhid Hussain. The two sides discussed way to enhance cooperation. The visit is an indication of the importance that India attaches to bilateral relations with Bangladesh and demonstrates India's desire to engage constructively with the government of Bangladesh.

India has concerns with regard to continued operation of north-east insurgents out of Bangladesh and has been pressing Dhaka to take action against them.

TOWARDS IMPROVEMENT

New Delhi realises its eastern neighbour is the bigger cause of concern than any other country along its borders. As Prime Minister Manmohan Singh told Prime Minister Khaleda Zia, "A strong and prosperous Bangladesh is in the interest of India, South Asia and the Asian region as a whole. Bangladesh also consolidate her ties with India.

The Indo-Bangladesh relationship is a complex one that requires nurturing. India can afford to be generous. Increased economic ties seem to be the best way out-break trade barrier, (fiscal, physical and psychological) promote investments on both sides and setup communications.

The joint Indo-Bangladesh boundary guidelines of 1975 is the key to the solution of all problems between the two countries. We should make use of these guidelines to solve our problems.

India-Bangladesh recently had a four day border coordination conference between BDR and BSF at New Delhi in March 2007. Bangladesh agreed to allow developmental activities within 150 yards of the border and barring a few stretches, tea plantations till the zero line. This marks a change in Bangladesh's stance as BDR previously was opposed to construction within 150 yards of zero line as also the barbed fencing of the 4096 km porous border.

The conference ended with an understanding to make "border dynamics more user-friendly and aimed at conflict resolution that aggravated. Bangladesh also pledged to check infiltration of its nationals into India and a check on touts involved in human trafficking.

The CBM's like increasing the area and frequency of simultaneous joint patrolling and feasibility of a joint retreat ceremony, exchanges of training facilities, exchange in the fields of sports and culture are also under consideration.

Both the countries are taking steps to build an understanding and confidence building measures.

Bangladesh is determined to not to aggravate the border and

infiltration disputes. The BDR Director General Major General Shakeel Ahmed committed at Border Coordination Conference of 2007 that:

> "We are determined to do the utmost to see to it that miscreants from India do not get breathing space in Bangladesh. . . . Any insurgents from India taking sanctuary in Bangladesh will be arrested and put through the law."

The Bangladesh also pledged to check infiltration of its nationals into India and a check on touts involved in human trafficking.

Prime Minister Sheikh Hasina, during I.K. Gujral's visit to Bangladesh in 1996, assured him that Dhaka would not permit any anti-India activity by a "third country" on its soil. This assurance was again repeated during Khaleda Zia's visit to India in 2003. But Bangladesh is still indulged in anti-India activities by giving shelter to terrorists and running training camps and madrassas along the border.

From April 14, 2007 (Bengali New Year) the Kolkata-Dhaka rail link is restored opening up yet another crucial cross border linkage with India's neighbour. The train will be operated by India and Bangladesh for six months each.

43 years after, rail links between India and Bangladesh were snapped during the 1965 Indo-Pak war, the Maitree Express from Howra rolled into Dhaka. The train between Kolkata and Dhaka has the potential of improving bilateral ties. It would facilitate easier and legitimate movement of people between the two countries, which is the first step towards better relations. In recent times, there has been a rise in Bangladeshi visitors to India, particularly to West Bengal, for business and medical treatment. But much more can be done to encourage legitimate Bangladeshi visitors. Dhaka, too, should make it easier for Indian visitors to get visas.

Indian companies have showed their interests to invest in Bangladesh. Recently the Tata company proposed $3 billion investment in Bangladesh including setting of a 2.4 million tonne steel plant, two power plants, a coal mine and a fertilizer plant. If Bangladesh Government agrees to it, it would be the single biggest foreign investment in Bangladesh. But the Tata's proposal of investment is facing a big protest in Bangladesh. The Bangladesh media has compared it with East India Company.

In fact, when the Bangla government decided to arrest ex P.M. Khaleda's son Tarique Rehman, India maintained a strategic silence following its non-interfering foreign policy.

India and Bangladesh have finalised a new trade agreement that will replace the quarter century old bilateral arrangement between them and more importantly pave the way for an early signing of the free trade agreement (FTA) between the two neighbours. The two countries are negotiating with the aim of freeing cross border, flow of goods, services and investments from duties and other barriers.

The new bilateral trade agreement has been finalised after sustained dialogue for two years. The agreement will be signed soon after the two government finalise the draft.

India already provides Bangladesh duty-free access to its market in a number of products. In mid-August, the two countries expanded the scope of their trade engagement beyond duties to cover other barriers which slowed down flow of goods. They had exchanged a list of these barriers. The Dhaka talks took that process forward. To eliminate barriers arising out of standards, India and Bangladesh have agreed to start negotiations immediately for recognising each other's standards.

Bangladesh is faced with many problems for which India could offer assistance for example shortage of 35,000 MW power and shortage of diesel. The Bharat Heavy Electricals Ltd. (BHEL) will invest in Bangladesh for generation of power and 1.2 lakh tonnes of diesel were being sent every year by vessel from Numaligarh Refineries in Assam.

The present caretaker government in Bangladesh has initiated positive steps to improve Indo-Bangla ties. The Bangladesh government has taken steps to prevent insurgents, operating in India, from using the soil of the neighbouring country. The two countries has renewed the pact on inland water transit in New Delhi in April, 2007, which would remain in force till March 2009. The pact will boost inland water trade between Kolkata-Pandu, Kolkata-Karimganj, Karimganj-Pandu and Rajshahi-Dhulln. Bangladesh recently has proposed to set-up special poles 10-20 m high on the international boundary in the Meghalaya sector as part of the exercise to demarcate the 443 km border. The international boundary pillars in the Bangladesh and Meghalaya sector have been washed away by the over flowing rivers. India is examining the proposal. This proposal came at the 127th Indo-Bangladesh Boundary Conference held in September 2008 at Shillong.

BSF-BDR TALKS

The BSF says it has concrete evidence of insurgent groups like ULFA, National Liberation Front of Tripura (NLTF), All Tripura Tiger Force, National Democratic Front of Bodoland (NDFB) and Kamtapuri Liberation Organisation (KLO) having bases in Bangladesh.

Other issues of disputes are voyage clearance for BSF watercraft on the Brahmaputra through Bangladesh, intrusion of BDR personnel into the Indian territory, speedy completion of the fencing process and construction work taking place within 150 yards of the border on the either side.

BDR opposes India's plans to fence the border, saying certain patches of the border are yet to be demarked.

The Director General of BSF-BDR, decided to talk bi-annually in April 2006 first time, which thrice postponed, meeting was held in March 2006.

- New Delhi should offer generous market access to Bangladeshi products and be prepared to setup development access.
- The trade deficit would be much reduced if Dhaka permits New Delhi to bring natural gas from Myanmar.
- Dhaka should allow transit for people and goods through Bangladesh to India's north-east. In turn India should offer transit to Nepal and Bhutan through Indian territory.
- Upgradation of communications and transport infrastructure in the region.
- A system of work permit could stop the illegal migration.
- Dhaka should respond to Indian sensitivities regarding terror and insurgent groups operating from Bangladesh territory.

NEED A POLICY ON BANGLADESH

Bangladesh relations with India became a source of fear. Small issues are souring the relations. There is a need to develop a policy on Bangladesh which needs clear understanding of the situation. What happens in Bangladesh has a direct impact on the security and stability of India's eastern and north-eastern states. It is in India's interest to ensure that Bangladesh does not become a failed state.

Problems arise when South Block sees relations with Bangladesh from the prism of a classic bilateral relationship, in which quid pro quo and equal mutual benefit are the fulcrum of policy-making. The issue is further compounded when Bangladesh takes intransigent and unreasonable positions on issues relating to India's national security. This is the result of a genuinely felt fear that too warm a relationship with India might dilute its identity. This in turn promotes anger and bitterness in South Block. In its own self-interest India must learn to accept asymmetry in evolving its Bangladesh policy. If this vital fact remains in focus, India will be able to respond wisely to the irritants from Dhaka.

Illegal migration (estimated at 15-17 million since 1971) and the safe heavens acquired by Indian insurgent groups in Bangladesh are the two main issues concerning India's security. For this, India must complete the fencing of the Indo-Bangladesh border, strengthen the policing of the borders and issue national identity card to its nationals in the states bordering Bangladesh.

West Bengal and Assam in particular have adopted an ostrich-like approach towards the issue of illegal migration, viewing them as vote banks rather than a threat to national security. The demography of the bordering districts of Assam and West Bengal has changed drastically and if this continues it will have disastrous consequences on the stability and security of the entire region shortly.

While taking necessary preventive measures to stem the illegal immigration, India must also enable Bangladesh to sustain its teeming millions by helping in its economic progress and political stability. In matters of economic cooperation, India must accept asymmetry and what may appear to be one-sided concessions. Once the goals of India's foreign policy towards

Bangladesh are clear, policy-making will not be as frustrating an exercise as it has been until now.

Both the countries share equal responsibility in controlling as well as containing human, drug, arms trafficking, narco terrorism across the borders and misuse of each others soil by a handul of extremists. No doubt, the perceptions of leadership of both the countries count in their bilateral relations. So leadership should show that maturity in forming a friendly policy. In a fast changing security, strategic and economic scenario, a long-term policy of a better understanding and stabilised relationship has become necessary for the peace, security and development of the Indian sub-continent.

The biggest hurdle for improved relations between Dhaka and New Delhi remains the huge and largely unaccounted flow of illegal migrants from Bangladesh into India along the highly porous 4,095 km. border. Though estimates of the number of migrants vary, some years ago an Indian government-appointed task force reported that over one lakh Bangladeshi migrants enter India every month. There are good reasons to believe that in recent years, terrorists, some of them trained by Pakistan's ISI, have set-up base in Bangladesh and have been infiltrating into India. However, the flow of migrants from Bangladesh cannot be stopped by building fences as India has been doing. It has been shown that fences such as those along the Indo-Bangla or the US-Mexico border cannot stem the flow of people.

It is far better to accept that there will be migration of people looking for better job opportunities from Bangladesh into India and to regulate the inflow. A formal agreement on migration, with some form of identification cards being issued, should be considered. Steps must also be taken to increase trade between the two countries and to address the trade imbalance, which is in India's favour. The Maitree Express could be the right place to begin a rethink of Indo-Bangla ties.

India and Sri Lanka: Love-Hate Relationship

Sri Lanka is an island situated in the Indian Ocean, south-east of India. It was known as Ceylon until 1972, when its name changed to Sri Lanka by the Republican Constitution on May 22, 1972. After nearly four and a half centuries of foreign domination of Portuguese (1505-1658), Dutch (1658-1815) and the British (1815-1948) it became an independent state on February 4, 1948. India is 50 times more than this tiny island state in size, population economic and military strength.

Sri Lanka island is centrally located in the Indian Ocean. A 62,627 sq. kms area of Sri Lanka is approximately half the area of Tamil Nadu state. A shallow sea Palk Strait separates Sri Lanka from India. Talaimannar on Sri Lanka's Mannar Island is only 22 miles away from Dhanushkodi on India's Pamabar Island. Laying around equator, the Sri Lanka Island is a detached portion of the mainland of India.

The proximity of both the countries is strategically very important. The island's position impart it a seminal importance for sea borne trade routes, naval activities and piracy. Sri Lanka is located in what Prime Minister D.S. Senanayake called the "strategic highway." Sri Lanka has two natural harbours Colombo and Trincomalee. Trincomalee facing the Bay of Bengal on the island's east coast is strategically very important.

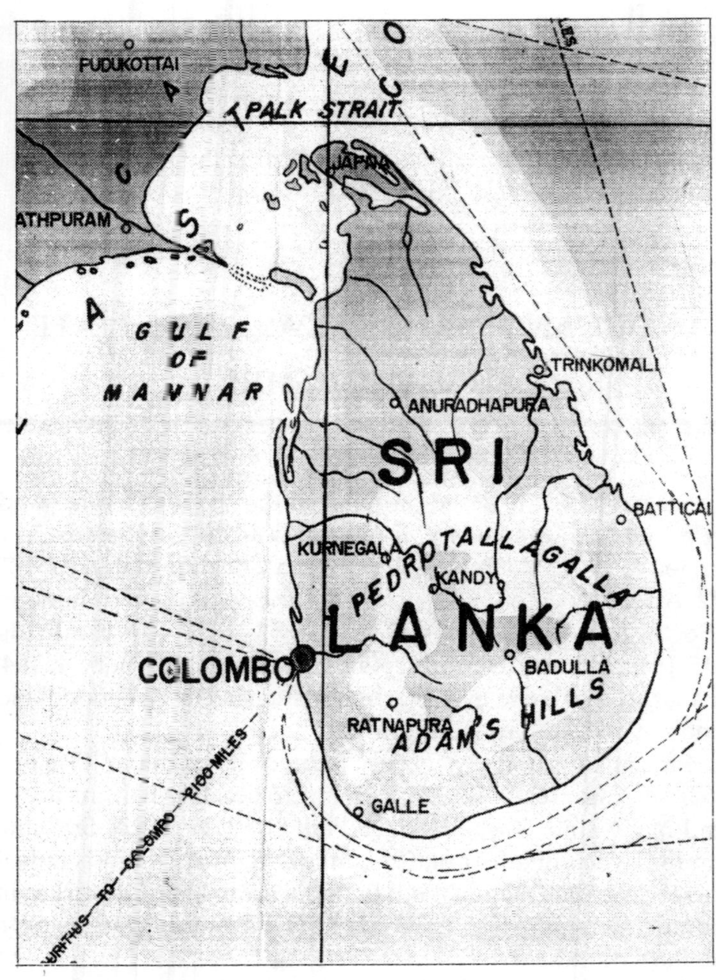
PUDUKOTTAI
PALK STRAIT
JAFNA
ATHPURAM
GULF OF MANNAR
TRINKOMALI
ANURADHAPURA
SRI LANKA
BATTICAL
KURNEGALA
PEDROTALLAGALLA
KANDY
COLOMBO
BADULLA
ADAM'S HILLS
RATNAPURA
GALLE

Sri Lanka and India are tied historically, culturally, religiously. Lanka people, whether they be Sinhalese, Tamil or Muslim belong to the same ethnic stock as India's population. The Sinhalese are the descendants of the Aryans of north India and the Tamilians are the descendants of the Dravidians of South India.

DETERMINANTS OF INDO-SRI LANKA RELATIONS

In the history of Indo-Sri Lanka relations, we find many twists and turns which can be described as their love-hate relationship. There are many important factors that have determined the relationship.

- The geo-strategic configuration of both the countries has been the most compulsive factor in their relations. India is Sri Lanka's closest neighbour. The implication of such a close proximity is that developments in any of the country have affected the other. Their bilateral relations have been influenced accordingly.
- Asymmetry of power in economic, technological, population, size, military strength make Sri Lanka deeply suspicious of India's hegemony and attack. The Sri Lankan elites in the past looked upon India as in the words of Ivor Jennings: "A mountain that might, at any time, send down destructive avalanches."
- Being a small nation, Sri Lanka knows that it could not defend its territory and security without foreign help and aid. But good neighbourly relations are equally important to it as far away friendly relations.
- Sri Lanka's economic dependence on foreign capital has intrinsic implications on India-Sri Lanka Relations.
- India is the dominant factor in Sri Lanka's security consideration and calculations, as Sri Lanka has no enough military strength for its defence, So 'India factor' 'fear and domination of India' is always there in its security perception.
- Understanding at the level of political leadership and regime has been an important factor in India-Sri Lanka relations. In the past Sri Lanka Freedom Party (SLFP)

government in Sri Lanka and Congress regime in India had good relations.

LOVE-HATE RELATIONSHIP

Sri Lanka has been one of India's assertive neighbour. In the past, its desire to assert its identity in international relations and to search for its security marred India-Sri Lanka relations. In the mid 80's, the bilateral relationship touched the rock bottom but never did they reach a point of breakdown or complete disruption. Both the countries have developed adequate strength to withstand the strength, stresses and strains is a notable feature of their bilateral relationship. This love-hate relationship has seen many changes in the pattern of relationship marked by mutual differences, irritants, cooperation and friendship. India-Sri Lanka relationship can be marked by a sort of ambivalance—an alternation between warmth, goodwill and cooperation on the one hand and fear, suspicion and political and territorial disputes on the other.

Based on the nature of relations and the issues dominating the bilateral agenda, the whole history of relations can be divided into four distinct phases:

- Decades of differences (1947-63)
- Resolving the disputes (1964-82)
- Troubled years (1983-90)
- Restoring friendship (since 1991).

In the decades of differences, three issues dominated the bilateral relations-statelessness of Indian Tamils, Kachchativu and divergent security perceptions and policies of both the countries. The second phase of India-Sri Lanka relations was noteworthy for the resolution of bilateral problems of citizenship of Indian Tamils and Kachchativu and demarcation of maritime boundaries.

The July 1983 ethnic violence in Sri Lanka and the subsequent civil war between the Sri Lankan army and the LTTE have started troubled years in the bilateral relations. The fear of India took Sri Lanka to the west for the search of security, which was against India's security sensitivities.

In the post-1990 period, India-Sri Lanka relation have

registered an all round improvement. The change and shift in policies started a new friendship era. The mutual common beneficial issues bring them together.

It cannot be ignored that Indo-Lanka relations over the years since independence stand out as a unique example of the manner in which two neighbouring states in South Asia have succeeded in resolving disputes and problems. Some of which carried out in a mutually cooperative spirit of give and take for example, citizenship of Indian Tamils, Kachchativu, maritime boundary and Indian Ocean.

SRI LANKA FEARS: SECURITY DILEMMA OF A SMALL STATE

India is the closest neighbour of Sri Lanka, in spite of historical and cultural links. India was a core factor in Sri Lanka security perception, and simultaneously Sri Lanka was feared with India because of its being so large in size and population and its close proximity with Sri Lanka.

Sri Lankan ruling elite had many fears, while recognizing centuries old ethnic, cultural and religious bonds, they were suspicious that India has an expansionist policy vis-a-vis Sri Lanka. India could take advantage of Sri Lanka's smallness, geographical proximity to India and military inferiority.

Besides, India's size, its economic potential and its role in trade and commerce have also created fear, mistrust, suspicion and insecurity in Sri Lankan perception of defense and security. Thus this asymmetry made the Sinhalese ruling elite looked upon India as "a mountain that might at any time, send down destructive avalanches." Even the fear of Indian aggression was in the minds of Sri Lankan leadership in 50s.

INDO-SRI LANKA RELATIONS: THE SECURITY DIMENSIONS

In the beginning Indo-centric security and defence system played an important role in strategic requirements of the two countries. And still India is by far the most dominant factor in Sri Lanka's security. The country's survival is related to India's fair play and sensitivity towards its ethnic internal problem. The 20 miles long Indo-Lanka maritime route gives an opportunity for the movement of militants and refugees. Much of Sri Lanka's fear of India arises from its proximity to Tamil Nadu, a state which articulated its ethnic demand for a separate Dravidastan in 50's and this provided the ideological strength and political support to Sri Lankan Tamil nationalism.

Nehru's ambition to make India a strong power, was thought by Sri Lankan leaders that it would lead to India's domination over the smaller countries of the region. Bandaranaike considered India friendly power but 'India factor' continued to play as an independent variable in Sri Lanka's security policy and a source of its insecurity.

Sri Lanka's suspicion was further increased when Indian leader-diplomat like K.M. Pannikkar and Pattabhi Sitarammaya proposed the idea of strategic unity of India, Burma and Sri Lanka in mid 40s. In 1949, Dr. Pattbhi, the president of Indian National Congress said in the Bombay session,

> "India and Ceylon must have a common strategy, common defence strength and common defence resources. It cannot be that Ceylon has no right to make its own alignments and declare its own affiliations—but if there are two hostile groups in the world and Ceylon and India are with one or the other of them and not with the same groups. It will be a bad day for both."

As Burma and Sri Lanka lie within the area of primary and strategic importance for India this idea frightened the Sri Lankan leader. This Indian thinking on the defence and security of the region alarmed the Sri Lankan leader. In 1954 Sir John Kotelawala, the Sri Lankan Prime Minister told, the Parliament that the writings of K. M. Pannikkar were tantamount to a proclamation of a 'Monroe Doctrine' for South Asia.

The fundamental concern of Sri Lanka was the protection of its independence, sovereignty and territorial integrity. This led it to take refuge under the security umbrella of western countries. The 'fear factor' of Indian hegemony and domination was also guiding her. The foreign policy of Sri Lanka looked pro-west. In 1950's Sri Lanka in its pro-American tilt was tempted to avail the membership of SEATO, but totally gave up its desire after India, Myanmar and Indonesia's opposition to the United State's sponsored treaty. But Sri Lanka's UNP (1947-56) government decided to follow the United States. A cabinet minister stated the position,

> "In this world today there are really two powerful factors, the United States and the United State of Soviet Russia. We have to follow either the one or other. There can be no half way. We have decided and we intend, as long as we are in power to follow the United States and its democratic policies."

But India was against bringing Cold War system on her southern flank. India accepted that Sri Lanka was free to use its foreign policy and security options only to the extent that it did not bring into the region the outside powers that would endanger India's security and defence. But Sri Lanka under Senanayake had allowed the use of its naval and air facilities by the United States. Sri Lanka's leaning towards the western powers gave insecurity to India.

Sri Lanka had a soft corner for Britain also. In 1947 both signed defence agreement. At the time of independence Sri Lanka had leased out the naval base of Trincomalee and the air base of Katunayaka to Britain. The Prime Minister Senanayake was convinced that "Ceylon's independence could be safeguarded only by maintaining good relations with Britain."

By 1957, Sri Lanka successfully negotiated a deal with the British government for the withdrawal of bases. Now Sri Lanka lost the external security guarantee that Britain was providing under the Defence Agreement for the past ten years.

Now there was a change in the security perception of Sri Lanka by 1957. India was no more considered a potential threat, but a friendly neighbour. During Bandaranaike's regime, non-alignment became the first line of Sri Lanka's defence and its national security got linked with global security. Friendship with all countries—in the neighbourhood as well as a far—was the objective of Sri Lankan diplomacy.

Initially Sri Lanka resisted the hegemonic relationship with India unlike the Himalayan states of Nepal and Bhutan but implicitly recognized India's pre-eminence in the region. Friendship with India was given high priority by the Sri Lankan leaders but they envisaged no collaboration on matters of defence and security or close economic links with India. "Friendship with a distance" was the core in the relations. Sri Lanka joined the camp of non-aligned nations. For Sri Lanka, neutralism and non-alignment provided it identity on the basis of equality. Sri Lanka accepted the leadership of India in non-aligned movement and agreed with Nehru on most issues of international importance-colonialism, nuclear arms, cold war, non-alignment and neutrality. Sri Lanka accepted Panchsheel as the code of conduct for resolving bilateral disputes and recognized Nehru's role in world affairs.

Sri Lanka's attitude of "friendship with a distance" was reflected at the time of Sino-India war of 1962 and the Indo-Pakistan conflicts of 1965 and 1971. Sri Lanka did not play a friendly role, rather acquired a degree of manoeuverability in regional affairs. The Sri Lanka Government took no sides and remained neutral, but made attempts to mediate in the dispute in order to bring about a peaceful settlement of the Sino-Indian border problem. After declaring ceasefire on November 21, 1962 by China, Sri Lanka came forward with Colombo proposal to prevent further deterioration in the relations between India and China. Colombo proposals was the result of attempts of six non-aligned countries—Burma, Ghana, Cambodia, Sri Lanka, Indonesia and United Arab. India accepted the proposals in their entirety.

During the early 1960's Sri Lanka evolved a regional policy calculated to serve its own security interests. The essence of the policy was a balanced relationship with the three main actors in the regional competition, India, Pakistan and China. When China tried to corner India in the non-aligned movement, Sri Lanka constantly backed the Indian position.

But Sri Lanka's refusal to brand China as the aggressor gave the message that Sri Lanka placed the neighbouring friend India on an equal footing with distant China. Later on Sri Lanka and China entered into a maritime agreement on July 25, 1963 providing facilities to Chinese warships.

During Indo-Pak war of 1971, Sri Lanka granted air transit facilities to Pakistan from west to east through Colombo and voted against India in the United Nations on Kashmir issue. Further nuclear explosion by India in 1974 and merger of Sikkim with India also made Sri Lanka suspicious. Sri Lanka did not recognize Bangladesh until March 1972.

During mid-80's, the security perceptions of Sri Lanka changed due to many reasons. First, the core 'India factor' in Sri Lanka's strategic thinking and security policy lost and fear and threat perception are replaced. A asymmetrical power relations and locational proximity caused fear and heightened the threat perception in the minds of Sri Lanka. Successive Sri Lankan leadership evolved a structure of defense against a vaguely formulated and perceived threat from India. Thus developing this, Sri Lanka became a strategic ally of the west. The idea of 'strategic unity and integration with India' became undesirable and unrealistic. And above all the outbreak of ethnic violence led to greater activation of the 'India factor' in the islands' security.

SRI LANKA'S LEANING TO FOREIGN COUNTRIES

During the ethnic crisis internally Sri Lanka adopted a pro-United States, China and Pakistan attitude as a counter balance to India, so that India could not convert the region as "Indian Lake" for India. To win the United States support, the Jayewardene extended refuelling and recreation facilities to visiting United States naval ships, granted a contract for leasing of oil storage tanks in the strategic harbour of Trincomalee to a Singapore based United States Company. Furthermore Sri Lanka entered into an agreement with the United States in December 1983 to setup a powerful Voice of America (VOA) station in the island.

All these developments were obviously considered a threat to Indian security. The presence of foreign powers in the island and any foreign military or naval base in the region were considered by India "as a threat to the peace and tranquility." Inspite of Indian protest, a cabinet minister of UNP put the argument, "when India signs treaty of friendship and cooperation with the Soviet Union, do they ask us. But when Sri Lanka wants to develop, there is a hue and cry."

On the other hand United States was finding Sri Lanka as an ideal place in the Indian Ocean for United States ships. Sri Lanka could get foreign assistance politically and militarily both but none of the country is prepared to become Sri Lanka's strategic partner. They could not go against the India's and littoral countries interests.

India's extensive 200 miles coastline is entirely open and needs strong defences. Sri Lanka's strategic location in the Indian Ocean area makes it as important strategically to India as Taiwan to China. As long as Sri Lanka is friendly or neutral, India has nothing to worry but if there be any danger of the island falling under the domination of a power hostile to India, India cannot tolerate such a situation endangering her territorial integrity.

INDIA'S PERCEPTION OF REGIONAL SECURITY

India's position in the region, no doubt is a position of pre-eminence and its leadership play an influential role in Asia as well as in international politics. In the early 50's India was compelled to recognise the geo-political realities of the Indian sub-continent region. The conflict with Pakistan and the task of safeguarding the Himalayan border made it insecure for its territorial integrity and national security. So India adopted a 'Indo-centric' security and defence system for the region. This made it imperative that India should exercise a close control over the external relations and defence strategies of neighbours or else receive their closest cooperation. So India expected from Sri Lanka to have common defence resources or like integration of Sri Lanka with India. This thought of India made Sri Lanka suspicious and threatened. The Indian thinking on the collective or collaborative defence and strategic arrangements was not acceptable to Sri Lanka. For searching security with neighbours, India succeeded in imposing unequal treaties on Nepal, Bhutan and Sikkim. But Sri Lanka looked to outside powers or associations of a wider international character to safeguard its independence and security.

INDO-SRI LANKA: SOME CONTENTIOUS ISSUES

The following contentious issues have created controversies and disputes between both the countries:

I. Citizenship of Indian Tamils

It was the first issue that arose after independence about the citizenship problem of Indian Tamil estate workers. The Indian Tamils were brought to the island by the British during 19th and 20th centuries to work in their tea and rubber estates in the

Kandyan hills. However the question of their permanent settlement and citizenship was left open by the British rulers. The Sinhalese held out the Tamil estate workers to be Indian and job opportunist. Therefore the Senanayake Government implemented the citizenship act No. 18 of 1948. As a result more than 9,75,000 Indian Tamils became stateless. The Indian government was not in a position to welcome them back to India and pressed Sri Lanka for restoring citizenship to them because of their long stay in the island.

Under Shastri-Sirimavo Pact of 1964, India accepted the responsibility of resettling 5,25,000 of 9,75,000 stateless Tamils and Sri Lanka granted citizenship to 3,00,000. The fate of remaining 1,50,000 was decided in 1974 by Indira Gandhi and Bandaranaike in which half number would be accepted by both the countries but the pact was not implemented. In 1988 Jayewardene Government granted citizenship to all stateless Tamils.

II. Kachchativu Problem and Maritime Boundary Dispute

Kachchativu is an uninhabited coral island about one square mile in area and located almost midway between India and Sri Lanka in Palk Strait. It is a barren, uninhabited and cactus-ridden place, which has been used by the fishermen as a resting place. It has no drinking water facilities and hence remains uninhabited. The dispute emerged in 1967, when Sri Lanka extended its maritime boundary from 6 to 12 nautical miles.

Both India and Sri Lanka claimed the island on the basis of historical sketch. The Tamil Nadu government claimed Kachchativu as belonging to Ramanathapur Samastham which had been taken over by the Tamil Nadu government under the Zamindari Abolition Act. Sri Lanka also produced evidence to prove historical rights over the island when during the second world war it was used as a naval bombardment range under Ceylon defence regulations. On 26 June 1974, India and Sri Lanka signed an agreement, demarcating their maritime boundary in Palk strait upon Adams Bridge, and Kacchativu was conceded to Sri Lanka. The 1976 maritime boundary agreement extended this boundary in Gulf of Mannar and the Bay of Bengal and gave each party a sovereign right over the continental shelf and the exclusive economic zones. Now Sri Lanka views Kachchativu matter settled and Kachchativu is no issue.

III. Indian Ocean as a Zone of Peace

Sri Lanka lies in the centre of Indian Ocean. That is why its regional security is attached to Indian Ocean politics. Sri Lanka has always perceived its vulnerability as a small island situated in the centre of Indian Ocean. One of the main reasons in doing defence pact with Britain in 1948 by Sri Lanka was that British naval power would protect Sri Lanka against any external threat from the Ocean. By the early 60's it was clear that Britain was no longer capable of continuing its role. The United States decided to fill the vacuum by sending its seventh fleet to Indian Ocean in 1963. This set the stage for a new big-power naval rivalry in the Indian Ocean.

Sri Lanka, apart from protesting United States action, initiated the Indian Ocean Nuclear Free Zone (IONZ) proposal at the Cairo Conference of the non-aligned nations. At the beginning the Indian attitude to the Sri Lankan proposal was lukewarm. Nehru's comments in the Lok Sabha was notable, "If the United States Government decides to do this, all we can say today is that outside territorial waters of India, the Ocean is naturally open to them as to the naval vessels of any other."

The anger of Sri Lanka was reflected during Chinese attack and its acceptance of military assistance from the United States. In 1968, the Soviet Union started its naval operations in Indian Ocean, which made the naval rivalry in Indian Ocean intensified and posed a threat of security to India as well as Sri Lanka. Now India had shown her interest in the proposal of Nuclear Free Zone.

After 1971 there was a radical change in the geo-political environment in sub-continent. The Indo-Soviet Friendship Treaty, Bangladesh war, rapid growth in India's military power and the intensifying superpower rivalry in the Indian Ocean had a marked impact on the power relations in the Indian sub-continent. The implication of these developments manifested in Indo-Sri Lanka relations also.

Sri Lanka raised again the proposal of Nuclear Free Zone at Lusaca non-aligned summit of 1970. But still India was against it as India till now had acquired nuclear capability. India was further irritated when Sri Lanka supported the Pak proposal for a nuclear-free zone in South Asia. Actually as a small state Sri Lanka began to look its security on the basis of IOPZ.

After 1975, both the countries made their pitch low. Mrs.

Bandaranaike took a softer line on the outstanding bilateral problems with India. This 'love-hate' relationship took a new turn when Indira Gandhi paid a visit to Sri Lanka in 1973 assuring Sri Lanka of India's friendship.

The Sri Lankan proposal of IOPZ softened in 1977, as victory of pro-western UNP in 1977 pushed the Jayawardene Government to accommodate western interests in its foreign policy. The western arms build up and Diego Garcia, in Sri Lanka's foreign policy almost disappeared. Its changed stand on the IOPZ was now directed towards general disarmament. But India opposed the Sri Lankan's offer to United States for base facilities in Trincomalee which India thought would severely constrain India's naval strategy in the southern Indian Ocean.

India stands committed to the objective of security and IOPZ, but is not willing to undertake any commitment involving the future security interests of India. It wants an unconditional acceptance of IOPZ and liquidation of super power military bases in the Indian Ocean. India wants Sri Lanka to collaborate fully for securing this objective. But Sri Lanka now appears to be not very enthusiastic about IOPZ.

IV. Ethnic Problem of Sri Lanka and Indo-Sri Lanka Relations

Sri Lanka is multi-ethnic, multi-religious and multi-lingual country. The majority of Sri Lanka's people-nearly 74 percent are known as 'Sinhalese', originally migrated from Bengal-Orissa region in the fifth century B.C. The Tamil, the largest minority in Sri Lanka (21.6%) are divided into two-groups—Sri Lankan Tamils and the Indian Tamils-both have been migrated from South India in the 5th and 4th century B.C. Other minor ethnic groups are Moors, Malays, etc. The conflict between the two ethnic groups-Sinhalese and Tamils has distorted Sri Lankan politics.

ETHNIC CONFLICT OF 1977

After coming to power in 1977, the UNP government under Srimavo Bandaranaike leadership went for 'open door' policies of a liberal, market oriented and free trade but could not solve the unemployment problem and also could not contain the Tamil's frustration and alienation which had begun to find militant and violent expression. The Tamil United Liberation of Front (TULF) formed in 1976 had started talking of independence for the Sri Lankan Tamils and a separate Tamil Eelam. The TULF claimed that the Sri Lanka government had discriminated against the Tamils in education, employment, land alienation, etc.

Ethnic violence erupted in August; 1977in Sri Lanka and TULF demanded the right of self-determination to solve their problems. The Government of India expressed its grave concern over the situation in Sri Lanka. This violence has been increased with time. The July 1983 ethnic violence which turned into communal frenzy and alike civil war was a great concern for both the countries. India's expression of concern over the killing of innocent civilians and its strong desire to protect the interests of Sri Lankan Tamils had created a strong sense of fear in the minds of the Sri Lankan government. Many incidents during 1983-87 led to the creation of such a fear complex. Firstly Tamil Nadu's demand for a Bangladesh type action in Sri Lanka was a great question of anxiety. Some Tamils had high expectation of India delivering a virtual 'Eelam' just as independent Bangladesh was created in 1971 with the help of Indian armed forces in East Pakistan. They were disappointed when this did not happen. Although the Indian leadership of Indira Gandhi and Rajiv Gandhi resisted such pressure and pledged to honour Sri Lankan sovereignty and territorial integrity. Second India supplied arms and extended sanctuary facilities to the Sri Lankan militants in Tamil Nadu. The entire Palk Strait became a major conduct for arms and militants. Thirdly, the operation Eagle of Indian Air Force dropped food and medicine in Jaffna on June 4, 1987, which the Sri Lanka government saw as a flagrant and naked violation of its air space and territorial integrity. These all actions led to Sri Lankan leadership to undertake a global search for security in 1983-84.

BILATERAL AGREEMENT

This security threat from India diminished on 29 July, 1987 when both the countries signed a bilateral agreement to restore peace on the island. Denial of base facilities to the militants in India and the Indian Navy's cooperation to prevent their activities, no use of Trincomalee port for military use by any country were the promises in the directions of restoring peace.

This India-Sri Lanka Agreement opened a new chapter in the relations between the two countries with cooperation rather than confrontation being the key element of policy which continues to this day. India had laid great emphasis on its regional security interests.

INDIAN PEACE KEEPING FORCE IN SRI LANKA

Under the July, 1987 agreement commitment of India that it would extend, as and when requested, military assistance to, Sri Lanka, India sent a contingent of peace keeping force of about 8,000 men on July 31, 1987 against LTTE on the request of Jayewardene. But the cost of intervention was very heavy for India. More than 1,200 soldiers were killed and about 2,500 injured. India spent more than $180 million on the operation. After the protest of Sinhalese, the Premadasa government asked India to withdraw. The IPKF in March, 1990 without fulfilling the objectives had to withdraw from Sri Lanka. The IPKF was sent to Sri Lanka as a part of Indo-Sri Lanka Accord to help Sri Lanka in restoring peace, order and civil administration in Northern and Eastern part of Sri Lanka.

With a view to resolving the ethnic conflict, India offered its good offices to bring the conflicting groups to the negotiating table at Thimpu. The talks proved a failure. Rajiv Gandhi and Jayewardene met in New Delhi for further talks. Along with the Sri Lankan press, the New York Times described India as "a trusted mediator." But President Jayewardene accused India of supplying arms and running terrorist training camps. But India in searching of a political solution of the problem, the Government of India even invited LTTE leader Prabhakaran for talks in New Delhi.

In total, India sent five dignitaries to commence its mediator role. They were G. Parthasarthy, Romesh Bhandari, Natwar Singh, P. Chidambaram and Dinesh Singh. India has been trying to resolve the problem by all means.

Resolution of the ethnic problem in Sri Lanka is vital to promote India's interests. Owing to its geo-political situation, India has a vital interest in defusing the situation. It is however a matter of concern that India's initiative is being failed. The ethnic conflict is, no doubt, Sri Lanka's internal problem. India is not in a position to dictate or even persuade Sri Lanka beyond a point. Domestic political pressures are at work, inhibiting Sri Lanka's option and jeopardising India's efforts for solution as well. Though the issue is complex, a way out in keeping with the larger cause of good neighbourly relations and reciprocal commitment to national sovereignty has to be arrived at. Sub-nationalistic and divisive elements are as destructive in case of India's national integrity as they are to Sri Lanka's.

The ethnic crisis of Sri Lanka has attracted worldwide attention. But India is directly affected since Tamil Nadu is separated by only 33 km from the north of Sri Lanka's Jaffna peninsula. This is one important reason why India figures prominently in the issue, wittingly or unwittingly.

India does not want to interfere in any country's internal affairs. India's concern for Tamil's welfare and interests should not be considered as interference. Actually India wants a legitimate political settlement of the ethnic conflict, India is not an external threat. The real threat to Sri Lanka emerges from within.

Tamil Tigers and Sri Lanka Government agreed to stop violence and renewed on February 24, 2006 a commitment to four years ceasefire to ensure that the country did not return to civil war. Both met in Geneva in April 2006 to talk after their first meeting in 2003. The Geneva talks could help in maintaining the ceasefire which has perhaps become the longest period of non-fighting between the state and the Tamil rebels.

The LTTE recently announced that the Cease Fire Agreement (CFA) is signed with Colombo has failed to deliver peace. The LTTE is again pitted in confrontation with Sri Lankan armed forces in the northern and eastern regions of Sri Lanka. India is worried with these developments. In the state of violence and war, the people will flee and seek refuge here. This will have an impact on Indian domestic politics, especially in Tamil Nadu. The LTTE has used these refugees to whip up passions and support for their militaristic campaign.

The Mahindra Rajapaksa Government in Sri Lanka intends to hold a referendum asking people to decide on whether or not it should continue to adhere to the Norwegian brokered 2002 Cease Fire Agreement (CFA). The international community is in favour of continuation of the CFA, though by the end of 2006, it has been violated over 4000 times.

Despite international mediation five years ago and a ceasefire agreement between Lankan Government and LTTE there is no solution at work. Both Colombo and LTTE have refused to think beyond the paradigm of a nation state based on ethnicity. The warning sides seem to believe in militaristic solutions even while pretending to be accommodative of each other's demands. As Indian interests are directly affected and the world looks to India to provide perspective on the Sri Lankan crisis, New Delhi needs to play a leading role in mobilising international opinion and assistance.

Sri Lanka blames India that Indian navy and coast guard do not vigil properly along the states' 1,076 km coastline to prevent militant infiltration from Sri Lanka. Since the collapse of the Norwegian sponsored ceasefire in January, 2006, the Sri Lankan navy had intercepted or destroyed nine trawlers and some smaller fiber boat and carrying explosives "all coming from the Tamil Nadu coast" in the Gulf of Mannar region, Sri Lanka sees increased LTTE activities along India coast.

Sri Lanka alleged India that the LTTE is procuring from India materials such as electric detonators, gelatins, ball bearings and metal bars. The Sri Lankan navy first detected in January 2006 a LTTE boat carrying more than 60,000 electronic detonators being brought from India.

On the other hand the security implications for Tamil Nadu following the collapse of talks between the Sri Lankan Government and the Liberation Tigers of Tamil Eelam are becoming only too evident. The State is witnessing not only an influx of Sri Lankan Tamil refugees, but also an increase in smuggling along its south-eastern coast. Besides fuel, medicines and callipers, components for making explosives figure among the item taken to the island clandestinely by boat from several "landing points" along the Ramanathapuram coast. Since January 2006, about 18,600 Tamil refugees have arrived at Rameswaram till June 2007.

INDIA AND THE PEACE PROCESS IN SRI LANKA

Peace is an essential pre-condition for regional cooperation. Peace is of over helming importance to the Sri Lankan people. Conflict has over the years afflicted hundreds of thousands of Sri

Lankan. Earlier attempts of ending conflict and bringing peace through negotiations had been unsuccessful. Four such attempts were taken by Sri Lanka-Thimpu talks initiated by India in 1985, the Indo-Sri Lanka Accord of 1987, the Premadass-LTTE talks of 1989-90 and Kumartunga-LTTE talks of 1994. They all began promisingly but failed. The LTTE who is involved in an armed struggle through war and terrorism guerrilla hit and run raids. Sri Lanka Government entered into the Ceasefire Agreement with LTTE in February 2002.

Sri Lanka considers India as an integral part of the peace process in ways that are mutually useful and sustainable. India wants to seek a negotiated settlement accepted to all sections of Sri Lankan society within the framework of a united Sri Lanka and consistent with democracy, pluralism and respect for individual rights. India confirmed its stand in the Joint Statement of 2003 during Prime Minister Wickremesinghe's visit to India.

> "India will maintain an abiding interest in the security of Sri Lanka and remains committed to its sovereignty and territorial integrity. India would welcome a resolution of the current impasse in the peace process and an early resumption of negotiations. Any interim arrangement should be an integral part of the final settlement and should be in the framework of the unity and territorial integrity of Sri Lanka."

India's support for peace talks is bi-partisan and shared by all political parties. This is confirmed from the UPA's Common Minimum Program (CMP) of 2004.

> "The UPA will support peace talks in Sri Lanka that fulfill the legitimate aspirations of Tamils and religious minorities within the territorial integrity and solidarity of Sri Lanka."

India is ready to help Sri Lanka to find a solution to the escalating violence. India preferred a negotiated solution to the ethnic problem in Sri Lanka and felt that a military solution was not feasible.

There is an opinion that India should consider a more pro-active role in Sri Lanka to manage the conflict and steer the peace process to a positive resolution. But for this to happen, India does not want to lift a ban on the Tigers.

FISHING AND VIOLATION OF MARITIME BOUNDARY

For fishing, the Indian and Sri Lankan fishermen openly violates the International Maritime Boundary Line (IMBL). And to Stop fishermen entering into IMBL, both the navies infringes into the territorial waters by crossing the IMBL, which often instigates firing. Both the navies uses harsh and strict measure to prevent illegal fishing and poaching. The fishermen are used for smuggling arms by the LTTE. India is very much concerned for the safety of fishermen. Many fishermen lose their life by gun firing on them.

It is not Katchativu island, located 12 nautical miles from Rameswaram, that has been drawing Indian fishermen in droves, but high-security zones like Kanakesanturai and Point Pedro in Northern Sri Lanka, where fishing is banned, besides Mannar and Talaimannar, in Jaffana's northern tip, provoking the Lankan Navy to open fire on them. Traditionally, the Indian fishermen are used to fishing in waters closer to the Sri Lankan coast, in places like Mannar and Talaimannar and the highly sensitive Kanakesanturai port and Point Pedro, which are rich in fish catch. But when they get close to Lanka's high security zone, its navy naturally opens fire because at night they cannot make out whether they are our boys or the LTTE.

After the death of a fisherman, due to fishing, by Sri Lanka navy near Kachchativu, which is very close to the International Maritime Boundary Line (IMBL). In February 2007, the Tamil Nadu Chief Minister M. Karunanidhi has written a letter to the Prime Minister drawing his attention to the incidents of "indiscriminate firing" by the Sri Lankan navy on fishermen. The Chief Minister said the firing was causing tension in the coastal areas and asked the Prime Minister to take urgent action to prevent such incidents.

Illegal fishing in the Sri Lankan waters by Indian fishermen normally become a question of irritance between the two governments. In this, many fishermen of both sides are caught up and sometimes the firing by Navies caused the death of fishermen. The Government of Sri Lanka assures that the Sri Lanka navy would not, under any circumstances, infringe into the Indian territorial waters by crossing the IMBL. Moreover the Sri Lankan navy, it claimed, has always strived to help Indian fishermen when in time of need, despite the fact that they enter the Sri Lankan waters for poaching. The Sri Lanka says that it is LTTE which is engaged in the practice of attacking Indian fishing trawlers with the sole aim of discrediting the Sri Lankan navy.

SRI LANKA'S CLOSENESS WITH UNITED STATES AND CHINA

Sri Lanka a small island country dangling from the southern most tip of the Indian peninsula has traditionally been a connecting link of the eastern and western trade route. Her strategic location in the Indian Ocean made China interested in the island. The unequal friendship of the giant and pygmy creates doubt and fear in the Indian mind.

The United States and China are interested in Indian Ocean—a major sea route of the world. The United States has a naval base-Diego Garcia-in the ocean and its fleets are moving in the Indian Ocean. China cannot leave the ocean for United States, so its presence is also noticeable. Both the powers have good relations with Sri Lanka. China has emerged as a big arms supplier to Sri Lanka.

Recently Sri Lanka and the United States on March 5, 2007 signed an agreement—Acquisition Cross Servicing Agreements (ACSA) valid for 10 years to facilitate transfer and exchange of logistics supplies, support and re-fuelling services during peace keeping missions, humanitarian operations, disasters and joint exercises. The ACSA will facilitate the exchange of non-lethal equipments and increase cooperation in the field.

The ACSA between Sri Lanka and US had been on hold for years because of India's objections. The great improvement in relations between India and the US in recent years, India shed its objections to the agreement. The US has ACSA with 89 other countries.

India from a long-term perspective is very much concerned with this agreement. No doubt, being a nation of 20 million, Sri Lanka does not have the capabilities or infrastructure for such ventures. But this agreement for United States is as good as acquiring a base in the Indian Ocean.

Sri Lankan President Mahindra Rajapakse paid a seven-day visit (February 26 to March 4, 2007) to China to participate in a series of events to celebrate the 50th anniversary of diplomatic relations between Sri Lanka and China. During the visit eight pacts were signed:

- China will develop a friendship city-Hambantota in Sri Lanka which includes developing a harbour, bunkering system and tank farm.
- China would encourage and facilitate financial institutions.
- China would assist Sri Lanka in the form of technical support and financial aid for major infra structure projects including the Puttalam Coal Power Project on which work has commenced in the island nation.

This agreement is significant as China is keen to enhance its influence in the Indian Ocean. During the visit a MoU (Memorandum of Understanding) on two-way investment promotion and an MoU on the film industry were also signed. Now China has come to Indian Ocean to establish a friendship city relationship.

It is immediately not clear if Sri Lanka intends to seek China's assistance to develop the Hambantota harbour on the same pattern as the Gwadar deep sea project in Pakistan undertaken by Beijing. China may announce the intention to take a major role in a planned $1 billion integrated harbour project in Hambantota on Sri Lanka's southern coast that would have an oil refinery, container port, airport. China is also participating in building a coal-powered power plant in Sri Lanka worth upto $500 million, which could address the severe power shortage faced by the island nation. Sri Lankan government may offer one block each to China and India out of the eight identified oil blocks in view of the country's close relations with the two countries. The Gulf of Mannar has been identified for the first phase of oil exploration.

The growing terrorism of LTTE has now turned Sri Lanka towards Pakistan and China for its weapon's needs. Only India in the sub-continent has the political and military leverage with both Colombo and the LTTE. But the Indian government appears afraid of even trying. So Sri Lanka has to depend on Pakistan and China for getting sophisticated weapons to face the LTTE threat. Though the U.S. had banned the LTTE in 1997 as a terrorist organisation, it was still operating there collecting substantial fund for procuring weapons.

Meanwhile, the United States has granted Sri Lanka Rs. 51 million ($474,000) as grant to promote "energy security" in the island nation through the development of the nation's oil and gas sector. Sri Lanka at present has no oil or gas production of its own and imports approximately 80,000 barrels per day. However, based on preliminary surveys, the Sri Lanka Government believes that there are oil and gas reserves in the Mannar basin.

INDIA AND SRI LANKA: RESTORING FRIENDSHIP SINCE 1991

In the post-1990 period India-Sri Lanka relations have an all round improvement in all areas—political, economic and culture. India's new policy of non-intervention in the ethnic conflict has also contributed to removing the cultivated fear complex of Sri Lanka. While refusing to play any direct role in the ethnic conflict, India is supportive of the peace process. India has extended its wholehearted support with the donor co-chairs to the peace process who are the United States, Europe, Norway and Japan. India has banned the LTTE and its Chief V. Prabhakran is wanted for trial in the Rajiv Gandhi assassination case. The demand of extradition of Prabhakaran still persists since 1995. But Prabhakaran is now declared dead.

Bilateral FTA has proven to be far more liberal

- ISFAT: Less than 14% of Sri Lanka's exports to India restricted under Indian negative list.
- SAFTA: Nearly 42% of Sri Lanka's exports to India restricted under Indian negative list.
- At present, 93% of Sri Lanka's exports to India enter under zero duty under ISFTA.

Spillovers into FDI

- Indian FDI in Sri Lanka accounts for 6% p.a. during 2004-06 compared to 1% p.a. earlier.
- Over 70% of Indian FDI now in services.
- Prompted moves to negotiate a bilateral CEPA.

India's Investments in Sri Lanka

- The India-Sri Lanka FTA has stimulated new FDI into Sri Lanka for rubber-based products, ceramics, electrical and electronic items, wood-based products, agri-commodities and consumer durables
- India is the 4th largest investor in Sri Lanka with FDI approvals of US$ 450 million.
- Indian Oil Corporation, Taj Hotels, L&T, Ambuja, Tata and Ashok Leyland are among the prominent Indian companies operating in Sri Lanka.
- With close to 120 flights per week including by Indian private airlines, tourist arrivals from India in Sri Lanka are the largest.
- Some of the important projects in the pipeline include a 500 MW coal-based thermal power plant at Trincomalee by NTPC, oil and gas exploration in Mannar blocks of Sri Lankan waters by ONGC and upgradation of the Colombo-Matara railway by RITESIRCON.
- Ceylon Biscuits and Oamro are the most visible Sri Lankan investments in India.

India's Imports from Sri Lanka

(Value in US$ million)

Sl. No.	*Commodity*	*1999-2000 Value*
1.	Coffee, Tea. Mate and Spices	13.9
2.	Iron and Steel	8.1
3.	Pulp of Wood or of other Fibrous Cellulosic Material, etc	3,34
4.	Animal or Vegetable Fats and Oils, etc.	2.74
5.	Plastic/Articles thereof. Lac; Gums, Resins/Other Vegetable	2.34
6.	Saps/Extracts.	2.13
7.	Edible Fruit/Nuts; Peel/Citrus Fruit/Melons.	2.11
8.	Rubber/articles thereof.	1.4
9.	Paper/Articles of Paper Pulp, etc.	0.85
10.	Products of Animal Origin, nes.	0.7
	Total	44.23

(Contd.)

	Commodity	*2006-07*
1.	Animal/Vegetable Fats and etc.	
2.	Copper/Articles thereof.	Value 99.93 87.63
3.	Electrical Machinery/Equipment /Parts thereof	44.13
4.	Coffee, Tea, Mate/Spices.	28.7
5.	Rubber/Articles thereof.	26.55
6.	Aluminium/Articles thereof.	24.31
7.	Articles of Stone, Plaster, Cement Asbestos, Mica, etc.	20.62
8.	Machinery mechanical Appliances like Dish Washing Mach./ Machnry for Fling, Sealing, Labeling Boxs, Bags/Containers	13.24
9.	Wood/Articles of Wood, etc.	
10.	Pulp of Wood or other Fibrous Cellulosic Material; Waste and Scrap of Paper	11.6 11.6
	Total	470.28

Structure of trade has changed. Sri Lanka is exporting more intermediate goods to India.
Source: DGFT.

AGREEMENT ON FREE TRADE

India and Sri Lanka joined in a new partnership with a Free Trade Area (FTA) agreement in December 1998, which became operational from December 15, 2001. India has committed to provide immediate duty free on 102 items and 50 percent duty concession is given on 400 items which would become duty free in three years. It was hoped that the FTA would give boost to Sri Lanka's exports.

INDO-SRI LANKA ECONOMIC COOPERATION

Sri Lanka has only two main industries—tea and tourism. Now both the countries are engaged in economic cooperation and want to conclude a Comprehensive Economic Partnership Agreement (CEPA). A Joint Study Group (JSG) set-up for this purpose. It is said that CEPA will cover services and investment. It will take the two countries to a "qualitatively new level of engagement by intensifying and deepening bilateral economic interaction, building on the advantages of close political and geographic proximity."

In June 2002, India offered a credit of $ 100 million to Sri

Lanka for purchasing capital goods, consumer services and food items from India. In October 2001, India also gave Sri Lanka a loan of 20 million dollar for its economic stabilisation. In June 2002, the Indian Oil Corporation and the Ceylon Petroleum Corporation signed a MoU under which the former is allowed to engage in retail oil trade in the island as well as to manage and operate, on a long lease, the Trincomalee oil tanks. Both the countries have planned to start a ferry service between Colombo and Cochin.

India is showing keen interests in developing the infrastructure of Sri Lanka. Trade and economic cooperation, both under the bilateral and the SAARC framework provides an important area for engagement. The scope for greater economic interaction arises from Sri Lanka's dependent economic structure and India's growing industrial and commercial sector. An Indian trade delegation visited Colombo in April 2007 firming up bilateral trade talks that include professional services, investments and trade in goods.

INDIA-SRI LANKA COOPERATION IN SMALL SCALE INDUSTRIES (SSI) SECTOR

India and Sri Lanka in January, 2004 signed a Memorandum of Understanding (MoU) to increase cooperation in six areas of the small scale sector-food technology, fisheries, light engineering, auto components, leather industry, IT and cottage industry. The MoU envisages carrying out industrial surveys and feasibility studies to identify thrust areas and opportunities for development of Small Scale Industries (SSIs) in Sri Lanka. Sri Lanka plans to allocate oil block in the Gulf of Mannar to India without the usual bidding process for the first phase of oil exploration.

The Tsunami of December 26, 2004, the biggest natural disaster in centuries faced by both the countries with worst results. The Tsunami directly affected millions in terms of damage to property or live hood. The disaster brought both the countries nearer in rescue and rehabilitation work. Now, both are exchanging informations about the sea and climate.

THE ISSUE OF FISHERMEN

The issue of Tamil Nadu fishermen, who often cross over to

Sri Lankan waters, is a major concern for India. Frequent arrest of the Indian fishermen by Sri Lanka has not however affected the bilateral relations. In order to end this irritant problem, India has made a proposal for the introduction of a system of licensed fishing in Sri Lanka's north-eastern waters. In view of the humanitarian dimension of the problem, India and Sri Lanka have agreed to deal with the fishermen issue in a "practical and comprehensive way."

Tamil Nadu Chief Minister Jayalalitha demanded India Government to take on lease Kachchativu Island from Sri Lanka so that fishermen could earn. But India has not accepted it as it has given this island to Sri Lanka accepting it sovereignty on it.

SETUSAMUDRAM SHIP CANAL (SSCP) PROJECT

The SSCP envisages the creation of a navigable canal from the Gulf of Mannar to the Bay of Bengal through a stretch of shallow sea in the Palk Strait separating India and Sri Lanka by dredging. Two channels will be created—one across Adam's Bridge, a chain of islets linking India with Sri Lanka, and another through the shallow Palk Bay, deepening the Palk Strait. The width of the proposed channel at the sea-bed level is 300 metres to facilitate two-way navigation.

Because of the rocky sea and less depth of sea water between India and Sri Lanka there is difficulty in transporting of ships near Rameshwaram. Indian ships from the Arabian Sea have to go to eastern ports through taking a round of Sri Lanka. This consumes more diesel and time. In this context India and Sri Lanka shipping ministry wants to increase the depth of sea. For this a canal like Panama and Suej Canal would be constructed in Palk and Bay of Manner. This project is named as Setu Samudram. The canal is expected to facilitate the movement of bigger ships and reduce travel distance by 254-424 nautical miles (about 465-835 km) and sailing time by 21-36 hour. It will reduce the steaming distances between the east-west coasts of India and improve the navigation within territorial waters of India. The channel is also expected to boost national defence by enabling easier and quicker access between the coast guard and naval ships will not have to circumnavigate Sri Lanka.

The project, to be completed by 2009, is expected to help spur industrial development, trade and commerce, promote coastal shipping and generate employment in southern Tamil Nadu. Tuticorin port could be transformed into a trans-shipment hub like those in Singapore and Colombo. The channel is projected to help not only in developing 13 minor ports in Tamil Nadu but also help currently languishing northern Sri Lanka ports like Mannar, Thalaimannar, Kankensanthurai (KKS), and Point Pedro.

The hypothesis of Setusamudram was first projected by a British commander A.D. Tailor in 1860 before 144 years, cleared first by Nehru's cabinet in 1955, 1983 and 1996. The project estimated to cost about Rs 2,500 crore was finally cleared by the present UPA government and was inaugurated on July 2, 2005 by Prime Minister Manmohan Singh. Setu Samudram Project is created for a continuous navigate route around India's southern tip and between Sri Lanka to Palk Strait to Gulf of Mannar.

As there is a cultural equality between India and Sri Lanka, this bridge will bring emotional love. It is building with joint collaboration. It will boost tourism and trade relations and will make easy transport of goods and people. The Indian businessmen now could bring their goods by trucks direct to Colombo port which could be then transported to other countries easily. Sending goods from Indian ports takes more time and fuel now.

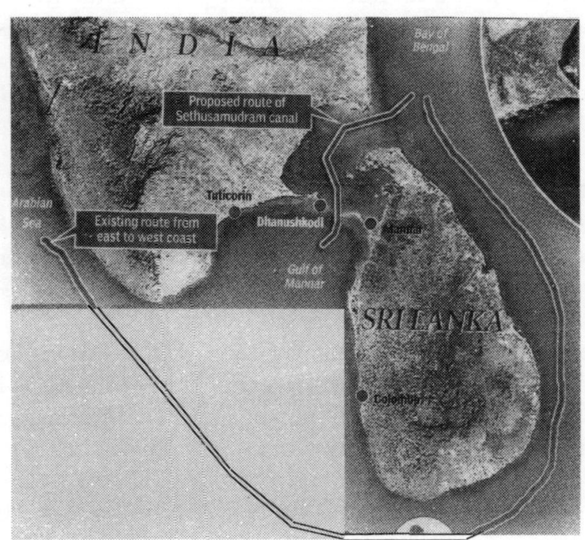

A GULF OVER RAM'S BRIDGE

The Sethusamudram controversy has flared up. The two canals to be dredged, a total of 89 km, are supposed to open new economic avenues. But, the proposal to cut through the bridge, said to have transported Ram's army, has environmentalists, politicians and Vishwa Hindu Parishad (VHP) up in arms. A look at the arguments and issues:

Environmental Factors

Official Claim: No major damage likely. Coral presence along route is negligible. Dredging not a threat to ecosystems like Mannar biosphere, coastal populations. Will increase opportunities for fishermen.

The Catch: Coral reef will be dredged, turbidity will be harmful. Bridge is natural defence against storms and tsunamis. Mix of hot-cold currents creates unique biosphere. Big ships will disturb fishing. Significant seismic activity.

Economics of the Canal

Official Claim: Siltation removal will not be prohibitive. Route will save 36 hours and 450 km for ships. It will provide transit for nine ships a day to begin with. Tuticorin port will be transformed into nodal hub. 13 minor ports planned.

The Catch: Sedimentation not accounted for. Ships will have to do a tightrope in shallow waters. Those displacing more than 10 mtrs cannot use canal. Maximum weightage is 30,000t, unlike 300,000t for Suez or Panama. Difficult to tow damaged ships.

Security Checks

Official Claim: Will allow swifter movement of small naval and coast guard craft. Will afford better control of east and west coast to check smuggling, terrorism. Direct Bay of Bengal-Arabian Sea link through Indian waters

The Catch: Ships, particularly commercial, are vulnerable to attacks by LTTE. If Tigers' security in north Sri Lanka is affected, they may target vessels. The narrow and shallow nature of the canal means an accident may block it for weeks.

OBJECTIONS AGAINST SSCP

The SSCP Project is against the environment. The Gulf of Mannar Marine Reserve is one of India's most biologically diverse coastal regions with over 3,600 species of plants and animals, including the globally endangered dugong. The coral reefs which surround the islands in the area, often referred to as "underwater tropical rain forest', are treasure house for marine ornamental fishes. Constant dredging to maintain the depth of the canal, it is feared, would damage the reserve. Green activists also point out that increase in shipping traffic will inevitably result in an increase in oil spills and marine pollution.

Hundreds of fishing villages along the coast will also be affected if the ecology of the fish is affected. They have expressed concern over increased movement of big ships in the area destroying their boats and nets and driving away marine life including fish. Activists have pointed out that the concerns of the fishing community have not been addressed by the project officials adequately. Other concerns include inadequate plans for disposal of the dredged material waste, water currents being altered due to the project construction and even greater impact of potential future Tsunamis from the construction of the canal. And recently, the BJP has protested against the project accusing the government of attempting to destroy evidence of the existence of the ancient 'Ram Setu', a bridge believed to have been built by Lord Ram linking India and Sri Lanka. The Shankaracharya of Dwarka Peeth too has threatened to move the Supreme Court if the government did not stop work on the project.

VISIT OF PRIME MINISTER MAHINDRA RAJAPAKSHE

The Sri Lankan Prime Minister came in July 2004 for a three day visit to India. This was his first visit other becoming Prime Minister. Both the states talked on establishing peace in Tamil majority north east province and India's cooperation in rebuilding of this province which is the main target of LTTE. Sri Lanka also asked for India's cooperation in the development of Sri Lankan infrastructure and rural development.

Both leaders expressed their satisfaction on the state of bilateral co-operation. Prime Minister Manmohan Singh extended

India's cooperation for the such solution of internal problem of Sri Lanka which could sustain regional sovereignty and safeguard interests of all citizens. Prime Minister also declared 10 million dollar aid to Lanka for the development of rural infrastructure and a credit of 15 crore dollar for the import of Petro products from India.

VISIT OF PRESIDENT KUMARATUNGE

The president Chandrika Kumaratunge came India on a visit of five days in November 2004. She met separately with President Kalam, Prime Minister Manmohan Singh, UPA Chief Sonia Gandhi, Lal Krishan Advani and Atal Bihari Vajpayee. The joint statement was issued after the talks which included:

- To set-up a Joint Working Group (JWG) for fishermen.
- Agreement on bilateral Defence Cooperation Agreement.
- Agreement on renewal of Palaly airfield.
- India was agreed on to refit the Sri Lankan naval war ship 'Sayura'.

India repeated again its old statement about the process to establish peace in Sri Lanka, acceptable to all the concerned parties. Both are agreed to call a meeting of technical experts who can exchange views on the economic and environmental affects of proposed building of Setu Samudram Project.

Mrs. Kumaratunge suggested to establish a Centre for India-Sri Lanka studies at Bhandara Naike Centre for International Studies (BCIS). She also offered a proposal to organise a Rajiv Gandhi memorial lecture every year. Again she visited India in June 2005.

VISIT OF PRESIDENT MAHINDRA RAJPAKSHE

The Sri Lankan president came to Delhi for a four day visit from 27 to 30 December 2005. This was his first visit to a foreign nation after taking charge of the post of president. In the background of ethnic violence and peace process, the visit was very important. The main objective of the visit was to talk with Indian leaders on the ethnic crisis. Both parties stressed on the re-start of the peace process with LTTE. For increasing mutual economic cooperation, both the leaders talked on some important issues. These were establishment of 500 MW electric center in Trincomalee with the help of India and building of a hospital in Dikoya for tea labourers. Both had talked on Comprehensive Economic Partnership Agreement (CEPA). India had also shown her interest in a Railway project of laying trek from Colombo to Matara via Gale. The Joint statement said that India is agreed to establish an electric center at Trincomalee under the joint venture of NTPC of India and Ceylon Electricity Board. India is agreed on issuing economic aid to Sri Lanka for the development of infrastructure, establishment of stadium and library in Jaffna and cooperation for establishment of a Information and Communication Technology park (ICT).

LTTE AIR ATTACK

The "Sea Tigers" (naval wing of LTTE) on March 27, 2007, did an air force attack on the Katunayake airbase near Colombo in which three airmen killed and sixteen wounded. The LTTE's new found air power is a grave threat to Sri Lanka, India and other South Asian countries. The LTTE is the only rebel group in the world with an air wing having bought up to four Czech-built 2 lin-143 aircraft. The Sri Lanka president Rajapakse found it a threat to the inter national community and called for concerted action to defeat terrorism.

Sri Lanka blamed the India-installed first generation radars for failing to detect LTTE aircraft. But India ruled out any possibility of the radars not working. India assured Sri Lanka of "full assistance" after LTTE attack. India's "threat perception" is increased with LTTE air strike. The Indian security establishment is worried that an aircraft in the hands of terrorists can be used as a missile against high value targets, which was demonstrated by the 9/11 strikes in United States in 2001. Other than Colombo, New Delhi is perhaps the one government that is surprised by the air strike of LTTE. Though the LTTE is declared as a terrorist outfit by India long ago, India is acutely aware of the significant upgrade of LTTE's capabilities in recent years.

From the beginning of coalition government at New Delhi, the political fear of offending the coalition partners from Tamil

Nadu stop the Delhi Government to take action against LTTE. Whether it is in letting its allies proceed with the controversial Setusamundram project or in failing to take timely steps to counter the LTTE. New Delhi have had to take into account Tamil political sensitivities in dealing with the civil war in Sri Lanka.

No political formation in India has a bigger grievance against the LTTE than the Congress Party because of the assassination of Rajiv Gandhi. But the Congress led UPA Government has not taken any firm action and has adopted such a dangerously permissive policy towards it.

The NDA too had its partners from Tamil Nadu. But in conducting its policy towards Sri Lanka, the Atal Bihari Vajpayee government was willing to explore sophisticated options, when the Sri Lankan crisis reerupted in 2000. Vajpayee moved quickly with arms supplies to Sri Lanka, but also pressed Colombo to embark on a negotiation with the Tamil Tigers. This even-handed policy helped strengthen the basis for a peace process.

MEETING OF RAJAPAKSE WITH MANMOHAN SINGH

Sri Lankan President Mahindra Rajapakse met Prime Minister Manmohan Singh and had a detailed discussion for about half-an-hour on bilateral and internal issues after the SAARC Delhi summit held in first week of April 2007. Following the LTTE aerial attack on 26 March 2007 at Katunayake air base, the Sri Lankan President Rajapakse called for SAARC to launch a "coordinated drive to curb terrorism in all its forms and manifestations." India assured Sri Lanka of "full assistance" after LTTE attack but also expressed that India prefers negotiated solution of the problem.

TAMIL NADU FACTOR IN INDO-SRI LANKA RELATIONS

The long stretch of Tamil Nadu coast, especially between Nagapattinam to Tuticorin is a key support base that the LTTE has. With thousands of fishermen having a traditional link with Tamils of Sri Lanka and sharing the waters for fishing, the bond is not easy to break. This bond assisted by geological, social and economical circumstances, extends to the LTTE, except for a brief gap post-Rajiv Gandhi assassination. Without the fishermen and the people of Tamil Nadu, LTTE could not have survived.

The island town—Rameswaram in Tamil Nadu is economically dependent on LTTE and offers a single window clearance to virtually all of the demands and requirements of LTTE from soap and clothing to machines and medicines and from armoured vehicles to aeronautical accessories. Lack of fish in Indian waters, debt and poverty has made Tamil Nadu's fishermen easy tools in the hands of LTTE agents. Rameswaram has long been known as a smuggler's haven, today it holds the lifeline for LTTE. The coastline and constant fishing traffic in the dark makes smuggling easy for LTTE. Smuggling is source of income for fisherfolks. Despite certain landing points near Tuticorin and Kodaikarai along the 1,076 km long coastline of Tamil Nadu are seen as safe havens for smugglers. Men and material are smuggled continuously.

INDIA'S ARMS SUPPLY TO SRI LANKA

India paid its 'moral support' to Sri Lanka to tackle its bloody ethnic strife by supplying four 'India' low flying detection radars, L-70 gun barrels. Playing upon India's fears about China and Pakistan making strategic inroads into Sri Lanka, Colombo has asked New Delhi to supply more air defence weapons and radars, artillery guns. Nishant UAV's and even laser detonators for precision-guided munitions (PCMs). India wants to refrain Sri Lanka from seeking arms from China or Pakistan. So India has been providing "largely defensive" equipments to Sri Lanka.

INDIA, SRI LANKA SIGN MoU ON TEA RESEARCH

The Tea Research Association (TRA), India, and Tea Research Institute (TRI), Sri Lanka, entered into a research collaboration and signed a Memorandum of Understanding (MoU) to cement their ties.

The collaborative research areas will include plant breeding, studies on maximum residue level, biological control of pests, mechanisation of field and factory operations, development of chemical index for quality tea, development of water harvesting techniques and development of soil health.

CONCLUSIONS

Sri Lanka as a small state obsessed with insecurity has recognized India's pre eminence and managed to contain its foreign policy behaviour within the security parameters of India. Its efforts to overcome this insecurity through collective security, non-alignment and disarmament were unsuccessful particularly in view of India's drive for military pre-eminence and nuclear capability in the region. Geo-strategic development were unfavourable to Sri Lanka's endeavour to adopt a policy of balancing external powers in the Indian Ocean as a guarantee of its own security. Sri Lanka was late in realizing this and when it realized this, it formed itself an integral part of the South Asia security system dominated by India. Though internal political competition and ethnic conflict and the security dilemma have brought India directly into the Sri Lankan foreign policy, but economic interaction links them more together. With time Sri Lanka was able to change the old paradigm that saw India as a threat to Sri Lanka. Now a new shift in the perception has taken place in the minds of Sri Lankans that India is a valuable opportunity towards achieving Sri Lanka's progress.

India was firmly against the presence of foreign powers in Sri Lanka and in Indian Ocean. That was why it firmly opposed the pro-western link in Sri Lankan defence policy. It could bring the cold war system on her southern tip. India opposed the Sri Lanka's move to enter in SEATO in 1954. The foreign powers in the region could endanger India's security and defense. Nehru and other Congress leaders were repeatedly assuring Sri Lanka that India did not want to dominate it but desired to have good relations and friendship with it.

'Harmony in perception' was necessary for India. The ideological harmony with this closest neighbour on the regional and international issues could bring peace and development to the region. The principles of non-alignment brought them closer on the international issues.

The Indian Ocean is strategically as important to India as Sri Lanka. The decade of sixties was a decade of insecurity for India. India was deeply involved in regional conflicts with China and Pakistan so India did expect Sri Lanka to play a friendly role. India was against the presence of foreign powers in Indian Ocean, so it supported the proposal of Sri Lanka for Indian Ocean Peace Zone (IOPZ).

During the ethnic crisis, India was against the interference or intervention in the domestic politics of Sri Lanka. Many Sri Lankans, including the LTTE saw the arrival of Indian troops as a move to make the Indian writ run on the island. They called the accord as an instrument of Indian hegemony. But India feels its security is linked to a solution to the ethnic crisis in Sri Lanka. But Sri Lanka takes it as an interference and India's showing self as a regional superpower which dictate the regional affairs. But this is not right. India could prove a model for Sri Lanka, which has managed to democratically govern a nation of even greater diversity than Sri Lanka.

Strategic harmony between India and Sri Lanka is essential for regional peace. Regional hegemony of India could only complicate the situation. A long-term strategic cooperation with India on an equal basis could protect the security and territorial integrity of Sri Lanka. India's stand on the Sri Lanka ethnic conflict has benefited Sri Lanka in a significant way, as it could concentrate on its internal defence preparedness without continuing its pro-active search for external defence cooperation and security assurances.

THE FUTURE PATH

In the last one decade, significant changes have taken place in India-Sri Lanka relations. The nature and pattern of relations are completely different. The credit goes to the leadership of both the countries for taking its bilateral relations to such a new height. The ending of mutual misperception and the increase in mutual understanding have brought about this desired change.

The real threat to Sri Lanka emerges from within. The internal sources of threat are more serious than external sources and their linkages create crisis. From the point of external security, India still remains a key factor even though the security perception of both the countries have tremendously changed in recent years.

It seems essential to analyse the prospects of evolving a framework. The experience of past shows that the mutual mistrust and misperception were the fundamental cause for strategic divergence led to the insecurity of the island. Hence a serious attempt at evolving a CCS framework could address the psychological issues which govern bilateral interactions. And no doubt, development of mutual trust will promote a constructive bilateral engagement between the two countries to the mutual benefit of both.

There is a deep-rooted fear of India in the minds of a majority of the Sinhalese. So the mobilizing and tuning the peoples of both countries for a harmonious relationship without fear and prejudice is a very important step. The people to people contacts could change the mindsets. There has, so for, been no systematic effort to develop a healthy interaction between peoples of India and Sri Lanka, even though the score and opportunities are plenty. The image of India as a destabilising and hostile force should be replaced with an image of a friendly and cooperative power which believes in peaceful coexistence. At the same time, Sri Lanka's image of an intolerant society dominated by the Sri Lanka chauvinistic forces, has to be changed.

We could not ignore the Tamil Nadu factor in Indo-Sri Lanka relations. The political forces in Tamil Nadu have always sought to influence India's policy towards Sri Lanka. No government in Delhi can afford to be indifferent to the opinion of Tamil Nadu on various bilateral issues in which the state's interests are involved. Any attempt at building trust and confidence between the two countries, therefore should take the Tamil Nadu factor into serious account. An understanding between Sri Lanka and Tamil Nadu is vital for India-Sri Lanka friendship and cordiality. At the governmental level, there should be an institutionalized framework for larger bilateral engagement. It need not be under a bilateral treaty arrangement but within the normal structure of foreign policy institutions.

There is scope for trade, commerce and maritime cooperation. Apart from policing the border along the Palk Strait, both countries can jointly exploit marine resources. As regards security matters, frequent consultations at higher political and official level and a permanent regulatory mechanism to deal with issues of mutual concern and misperceptions will contribute to bilateral trust and understanding.

Recently on the death of an Indian fisherman in firing, it reiterated the proposal for joint monitoring and patrolling of the International Maritime Boundary Line (IMBL) by the Indian and

Sri Lanka Navies. Sri Lanka had told the Indian authorities that it was willing to work out an arrangement to jointly monitor the IMBL and share information on fishermen movement. But the Indian navy has virtually ruled out the possibility of conducting any joint patrolling with the Sri Lankan navy, saying it could have unpleasant consequence on the Indian side. The Indian navy had decided to setup nine sea surveillance radars along the coast from Nagapattinam to Rameswaram to bring the entire region under direct surveillance. After the LTTE attack on Katunayke, Indian air Force set-up eight radars in Sundarmudaiyan village.

Sri Lanka should go for multilateral diplomacy to create a security regime for small states under the auspices of SAARC. India resists to incorporate in the SAARC agenda the task of creating a regional security framework. It wants it to be based on socio-economic goals. But meaningful economic cooperation will provide greater impetus to regional security. No doubt, that India's security interests in the region lies in the security of small nations.

Militancy and terrorism are the big problems and threat of the sub-continent. Almost all the nations are facing its ugly face. Apart from this, poverty, ill health, illiteracy, natural disasters are another challenges, which can be solved with joint efforts only.

In an interview to the Hindu on September 12, 2008, Sri Lankan foreign affairs minister Rohitha Bogollagama said:

> "Bilateral ties with India are at the highest levels of trust confidence and friendship . . . "Continuous dialogue" at the bilateral level had helped us to communicate better toward finding solutions effectively and towards sustaining our relationship at the highest level."

India and Her Neighbours under the SAARC Framework

International politics is the politics of the unequal. No international organisation has the power to compel the stronger nations of the world to conduct their relations with weaker states according to the precepts of "fair play." However the weak are not completely at the mercy of the powerful. The primary force in international politics is competition among the strong and this affords weaker states an opportunity to assure their independence by establishing economic and political ties with a powerful national or regional organisation.

Nations pursue their interests through alignment with powerful or in coalition with others, for example Cuba influence western hemisphere politics with ties with Soviet Union. Similarly OPEC states control the flow and price of world's crude oil supply with its combined strength than they would posses individually. Similarly the originally South Asian states gives birth to SAARC-South Asian Association for Regional Cooperation in 1985. The original seven states were—India, Pakistan, Bangladesh, Nepal, Sri Lanka, Maldives, Bhutan and Afghanistan is the latest entry in the SAARC in 2007.

SAARC is a small organisation, but this does not lessen its importance. It is a regional entity, confined to South Asia only. It may not be as big as Arab League or African Union or as important as European Union but its significance lies in the strategic location of the region.

All the SAARC member countries are separate nation, independent and sovereign and have their own identities. But these nations have a common history. The region of SAARC lies in the south of Himalayas as surrounded by Hindukush mountains. The SAARC countries are of different sizes both geographically and population wise and have different resources. They are the less developed states (LDS) of the world. They account about 21 percent of the world population and only 3.5 percent of total land area. However their share in world output is a mere 1.3 percent.

SAARC—BIRTH, OBJECTIVES AND PRINCIPLES

The idea of regional cooperation in South Asia was first mooted in November 1980. In August 1983 in New Delhi, the foreign ministers of seven countries adopted the Declaration on South Asian Regional Cooperation (SAARC). First SAARC summit held in Dhaka on 7-8 December 1985.

The objectives, principles and general provisions as mentioned in the SAARC Charter are as follows:

Objectives

- To promote the welfare of the peoples *of* South Asia and to improve their quality of life;
- To accelerate economic growth, social progress and cultural development in the region and to provide all individuals the opportunity to live in dignity and to realise their full potentials.
- To promote and strengthen collective self-reliance among the countries of South Asia.
- To contribute to mutual trust, understanding and appreciation of one another's problems;
- To promote active collaboration and mutual assistance in the economic, social, cultural, technical and scientific fields:
- To strengthen cooperation with other developing countries;
- To strengthen cooperation among themselves in

international forums on matters of common interests: and

- To cooperate with international and regional organisations with similar aims and purposes.

Principles

- Cooperation within the framework of the Association is based on respect for the principles of sovereign equality, territorial integrity, political independence, non-interference in the internal affairs of other states and mutual benefit.
- Such cooperation is to complement and not to substitute bilateral or multilateral cooperation.
- Such cooperation should be consistent with bilateral and multilateral obligations of member states.

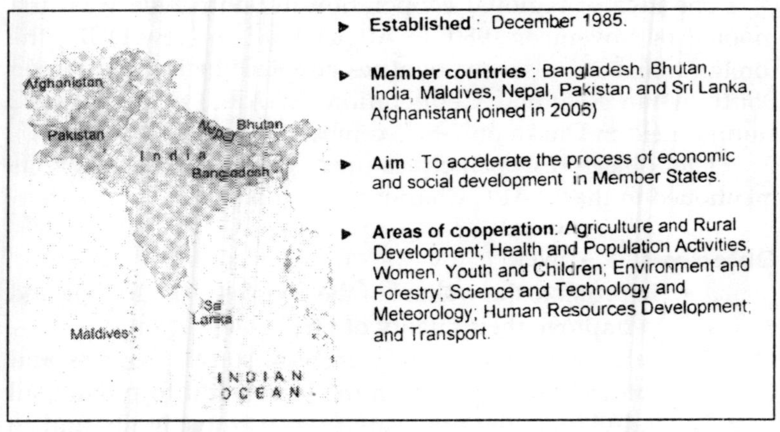

SAARC : SIGNIFICANCE FOR SUB-CONTINENT

The regional cooperation among these countries would not only lead to rapid economic development, but also strengthen their mutual relations. Normally the economic system among the SAARC countries is the same as that of mixed economy because of their underdevelop characteristics. These countries are having various economic features in common like poverty, income inequality, large population, dependence on agriculture, low productivity and mass unemployment. The emergence of regional trade blocks like WTO, EU, ASEAN, NAFTA, APEC, etc. have compelled the SAARC countries to operate in the global market with their increased economic strength. In this changed economic scenario, SAARC is expected to augment the intra-regional trade of the region for the benefit of the people of the region.

The region represents one of the poorest parts of the world. The region belongs to developing and less developed states (LDS) of the Third World. The region is facing some common problems like food, unemployment, poverty, health, law and order, terrorism, environment, water and energy which can be solved by only common strategy. And no doubt, SAARC is an institutional arrangement to encourage mutual cooperation among its member states. Under the aegis of SAARC, so far 13 broad areas have been earmarked for intensive cooperation including drug trafficking, suppression of terrorism, protection of environment etc.

These SAARC nations can come forward for collective interests and take initiative for establishment of "SAARC Food Reserve", "SAARC Children and Women Forum", "SAARC Environment Forum", "Regional Technology Transfer Centre", etc. The full utilization of the existing human and material resources of the region is the need of the hour which can be fulfilled by the professional approach only.

The 21st century's main problem is water and energy. These sub-continent powers can cooperate in oil exploration, power generation, bio-gas production and the development of wind and solor energy. Himalayas are rich in forestry and mineral resources. The development of Himalaya's mineral can benefit five countries of the region namely India, Pakistan, Bangladesh, Bhutan and Nepal.

Another resource which yet to be explored is the sea and sea bed. Exploration and drilling of oil and gas in the sea and development of common fisheries and marine based industrial complexes have good potentialities for collaboration between sub-continent powers.

The transfer of technology may be useful for small countries like Nepal, Sri Lanka and Bangladesh, which are not in a position to invest large amounts on industrial and scientific research.

SAARC can be used as a mechanism for "crisis management" at the regional level. The crisis management and tensions can be defused through the formal and informal talks and meetings among the nations and leaders. Exchange of views at informal meeting during SAARC summits between the leaders play an important part in defusing the tensions in their bilateral relations.

The 12th SAARC summit held in Islamabad in 2005 and adopted the Islamabad Declaration and signed a historic agreement on free trade and additional protocol on terrorism and a social charter. The commitment of member states to fight terrorism is a welcome step. The additional protocol reiterates the condemnation of terrorism by all SAARC countries and showed their commitment to implement all the relevant international conventions to which they are party. Under the agreement the member states pledged to create a "just and equitable partnership" in the region and to work towards the creation of a South Asia Economic Union.

Under the social charter the nations have pledged to work together for poverty alleviation, population stabilisation, empowerment of women and Human Resource Development.

There are many fields in which SAARC nations can cooperate eg. telecommunication, meteorology, transport, shipping, tourism, agriculture, rural sector, joint ventures, market promotion, science, technology, education, technical and culture.

13TH DHAKA SAARC SUMMIT, 12-13 NOVEMBER, 2005

The 13th SAARC Summit held in Dhaka on 12-13 November 2005 after the two times cancellation to strengthen the organisation. Manmohan Singh proposed for increasing daily air flights, developing planned system for disaster management, develop transport facilities. South Asia University and regional food bank, organise South Asia car rally and to form SAARC textile and handicraft museum.

Three important agreements were declared in Dhaka:

- Rescue from double taxation.
- Relaxation in visa rules.
- Formation of SAARC Arbitration Council.

14TH NEW DELHI SAARC SUMMIT, 2-3 APRIL, 2007

In the 14th New Delhi SAARC Summit, India unilaterally announced that it will open its market to poor South Asian neighbours with duty free access liberalising visa regimes. The duty exemption will help Nepal, Bangladesh, Maldives and Bhutan.

As a step towards improving people to people contact, Manmohan Singh announced that India liberalise visas for students, teachers, professors, journalists and patients from the SAARC countries.

Again the SAARC members declared their desire to implement the South Asia Free Trade Agreement (SAFTA) in "letter and spirit." Highlighting the importance of enhancing regional trade in South Asia, SAFTA should be made fully operational. Calling SAFTA a "spring board" for economic-development of the region, Maldives President Abdul Gayoom said it "should be made fully operational". He said that more open global economy had not resulted in equitable benefits for the region. So the regional cooperation should address issues affecting the quality of life.

A declaration issued by the leaders emphasised the need to develop a road map for a South Asian Customs Union and a South Asian Economic Union in a "planned and phased manner." The leaders also called for finalising an agreement in the 'services sector' at the earliest.

They stressed the need for ensuring market access through smooth implementation of the trade liberalisation programme and directed the SAFTA bodies to review the progress on a regular basis. Successful implementation of SAFTA will catalyse other areas for regional economic cooperation, the document said.

Participation in World Economy (2005): A Comparison

Indicator	*SAARC*	*ASEAN*	*CAREC*	*CAREC (Excl. China)*
Surface area	3.8	3.3	11.5	4.3
Population	22.8	8.6	21.3	1.0
GDP	2.3	2.0	5.4	0.2
Merchandise exports	1.2	6.3	7.7	0.4
Merchandise imports	18	5.6	6.5	0.3
Total reserves minus gold	36	7.1	19.8	0.2
FDI Inflow	1.0	3.9	8.5	0.4

Source: WDI, 2007.

Business Environment in SAARC Countries

Country Ranking (1-175)	Country	Starting a business	Dealing with licenses	Employing workers	Protecting investors	Trading Across borders	Enforcing contracts	Closing a business
53	Maldives	31	9	5	60	91	83	114
74	Pakistan	54	89	126	19	98	163	46
88	Bangladesh	68	67	75	15	134	174	93
89	Sri Lanka	44	71	98	60	99	90	59
100	Nepal	49:	127	150	60	136	105	95
134	India	88	155	112	33	139	173	133
162	Afghanistan	17	—	74	173	152	165	151

Source: World Bank, 2007.

Intra Regional Trade Among SAARC Countries: A Profile (Average Over 2002-06)

	Intra Regional Exports			*Intra Regional Imports*		
	Value (US $ mill)	*Share in*		*Value (US $ mill)*	*Share in*	
		Region	*Own Total Exports*		*Region*	*Own Total Imports*
Afghanistan	83	1.2	41.9	896	13.2	39.8
Bangladesh	145	2.1	1.8	1836	27.1	15.2
India	4474	86.2	5.5	984	14.5	0.9
Maldives	17	0.2	13.9	127	1.9	20.0
Nepal	319	4.7	51.9	762	11.2	45.9
Pakistan	1209	17.9	8.9	573	8.5	2.8
Sri Lanka	508	7.5	8.7	1598	23.6	19.4
SAARC Region	6754	100.0	6.2	6776	100.0	4.4

Estimated from data from DoTS.

Composition of Intra SAARC Trade—Exports

(percent)

SITC	*Description*	*1991*	*1995*	*2001*	*2005*
0	Food & Live Animals	20.8	29.3	28.6	17.4
1	Beverages & Tobacco	0.8	0.9	0.6	0.5
2	Crude Materials ex. food/fuel	13.1	5.5	4.7	4.7
3	Mineral fuel/lubricants	3.1	1.7	2.8	19.1

(Contd.)

SITC	Description	1991	1995	2001	2005
4	Animal/veg oil/fat/wax	0.1	0.2	0.6	4.5
5	Chemical/products n.e.s.	9.4	10.0	11.5	11.5
6	Manufactured goods	37.3	34.8	30.0	26.8
7	Machinery/Transport equipment	13.2	14.8	14.3	10.5
8	Misc. manufactured goods	1.7	1.7	5.0	4.8
9	Commodities n.e.s.	0.6	1.0	1.9	0.3
	SAARC Region	100	100	100	100

Calculated on the basis of data from VATS.
Countries considered: India, Pakistan, Sri Lanka and Bangladesh.

15TH SAARC SUMMIT, COLOMBO, 2-3 AUGUST, 2008

A Partnership for Growth for the Peoples of South Asia

The Heads of State or Government were convinced that the process of regional cooperation must be truly people-centered, so that SAARC continues to strengthen in keeping with expectations as a robust partnership for growth for the peoples of South Asia. They accordingly directed all SAARC mechanisms to abide by the Charter objective of promoting the welfare of the people and improving their quality of life. In this regard they directed the Council of Ministers to ensure that SAARC mechanisms identify further areas of cooperation where people-centric partnership projects could be initiated.

The Heads of State or Government observed that an effective and economical regional tele-communication regime is an essential factor of connectivity, encouraging the growth of people-centric partnerships. They stressed the need for the Member States to endeavour to move towards a uniformly applicable low tariff, for international direct dial calls within the region.

The member countries reaffirmed their commitment to the principles and objectives enshned in the SAARC Charter. They removed their resolve for collective regional efforts to accelerate economic growth, social progress and cultural development.

Addressing the inaugural session of the 15th SAARC Summit, PM Manmohan Singh said:

> "With globalisation, our economies are ever more inter-connected with our neighbours and with the world as a whole."

He also reminded that the success and prosperity of each provides opportunities to the others to promote their own success and prosperity. This mutuality of interests is the central driving force of regional corporation everywhere.

The 15th SAARC Summit theme of the year 2008 was "Growth through Partnership". Economic cooperation, connectivity and integration can lead to a peaceful and stable South Asia. The SAARC Development Fund, development of SAARC Model Villages in each country, SAARC Cultural festival and SAARC Youth Cooperation, establishment of SAARC Food Bank in 2007 are the forward looking steps to address new challenges. India stands ready to play her part in the evolution of a stable, vibrant and prosperous South Asia.

DEVELOPMENT FUND

The leaders held that the SAARC Development Fund should be "made operational" at the earliest and resources mobilised from both within and outside the region. They emphasised the "importance of decision-making and working of the fund being consistent with the SAARC Charter."

In a strong statement against terrorism, the leaders called for the "urgent conclusion" of a comprehensive convention on international terrorism. They agreed to "work on the modalities" of implementing the provisions of existing SAARC conventions to combat terrorism, narcotics, smuggling and other transnational crimes.

"They expressed their commitment to take every possible measure to prevent and suppress, in particular, financing of terrorist acts by criminalising the provision, acquisition and collection of funds for such acts, including through front organizations and also to counter illicit trafficking of narcotic drugs, trafficking in persons and illicit arms," the declaration read.

In the 14th SAARC summit, SAARC nations have decided to implement concrete projects in the next six months in four areas that affect their people's daily lives—water, energy, food and environment with international agencies.

Iran was formally accorded 'observer status' by the regional grouping. Two Agreement were signed in this summit:

- Setting up a South Asian University in India.
- Forming a regional food bank.

SAARC countries (India, Pakistan, Sri Lanka, Bangladesh and Nepal) agreed to launch "Southasian" a weekly programme that will be packaged in Kolkata and edited by Bangladeshi journalist Rubana. Efforts would be made to evolve a South Asia vocabulary to address ticklish issues on the programme.

In 14th summit, India took initiative to draft a SAARC convention on mutual assistance in legal matters. India also unilaterally announced measures to open its market to poor and least developed South Asian neighbours with duty free access and liberalising visa regimes. The duty exemption will help Nepal, Bangladesh, Maldives and Bhutan.

The Prime Minister also made a proposal for linking all SAARC capitals through direct flights.

INDIA AND SAARC

India among the SAARC nations, has the largest area, population and GDP. It is bordered by four SAARC countries namely, Pakistan, Nepal, Bhutan and Bangladesh. The other two countries namely Sri Lanka and Maldives, though not connected by common border being islands, can be also considered as border countries. Thus India stands as a centre of the SAARC region both location-wise and area-wise.

For the success of SAARC, the great responsibility lies with India, the predominant power among the sub-continent powers to develop greater under standing with its small and sensitive neighbours. This was reflected in the speech of former Sri Lankan president Jayawardene at Dhaka Summit,

> "India, larger than all the rest of us combined can create the confidence among us so necessary to make a beginning."

Never the less the neighbours also need to maintain goodwill and understanding.

A country of India's size and potential has its own compulsions and problems, some of its smaller neighbours are triggered by the insecurities. Big countries like India have traditionally used the carrot and stick approach to establish their standing with smaller neighbours.

In sub-continent, India possesses economic, military, technology and ideology power but not in as generously. Though a strong military power, its ability to influence Pakistan has always been limited.

The smaller countries in the region are intimidated by India's size and economic might and harbour fears about their domestic industries begin undermined in the event of free trade. But this is not a valid argument.

WHY SHOULD INDIA SUPPORT SAARC ?

- Make de facto the dejure
- For greater inflow of FDI
- Dynamic trade gains
- Regional security
- Promotion of development of least developed countries.
- Returns to scale.
- Increased efficiency in the provision of public goods and services.
- Connectivity payoff with the rest of Asia
- Achieving greater social cohesion within India.
- Defining and defending our regional space.

As the largest country in sub-continent, efforts must be towards a process that will lead to closer economic integration as well as a harmonisation of the political perspectives of the countries of the region.

Among the SAARC nation's community, lack of mutual faith and trust, cooperation and support system are the main factors which are responsible for not smooth working of SAARC. There are many issues on which there are disputes among the nations.

Afghanistan blames Pakistan for the resurgence of Taliban and spreading terrorism in Afghanistan, so that it can use the Taliban, to turn Afghanistan into a colony and a helpless puppet of Pakistan.

India and Pakistan are in dispute since the independence and the Kashmir is the core issue on which both have fought three wars. Pakistan reluctance to grant MFN status to India, even under the ratified SAFTA is noteworthy.

Pakistan utilised the 14th summit to raise Kashmir issue and linked free trade with India to progress on the 'core' issue of Kashmir. The Pakistan Prime Minister Saukat Aziz said "Trade is linked to progress on Kashmir."

Pakistan refused to implement SAFTA in relation to India. Pakistan is the country in the region with whom India does not have a FTA. Pakistan is also not cooperating in the Iran-Pakistan-India gas pipeline project.

Terrorism and Maoism in Nepal, Naxalism in India, fundamentalism in Pakistan, Bangladesh and Afghanistan creates the unpeace, unrest and communal frenzies in the region. Above all US interference and favourism to Pakistan is the issue of great concern for region. The open geo-political boundaries between the states have created many problems like smuggling, drug trafficking, women and child trafficking, security and border disputes. SAARC regimes are of different types—autocrat, military, democratic, royal in nature which have different perspectives on different problems. The growing arms race among the nations has given growth to arms collection and modernisation of military. The nuclearisation of Pakistan and India has more worsened the situation in the region and blocked the peace process.

SAARC could not work smoothly because of the differences among the nations. India, seeing the unrest in Nepal, declined to participate in the SAARC Dhaka conference going to be held on 6-7 February, 2005, so the summit had to be cancelled.

As the largest member of SAARC, India should give duty-free market access to its smaller and less-developed neighbours like Bangladesh, Maldives, Bhutan and Nepal while Pakistan needs to implement the South Asia Free Trade Area (SAFTA) agreement.

The size of our industry and economy is large enough to accommodate the requirements of these countries, if our government comes out with any package for our smaller neighbours. We should share the fruits of growth with smaller members of the SAARC. The SAARC region accounted for a mere 2.5 percent of India's total foreign trade in April-October 2006. Therefore the opening up of India's market is important for growing trade and commerce in the region.

INDIA VISION FOR SOUTH ASIA

India's vision is for sub-continent is an integrated, prosperous and peaceful subcontinent. Three developments—terror and counter terror, corporate globalisation and political violence—have been deeply impacted the region. In Bangladesh, politically motivated misuse of institutions of the state, including the police and the judiciary, the frequent use of violence against political opponents and the growing Islamic fundamentalism have had grave impact on respect for human rights.

South bloc has a new vision for South Asia—Lets Get Together:

1. Future lies in having a **common market**. South Asia should strive towards **common economic goals**.-India invites neighbours to share this vision as equal partners.
2. **Free trade** is possible only when cross border links, including transport and other means of communication are developed.
3. South Asian confederation on the lines of EU.

India has free trade agreements with Sri Lanka, Nepal and Bhutan.

SOME RECENT INITIATIVES BY INDIA

- India has unilaterally reduced negative list of trade items from 744 to 500 for least developed countries (LDCs) of SAARC.
- India has advanced the trade liberalisation programme in respect to LDCs by one year and with effect from 1st January 2008, the import duty on all items other than those in the negative list has been reduced to zero.
- A task force has been set-up to address Non-Tariff Barriers faced by partner countries in India.
- To promote people to people contact, trade and commercial interaction within the regions, India's initiatives include, opening up of road, rail and ferry links with Pakistan; the Open Skies arrangement with Sri Lanka; Integrated Check Posts along the borders; the optical fiber backbone across the Nepalese Terai as well

as, the Rail Agreement with Nepal, hydro-electric projects in Bhutan and Nepal, etc.
- Under the chairmanship of India an Intergovernmental Agreement to establish the South Asian University was signed during the 14th SAARC Summit. The main campus of the University will be in India.
- To enhance cultural connectivity in the region, India hosted a SAARC Cultural Festival in November 2007.
- To focus on issues relating to women, India hosted meetings relating to Home-based Workers, Trafficking in Women and Children and, Micro Financing and women Economic Empowerment.
- India will contribute $100 million of the $300 million initial corpus of SAARC Development Fund established to finance projects related to poverty alleviation, infrastructure development, etc.
- India has offered SAARC nations access to free-of-cost remote sensing data collected by various satellites launched by the Indian Space Research Organisation (ISRO) during major disasters in the region.
- India is now sharing remote sensing data collected by various satellites launched by the ISRO with entire SAARC region free of cost. The idea is to use geo-informatics in risk mapping, risk assessment and risk monitoring under diverse settings.

INDIA'S POSSIBLE ROLE

- Take a long-term strategic view of South Asia and be seen to be doing.
- Committing greater resources by both Central and State Governments to regional cooperation.
- Clarify that security is a concern but will not come in the way of promoting regional cooperation.
- Further Encourage the private sector to take up cross border projects.
- Invite multilateral and bilateral support in key sectors: Transport, Energy, Tourism, Environment, Irrigation.
- Listen as an equal partner and report back on suggestions implemented.
- Actively strengthen SAARC Secretariat.

INEFFICIENCIES OF SAARC

- SAARC could not adopt pro-people policies like democratic freedoms, denial of rights, commercial exploitation and sexual abuse of women and children in the region, trafficking, poverty, social inequalities, land reforms, etc. Largely SAARC has remained an organisation of interactions among the governments.
- SAFTA is still not fully operational despite this that it is a 'spring board' for economic development of the region. All the member countries should strive to take concert and interlocking steps in an accelerated pace to operationalise the FTA. The economic cooperation had so far failed to strengthen regional cooperation and the benefits of the more open global economy has not resulted in equitable benefits for the region.

India being the largest economy among the SAARC countries, has the largest volume of trade. But India's trade with SAARC nations is not substantial. The intra-SAARC annual trade of $ 3 billions is only 3 per cent of its total imports and 4 per cent of the region's exports. This shows the SAARC government's non-cooperation in trade. Presently South Asia is lagging behind every other world area in cooperative arrangements including economic cooperation. There has been a consistent decline in South Asia's share in world trade

Trade among the nations, can strengthen the relations. India's potential of aluminium, Pakistan's of copper, Bhutan, Nepal and Sri Lanka of tourism, could be beneficial for all the nations. The intra-regional trade at present in manufactured goods is very small, there exist a vast potential for increasing it. Rice, jute, tourism, tea, coal, technology, medicines, water and energy are some of the areas where mutual trade can be expanded. The regional management of water resources can check the wastage of river water and produce the energy. The Ganga and Brahmaputra-Barak-Meghna water management can provide a face lift to the region.

The World Bank is also in favour of more open trade in the South Asia region saying there was potential for $20 billion commerce by 2010 if barriers were reduced. Trade can more than double if appropriate regional agreements on roads, rail, air and shipping are put in place enabling seamless movement.

- The economic integration of the region is a condition for economic growth of the region. The international aid and trade environment help in growing burden of debt, deteriorating terms of trade.
- A cooperative approach is necessary for solving regional problems. Exchanging of experiences and technologies, know how is a condition for development and reducing economic disparities. All the nations are facing common problem of terrorism.

Promoting people to people contacts in the sub-continent is essential for establishing peace, law and order. The educational, cultural, tourist, businessmen exchange is also beneficial.

Factors Inhibiting Intra-Regional Trade

- Low trade complementarities.
- Export basket not diversified (exception, India).
- Restrictive Rules of Origin and destination.
- Services not Included in the regional trade agreement.
- High trade barriers (large negative list, non-tariff and para-tariff barriers).
- Lack of communication links (Poor transport infrastructure).
- High transaction costs (Corruption, custom delays, etc.)
- Inability to build a relationship of mutual trust and confidence.
- Politics and lack of commitment.

Bilateral Trade Restriction under SAFTA

%NL	*BAN*	*IND*	*MAL*	*NEP*	*PAK*	*SRI*
BAN		11.2	0.0	29.7	31.3	45.2
IND	66.0		65.2	64.2	14.5	53.5
MAL	72.9	3.6		0.0	0.0	59.2
NEP	87.8	46.2	0.0		25.4	17.6
PAK	54.5	16.4	15.5	30.0		28.4
SRI	66.6	41.5	85.4	37.6	29.7	
Total	65.0	38.4	74.5	64.0	17.2	51.7
Intra-SAARC Imports	16.7	0.8	21.1	42.4	3.1	25.9

Source: Weerakoon and Thennakoon, 2008, "SAFTA: Which Way Forward?", *Journal of South Asian Development*, Vol. 1, No. 3 (forthcoming).

SUGGESTIONS FOR EFFECTIVE SAARC

Lack of democracy and inconsistencies in trade have prevented the SAARC from realising its full potential. There is enormous potential if we can overcome problems of trade, problems of security and problems of democracy.

Beyond the compulsions of politics and the imperatives of economics, there is a cultural dimension to unity within SAARC. The eight countries that constitute SAARC today—Afghanistan, Bangladesh, Bhutan, India, Maldives, Nepal, Pakistan and Sri Lanka have several examples of shared culture, which is dynamic factor for greater interaction and understanding.

The cultural dimension flows from a joint civilisational history as well as the legacy of colonial rule. Hindu and Buddhist temples are to be found throughout this region, all the way to Afghanistan, where, tragically, in a frenzy of iconoclasm, the Taliban blew up two gigantic rock-cut statues of the Buddha. There are also a number of Sufi centres in this region, the most important of which is the dargah of Khwaja Moinuddin Chisti in Ajmer, which millions visit every year regardless of religious affiliation.

If Hinduism is the predominant religion linking India and Nepal, Islam is the common thread running through India, Pakistan, Afghanistan and Maldives. Buddhism bridges India, Sri Lanka, Bhutan and Nepal. India is a land of the Buddha and apart from the place of his birth in Lumbini, Nepal, all the monuments and sacred places associated with his life are in India.

For the Sikhs, the most holy shrine, of course, is the Golden Temple at Amritsar, while Jain temples include Ranakpur, which, in its own way, rivals the Taj Mahal. This last, of course, is the best known monument in the entire SAARC region.

Striking commonalities exists too in the traditions of music, in sartorial wear and in cuisine. There is also a powerful shared linguistic and literary dimension to SAARC. We share Urdu with Pakistan, Nepali with Nepal, Bengali with Bangladesh, Tamil with Sri Lanka. Both India and Bangladesh sings Rabindranath Tagore's songs, who also wrote the national anthems of both the countries. Mirza Galib, Meer, Souda and Iqbal are recited both in India and Pakistan, and English is the link language for the entire region.

- Maldives had proposed the idea of a social charter for the area.
- SAARC must adopt a single currency to improve trade without barriers.
- Trade can more than double if appropriate regional agreements on roads, rail, air and shipping are put in place enabling seamless movement.
- Democracy is the key ingredient for regional cooperation.

SAARC made history by choosing the girl child as its theme in 1990 and declared 1991-2000 the SAARC Decade of the Girl Child. Other themes that SAARC have brought into focus had a gender dimension, like trafficking, violence against women and more recently, home-based workers and network. Now SAARC should go for peace and security in the region by eliminating terrorism. The member countries should show their commitments to "take every possible measure to prevent and suppress, in particular, financing of terrorist acts. There should be a regional agreement of Mutual Legal Assistance in Criminal Matters to deal with terrorism and organised crime.

SAARC NEEDS A SHIFT IN FOCUS

In today's world SAARC needs a paradigmatic shift. It came into being with the aim of accelerating the process of economic and social development among members. Today, however, it requires each member state to promote and protect human rights, equality between men and women and condemnation of unconstitutional changes of government. The governments in the region are shaped through military dictatorships, ethnic and religious conflicts, emergencies and political violence. Governments today continue to violate human rights and justify their actions on grounds of 'security'. It is up to the regional community as a whole to protect these rights on behalf of the people of sub-continent region. This is resulted into the formation of people's SAARC.

PEOPLE'S SAARC—ALTERNATIVE SYSTEM

The people's SAARC comprising parliamentarians, writers,

women's rights activists and civil society organisations from across the region was formed in 2000. The people's SAARC is an attempt to create a vision of an alternative political, socio-economic and cultural system free from the baggage of history and artificial boundaries.

The people's SAARC was formed as an alternative as the people of SAARC countries felt that SAARC had failed to fulfil the aspirations of the common people. The SAARC has become an organisation of interactions among the governments, where the common people's interests were totally ignored.

The people's SAARC is holding its summit parallel to the SAARC summit since 2000.

Describing the SAARC meets as mere ceremonial occasions, the people's SAARC urged the official SAARC in its Delhi Summit to:

- Combat poverty and social inequities, demand for regional security council to curb nuclear proliferation in the region.
- Work towards a meaningful unification of the region.
- Combat trafficking, commercial exploitation and sexual abuse of women and children in the region.
- Ratify the regional Victim/Witness Protection Protocol.
- Declare the region visa free to facilitate free movement of people.
- Work for land reforms and land right for indigenous people. President Gayoom of Maldives also had proposed the idea of a social charter for the area.

SUB-CONTINENT TOWARDS SUB-REGIONALISM

BIMSTEC is established in 1997 as a sub-regional group. BIMSTEC identified regional cooperation broadly in six areas-trade and investment, technology, transportation and communication, energy to tourism and fisheries.

BIMSTEC is a sub-regional organisation of seven countries—Bangladesh, India, Myanmar, Sri Lanka, Thailand Economic Cooperation. Originally it was BISTEC (Bangladesh, India, Sri Lanka, Thailand Economic Cooperation). The actual initiative for establishing a regional forum came from Bangladesh President

Zia-ur-Rehman in 1977 and after the talks to Pakistan and Sri Lankan leaders, he suggested a summit level meeting. Though all the countries of the region supported President Zia's proposal in principle, but India and Pakistan were not enthusiastic. The organisation took place on the initiative of Thailand. It is a speculation that India considers it as an alternative of SAARC for the regional cooperation. In February 2004, Nepal and Bhutan became the member of BIMSTEC. As now it was not representing the first alphabet of all members, so its name was changed in the Bangkok session (July 2004). Now it is considered as Bay of Bengal Initiative for Multi Sectorial Technical and Economic Cooperation.

The 1st session of BIMSTEC was held in Bangkok on 30-31 July 2004. Addressing the meeting, Manmohan Singh called the member states to use their internal resources and powers in such a way so that the whole area can make powerful. He stressed on to develop India-Myanmar-Thailand route, importance of Internet networking, reforms in United Nations, reorganisation of UNSC, end of religious fundamentalism and terrorism. He called the member states to show solidarity in facing terrorism and the smuggling of arms and narcotics. In the joint statement all the nations promised to:

- Increase mutual trade.
- Implement free trade agreement.
- Combat international terrorism.
- From joint action group to face inter-state crimes.
- No use of land for activities against member nations.
- Exchange secret informations.
- Establish a BIMSTEC centre on weather and environment.

BIMSTEC 8th ministerial meeting held in Dhaka on December 19, 2005. Talks on increase of mutual trade and investment and FTA were held.

Out of the seven members of BIMSTEC, five are also members of SAARC. The total trade of India with BIMSTEC nations is 3.7 billion dollar.

SAARC within SAARC

Nepal first mooted the idea of a sub-regional block in May 1996 with Nepal, Bhutan, India and Bangladesh. The purpose of the project is to form the sub-regional group outside SAARC or to say "SAARC within SAARC". India is not against the idea. This whole idea is only to make an economic alliance. This logic of economic cooperation makes some sense. The proposed group will strive to develop the area which forms an ecological economic unit. People of Nepal, Bhutan, Bangladesh and India's north-east share a common culture of wreathed poverty. The unique way of life is trapped in the vicious circle of drought and deluge. The region has common rivers and other natural resources which can be developed for the general good of the region's people.

But because of the objections raised by Pakistan and Sri Lanka and some sections of public opinion in Bangladesh and Nepal, the idea has got bogged down in the legality of SAARC charter and procedure.

The Pakistan, Maldives and Afghanistan do not want any such arrangement within SAARC. They are again charging India that the big brother is again trying to bully the younger ones. Begun Khaleda Zia of Bangladesh was accused by Sheikh Hasina's regime of selling out to India by agreeing to "SAARC within SAARC". Islamabad, as usual, alleged that New Delhi was using dirty tricks to isolate it in order to dominate the region. Pakistan accused India of trying to kill two birds with one stone-dominating its smaller neighbours and isolating Pakistan.

Though the SAARC charter allows the formation of sub-regional groups on specific issues. But there is no doubt that a sub-regional group in the region can really weaken the already fragile SAARC.

CONCLUSIONS

Indian foreign policy is going through many challenges in today's world-economic, political, technological, military, etc. Post-cold war sub-continent is feeling the strong presence of many powers, i.e.—US, Russia, China and Japan. In the post-cold war period not geo-politics rather geo-economics characterising the strategic scenario. So the sub-continent region became significant for Washington mainly due to economic reasons. In the post-cold war period the need for economic cooperation has become quite vital for every country. Therefore, the US is acquiring benefits from the changed geo-political landscape through free market forces, promotion of democracy, human rights and protection of environment from rapid degradation. So the US strategy in the post-cold war period reflects its policy of engagement and enlargement, especially in South Asia. The US presence in South Asia and in the sub-continent countries is posing many threats and encouraging other powers also to be here to counter the US hegemony.

On the other hand, the process of globalization has proved positive for India. It has not only opened up Indian economy for global world, but thrown open opportunities for building strategic and political relations with the outside world that could be of benefit to India.

The Liberalisation, Privatization, Globalisation (LPG) age has thrown open opportunities before India for building strategic and political relations with the outside world and neighbouring countries that could be of benefit to India. An economically stable and prosperous India is increasingly involved in global and regional economics and is more likely to build webs of economic interdependence which offer it greater political security. Prosper and stable economy of our neighbouring countries would able to provide India strategic choices in the course of its development. If US and China can become friends, why not India forgive the hostile relationships of yesteryears. Economic cooperation must take precedence over political issues in the region. Only this is the sound approach.

During the last some years, the political climate for regional cooperation in the region has improved vastly. These include the water sharing agreement with Bangladesh, FTA with Sri Lanka, the Lahore Declaration, etc.

Globalisation has on the one hand, opened new opportunities for sub-regional countries and on the other hand made them more vulnerable to outside forces.

There is a direct correlation between security and development. This requires sub-regional powers to resolve the difference and disputes within and between the countries through dialogue and compromise.

The SAARC nations have remained mired in conflict management. The consequent drain of our energies has hold us back from achieving the goals that we set for ourselves in the SAARC charter.

We must come to grip with our challenges both individually as nations and collectively as members of SAARC. We need to evolve a road map for the region that will enable us to leverage our assets and advantages while overcoming our limitations. Only then will we be able to make a difference in the lives of our people. A shared desire for regional cooperation can convert the region into a region of peace, security and development. SAARC could open up vast possibilities and opportunities for mutually beneficial cooperation.

SAARC which was formed in 1985 had not been able to realise its potential yet. The entire SAARC area suffered from poverty and disease. For most people in the region life is far from satisfactory. We can look at SAARC as a catalyst for regional growth and sustainable economic development. SAARC development goals can be realised with a common effort. Beside these, SAARC is the 'correct vehicle' to undertake counter-terrorism operation in the region. The obligations under SAARC had not been translated into law enforcement action by grouping.

Today the economic and political issues should not be considered in a sectoral way. Every foreign policy has two core goals—national security and economic betterment. The Indian foreign policy is also based on these two principles in today's global world. Indian national security today is based on its economic growth. India's economic growth in itself holds the key to India's global profile and power, its strategic role and relevance and its national security. India's economic policy can be an instrument of foreign policy. Business and economic cooperation can help ease political tensions and reduce the relevance of border disputes.

Trade and investment flows among countries create an interdependence and countries are more willing to downgrade bilateral political differences when economic prosperity is at stake. The changed relationship between China and US in recent years is good example of this. China has locked the United States into a relationship of mutual dependency whereby the US middle class households would be hurt if the US-China trade relationship is interrupted. Indeed China has used trade as a strategic policy weapon building a relationship of mutual benefit, not just with the US, but also with other countries world wide.

India should use trade as a lever for closer political understanding in sub-continent And that India should take the lead in this, as it enjoys a considerable trade surplus with many of her neighbours e.g. Bangladesh and Sri Lanka. This line of thinking much to be commended. India has already signed a free trade agreement with Sri Lanka and this is resulting in greater confidence of Sri Lanka and expanded trade and investment flows between these two countries.

However India's ability to achieve closer economic integration in the SAARC countries is stymied by Pakistan's spoiling attitude. But the emergence of a Bay of Bengal community known as BIMT-EC is a promising development and India should nurture it as a way of breaking out of the gridlock that has developed in the SAARC.

This is not to say that we can ignore Pakistan or that it is unimportant in our own economic calculation. No doubt, that improved relations between India and Pakistan can alter the whole scenario of the sub-continent.

"The Sub-continent can Rise and Shine Together." So India requires adequate mechanisms for coordination and cooperation of economic, foreign and security policies. No doubt there is political, economic, cultural, ethnic, military disputes among the sub-continent powers. But it can be solved through India's mature thinking and acts. Indian foreign policy needs some internal restraints and effective internal mechanism for effective and smooth operation of foreign policy.

The business sector, people to people contacts, more trade and investment, cultural and educational exchanges, etc. are some of the areas where more cooperation and joint ventures will reduce the barriers of boundaries.

No doubt, the sub-continent is facing many political, social, economic problems. But the region possesses the factors of positive strengths also. The region is very close to China, Japan and Singapore which are emerging economic powers. It has a great source of human capital. The large population of the region is its capital and a source of cheap labour.

India has proved a big consumer market. India's proven strength is its great educational institutions like IITs and IIMs. Large English speaking population has proved the asset of the nation. Indian Ocean is full of natural resources.

No doubt economics has become the cornerstone of diplomacy. As Musharraf said during his visit to India that business and economics has now become drivers of politics all over the world. After decades of war and conflict, the sub-continent region wants peace and development go simultaneously. Trade and business are emerging as the most effective Confidence Building Measures (CBMs) the world over. So why it can not be happened in this sub-continent. Prime Minister Manmohan Singh proposed a pan-Asian free trade area embracing major economics to drive the region's growth. India has a vital stake in the prosperity and stability of Asia. The Prime Minister said on 5 May 2006 at Hyderabad while inaugurating the ADB meeting that future of Asia lies in pan-Asia FTA.

Today more than half of global trade takes place through regional cooperation arrangements such as regional trade agreements, free trade agreements and customs union. If Indian sub-continent goes for FTAs, firstly, it can benefit member countries in various ways. FTAs provide time to the domestic industry to adjust, besides allowing countries an arena to tackle difficult issues like agricultural subsidies and trade in service. Secondly, the political and ethnic hostility between various member countries can be minimised with the signing of FTAs. The formation of FTAs can be seen as a strategic move to consolidate peace and increase regional security among member countries. The FTAs are more beneficial to smaller countries as they can offer domestic firms the advantage of economics of scale. It can also resist the hegemony of large powers. So India should go for more FTAs with the neighbouring countries. Presently India has FTA with Sri Lanka only in the sub-continent. The full implementation of SAFTA would pave the way for further integration of regional economics. The agreement on SAFTA came into effect from January 1, 2006. India being the larger economy among the sub-continent powers, has to play a big brotherly role to provide a boost to the Least Developed Countries (LDCs) of the sub-continent which are Bangladesh, Nepal and Bhutan.

Days before the New Delhi SAARC summit, Assocham President Venugopal Dhoot said,

> "Our economy, which is expected to reach a size of a trillion dollar by March 2008, should share the fruits of growth with smaller neighbours. Since the size of our industry economy is large enough to accommodate the requirements of these countries."

There is no issue that cannot be resolved through dialogue and discussion. The approach of seeking an eye for an eye, as Mahatma Gandhi taught us, can only leave us blind. Violence and force have never offered lasting solutions. Amartya Sen has written about the "Argumentative Indian" but our real strength has always been our willingness to live and let live. We must be more open to our neighbours. Prime Minister Manmohan Singh emphasized on this while addressing the India Conclave on April 9, 2007,

> "I want India to be more open to all our neighbours. I want our neighbours to feel secure and confident that in India they

have a well-wisher. We see their prosperity as a guarantee of our own prosperity. The destiny of the people of South Asia is inter-linked and inter-dependent. I see a similar mutual beneficial inter-dependence between India and the wider neighbourhood of the Indian Ocean and the Asia-Pacific regions. For centuries our forefathers sailed westwards and eastwards—as teachers and traders, as merchants and monks. That is how we would once again approach the world at large."

A shared desire for regional cooperation, with real and tangible benefits that accrue equally to all sides will make such cooperation possible. As a first step, this would require a truly open environment for regional trade-devoid of all types of barriers to free trade. There is a direct co-relation between security and development. This requires to resolve the differences and disputes between the neighbouring countries through dialogue and compromise. During the visit to New Delhi, Pakistan Prime Minister Shaukat Aziz said on April 3, 2007,

"There was a need to build mutual trust and confidence, thereby removing the obstacle of the trust deficit that had hampered meaningful cooperation in the region."

Security can be achieved today in sub-continent only when its rival nations hold it as an objective "in common" and only when policy makers take a comprehensive view of security threats en-compassing demographic, economic, environmental, political, psychological and religious as well as military problems that jeopardize the future of their people. No country in sub-continent can maintain its own security ignoring the security of neighbouring societies. How to Facilitate Regional Cooperation?

To promote government to government understanding and cooperation we suggest three approaches to inter-governmental cooperation:

- Cultural Approach
- Functional Approach
- Political Approach

Through cultural exchanges creation of goodwill and inter-people and inter-elite cooperation can be gained.

Under the functional approach inter-governmental cooperation through SAARC, etc. should be developed.

Through political approach, the political will of the ruling elites and skilled diplomacy could play a decisive role. It should include:

- Cessation of all overt and covert interventionary operations.
- Establishment of confidence and security building measures.
- Arms control and force reductions.
- Management, containment and resolution of inter-state conflicts.

What to do?

- India should redefine its foreign policy interests and role more specifically in sub-continent.
- India should exhibit greater sensitivity and understanding towards these neighbouring countries.
- Defence cooperation should be increased.
- India should also maintain a political dialogue with all individually at all levels.
- Economic interactions in sectors such as trade, tourism, joint ventures should be initiated. Economic policy can be an instrument of foreign policy. Business and economic cooperation can help ease political tensions and reduce the relevance of border disputes.
- India should revive the policy of non-alignment which is one of the largest global diplomatic fora of 116 nations. It is still relevant even after the end of bipolarity in the international arena to resist the only super power's unilateral attempt to control the world. The doctrine of preventive war and the imposition of regime change on the pretext of combating terrorism, promoting democracy and controlling rogue states have made the world a more dangerous place. So in these circumstances, the revitalization of NAM could be a ray of hope. NAM could focus on urgent sub-regional and transnational issues such as terrorism, health, energy security and environment.

Index